FEAR AND
LOVING
IN SOUTH
MINNEAPOLIS

FEAR AND
LOVING
IN SOUTH
MINNEAPOLIS

. . .

JIM WALSH

FOREWORD BY TOMMY MISCHKE

University of Minnesota Press
Minneapolis
London

Published by the University of Minnesota Press
111 Third Avenue South, Suite 290
Minneapolis, MN 55401-2520
http://www.upress.umn.edu

Printed in the United States of America on acid-free paper

The University of Minnesota is an equal-opportunity educator and employer.

25 24 23 22 21 20   10 9 8 7 6 5 4 3 2 1

Library of Congress Cataloging-in-Publication Data
Walsh, Jim, author. | Mischke, Tommy, author of foreword.
Fear and loving in South Minneapolis / Jim Walsh ;
foreword by Tommy Mischke.
Minneapolis : University of Minnesota Press, 2020.
Summary: "A veteran Twin Cities journalist and raconteur summons the life of the city after reporting and recording its stories for more than thirty years"—Provided by publisher.
LCCN 2020024739 (print) | ISBN 978-1-5179-0605-4 (pb)
Subjects: LCSH: Walsh, Jim, 1959– | Journalists—Minnesota—Minneapolis—Biography. | Minnesota—Biography.
LCC PN4874.W2835 A3 2020 (print) | DDC 070.92 [B]—dc23
LC record available at https://lccn.loc.gov/2020024739

FOR MY FAMILY

CONTENTS

Foreword *Tommy Mischke* xi

Prologue 1

1. Stay Warm 9

Twenty-five Years of the Good Craic 12

"It Feels Like a Brighter Day" 13

Citizen Berquist: The Man with the Van 18

Misanthropes for $500, Alex 21

Confessions of a Commodore 25

The Santa Claus Diaries 28

2. Nature City 37

Stop and Smell the Rose Gardens 38

Lucky Us 40

Summer of the Super Sunsets 42

Seize the Light 44

Loving Lake Harriet 46

Harriet Lovejoy Was Here 48

Nightswimming 51

3. Family Ties 55

From Colombia, with Love 56

Thanks Given 65

Finding Henry 68

Police Off My Kid's Back 71

Fire Alarm Fluffy 74

An Ambulance Chaser Is Born   77

Letter to a Young Soccer Parent   79

4. I'm Only One   83

Thanks for the Skerch, Dad   89

Father Fantastic   91

Why Sylvia? Why Now?   93

Gold Experience at First Avenue   96

The Tao of Spring Forest Qigong   97

Krista Tippett and the Wisdom of *On Being*   101

Fear and Loving in South Minneapolis   105

Walking the Path   108

Being the Buddha at Mile Eight   111

5. Hootenanny   115

Peace, Love, and Bobby Sherman   118

When in Doubt, Hoot   121

Rings of Fire (Brothers United)   122

Sing Out!   126

"Possibly the Most Awesome Place on Earth"   128

The First Dad Rock Column in the History of Rock Criticism   130

They Sing 'til They Drop   134

This Week's Best Bet: Shhh . . .   135

Can You Even Still Hear This Song?   138

Dan Israel and the Struggle   140

Free and Grateful   144

That Thing You Do!   145

The Magic of the Mad Ripple Hootenanny   149

Inside the Hollow Square: Shape Note Singing from the Heart   152

Gather 'Round, Children, and Ye Shall Hear a Tale of
Standing in Actual Physical Line for Tickets   156

In Praise of Great Expectations   158

6. Famous Lasting Words   163

A Lesson before Dying   165

Famous Lasting Words   168

Working Stiffs   169

Tears in Heaven 172
Family Man 174
Notes from Karl's Bench 176
The Day David Bowie Died 178
The Funeral Singer 181
Zero Our Hero 182

7. Falling in Love with Everything I Have 187
Two Hearts Are Better Than One 190
Brilliant Disguise 192
Because the Night 194
I Wanna Be Where the Bands Are (The Autograph Man) 198
She's the One 202
Reason to Believe 205
Drive All Night (Desperately Seeking Denise) 209
Glory Days 212
Back to Minneapolis 214

Acknowledgments 217
Publication History 221

FOREWORD

TOMMY MISCHKE

One of life's great questions is to what extent are we all seeing the same thing when we look out at the world. To what degree is the engineer across the street seeing the same world as the poet on the corner? Each takes in similar surroundings and processes it all, but how similar are the minds doing the processing, or the hearts? What individual perspectives remain forever thus, and what experiences can be wholly communicated, and shown to be universal, through the tools of language?

For most of us, it's rarely enough just to know something for ourselves. There's a longing to share a perspective with another, and, together, see the same thing in the same way at the same time, if only for a moment. It's how we come to feel less alone, less locked away inside our skin. But getting there can be arduous. How does one persuade another to fully share a unique state of amazement or a moment of profound heartache? Writers ask themselves this all the time. They take their poetic insight and that handbag of words and spend their lives trying to create such moments. They say, I'm going to tell you a story, and at the end of this story I want us to be in the same place with the same sensations and to bask there momentarily.

"Connection" can sound so mechanical. There's no romance in the word. Yet it's the story of our time here on earth. Some force in the universe has seen fit to create a grand play where we are born alone and die alone. In between, we pierce the loneliness by forming tethers to some other intellect, some other heart and soul. When we do it well, it works like a salve. And when we fail to fasten the knots across that human divide, due to a lack of patience, lack of desire, or lack of skill, we remain with the ache of our isolation.

My friend Jim Walsh has spent his working life seeking to connect in a very specific way. He's tried to do what's been attempted since humans first gathered around a tribal fire and heard: this is what I saw, this is what I felt, this is what I know. He has a yearning to know life intimately, and he carries the writer's blessing and curse of needing to bring that intimacy to others—not selflessly, but so he too can know connection. All he has is words, and a poet's eye, and the daunting vista of all our wildly varied hearts and minds, spread out across the prairie, living separate and solitary lives. I share with him this love of storytelling. We have sat together in diverse settings and taken notice of the sudden light in the eye that sparks when we hear the other begin yet another tale— one that if told well, with a storyteller's craft, will give others something to marvel at.

And that's the endgame, always, it seems to me. Getting us all to marvel together, for just a little while, and to share the wonder of life's spectacle: her truths and her mysteries, laid bare in a single tale of existence, delivered with a writer's flourish.

Jim's writing reveals as much about setting as story. Place matters. Hometown is no mere location; it's a sensation in the heart, a handrail to lean on, a lawn chair to slide into, a patient mentor, and a loving nanny. His town has always been Minneapolis, mine has always been St. Paul. I read his words and find my way out of my neighborhood treehouse and into his. He takes me there with a single guiding principle: empathy. Not all writers hang on emotion as much as Jim does, not all of them bleed on the page the way he can, not all of them need to feel with that ache of human recognition. But the best ones do.

So, for the next two hundred pages, escape your isolation. Connect with a storyteller, and with all the other readers, me included. Connect with the town Jim has come to love so well. Bathe in those sudden moments of shared understanding and shared experience that too often elude us. You're not reading this book by yourselves. We're all in this together.

PROLOGUE

ON THE GRAY LINE IN DUBLIN ("THE ORIGINAL HOP-ON HOP-OFF Sightseeing Dublin!"), it was either near the James Joyce statue in the center of the city, or by Trinity College, or tooling past the Temple Bar, the Epic Irish Immigration Museum, or St. Patrick's Cathedral on our way to the Guinness factory and Jameson Distillery, I'm not sure, but what came out of the tour guide's mouth in that lovely, lilting, singsongy Irish burr at the end of his short Joyce bio gave me a start and something like the focus for this book.

"James Joyce was born in Dublin. Joyce's most enduring books, *Dubliners, A Portrait of the Artist as a Young Man, Ulysses,* and *Finnegans Wake,* are all based in Dublin," chirped the tour guide. "Joyce spent the first twenty-two years of his life in Dublin, and the last thirty-six years of his life in self-imposed exile, but he never wrote of any other place. Joyce once famously bragged that if Dublin were destroyed, the city could be rebuilt in its entirety from his written works."

The city could be rebuilt in its entirety from his written works.

Now, I am no James Joyce and Minneapolis is not Dublin, but in that moment—and I'd heard the quotation before, but not like this—it struck me that that is what I've been trying to do all my writing life: put into words what makes this town and its people special to me and illustrate the soul of the place, if not the sociology. In my writing I've hoped to explain and preserve some of the reasons why this area has been so important to me as my home, my muse, my salvation, my anchor, my ball and chain (winter sucks, and I often dream of trains going West, as a young old man).

The name of the column I wrote for more than a decade in the *Southwest Journal* was "My Minneapolis," named in honor of the Mill City, not to mention the great Stook & the Jukes album of the same name. Like so many lovers of this hotbed of hard work and forward progress, I've claimed the city as my own, told many stories of its people, and with this collection I aim to chronicle some of it for current and future readers and residents, and somehow bid goodbye to Old Minneapolis so I can say hello to New Minneapolis and beyond.

Let this book be a mix of both, then, and a history lesson from a quieter, if not more peaceful time. All of what follows was written before the Covid-19 pandemic, and I'm happy to have a few reminders from a time when impending doom wasn't part of our daily communion. So consider these to be my hieroglyphics on the pyramid wall, my tag on the boxcars, my messages in a bottle of hope, love, light, darkness, confusion, truth, and testament to what I've borne witness to for the next flounder discovering the Land of Ten Thousand Lakes.

The good news is that this guy works a lot and learns a lot. And he hears amazing stories. Two or three times a week, as a columnist, hustling freelance writer, and genuinely curious person and reporter, I find myself in a coffee shop or bar, or on the phone, asking strangers about their lives and their work. I've had great conversations, and I've learned so much about life by just asking the questions I need answered for myself, and so I ask questions that I think will evoke an answer that will be meaningful and useful to me and the reader, and that we'll all have a human moment together.

What comes next for you and me in these tumultuous times remains to be seen, but what comes next in these pages are stories, interviews, history, and ruminations from a time when a single hometown columnist could reach across your coffee cup and cereal in the morning and say, "I feel you. Me, too. Here's a story."

As such, the original full title for this collection was *Ancient Celtic Banshee Wail*, after a chant-song I came up with one night a couple of summers ago, sitting around the campfire in northern Minnesota playing music with my nephews, son, and brothers. I figured it was a good name for the spark of primal inspiration that has been at the heart of all the columns, essays, liner notes, songs, and other various stories that have spilled out of me since I first started writing in my journal and diary as a kid growing up in South Minneapolis.

That wail first made itself known and rose up in me when I was in fourth grade at Annunciation Catholic Grade School. Some visiting nuns admired and requested copies of a poem I'd written, which I happily and dutifully wrote out for them one day after school. It was the first time anyone had asked me for a copy of anything I'd written, and my nine-year-old writer's heart sprang into action. I was a little clueless kid, but writing and reading grabbed me.

The nuns' encouragement made me feel like I'd discovered something I was good at, and as they stood by patiently and admiringly, hovering over me as I rewrote my words—not for an assignment but for posterity on convent bulletin boards or keepsake drawers—I recognized that I liked that feeling of connection, and of a kindred-spirited recognition for expressing something so personal and inner.

Much in the same way the late, great Roger Ebert talked about the magical feeling he got as a kid when he received as a birthday gift from his parents a stamp with his byline on it with which he could stamp "by Roger Ebert" all over the place, I realized that this poem, printed out on a piece of paper by my own hand, was something that I alone had made and duplicated four times over as my gift to the world. The fact that the nuns actually wanted copies of my and no other student's poem that day made me feel like I'd been given a gift to use, and it set me on a path. The discovery that not only could I get my feelings out onto the page, but that writing could help me make sense of those feelings and also engage with the larger world was powerful and new, so I kept going.

I've been an author, writer, journalist, columnist, and singer/songwriter for almost thirty years. I get up every day and write something, anything, to keep the muscles and gray matter moving, to connect and make community, and to make a living, and I know I will until the day I die. I've written for scads of publications, and I'm currently a freelance writer, versed in stories about life, love, music, art, law, politics, and this mad, mad, mad, mad world.

At the moment, I'm covering how the pandemic is affecting Minnesotans, and from the looks of things that beat will continue indefinitely, and precariously. In March 2020, like millions of other Covid-crushed workers, I got laid off from my *Southwest Journal* column, along with the rest of the neighborhood newspaper's freelance staff, but I won't stop writing, as I believe the times demand it. Here's part of what I wrote in my farewell column to my readers:

> More than anything as I embark on yet another new chapter with all the rest of the gig economy warriors, I want to take this opportunity to, at this crazy juncture in our collective lives, put in a crucial word about supporting local journalism, and in particular homegrown/local columnists.
>
> I got the pink slip Friday, but the loss of it didn't hit me until later that night, when I was hanging out in front of the Lowbrow, waiting for my take-out order. Cars were lined up six deep, filled with hungry shelter-in-placers picking up dinner. Inside the shutdown restaurant on the front wall hung a framed column I wrote a year ago this month, about the Lowbrow's baseball card bar and its owner. On the street, as I chatted from a safe distance with a couple of families and made the kids laugh, a little blue Subaru pulled up. Out popped a guy who gave the Lowbrow server who was running take-out orders two big bottles of hand sanitizer.
>
> "Free! Courtesy of Tattersall," the server told me with a huge smile, of the local distillery that started making hand sanitizer last month. It was a beautiful moment of local business camaraderie and an example of the organic chain that makes a community thrive, and I realized I had the perfect place to write about it, that little place where I could once again make minutia into something meaningful—in my neighborhood newspaper.
>
> Then I remembered. As I write this, the unemployment rate is at an all-time high, and I'm just another flounder, collaterally damaged by the pandemic and making it up as I go along. I'll keep

writing and reporting, but my thirteen-year run of landing on your doorstep ends today.

Sigh. I've been the staunchest proponent for the job of columnist I know, and that won't change. There's a rich history of columnists writing personally in newspapers, but at the moment in these back-to-basics times, I fear that their value will be lost. So for the next columnist in this space, and for all working/surviving columnists out there, a few parting words of advice:

Writing a local newspaper column is one of the best jobs in the world, so act like it. It takes some guts, but do your thing. Your colleagues and editors might not even get it, but your readers will. Take risks. Show us your heart, your mind, your weaknesses. Write like no one's reading. Tell us something silly, profound, funny, or serious about yourself. Tell us a story about something, anything, that happened to you or your family or friends, no matter how insignificant it might seem as a germ of an idea. Write it out. See what happens. Don't leave the heart and snark and alt-storytelling to social media; develop your voice and use it and write, write, write. I, for one, will be reading.

When Governor Tim Walz issued the state's stay-at-home guidelines last week, "news organizations" were deemed part of the essential workforce, and there's a reason. We need information gatherers, storytellers, photographers, editors, columnists, and journalists to help make sense of these times. The good news in the Twin Cities is that there's an army of great journalists doing good and sometimes thankless work these days, and they deserve your support.

Ironically and tragically enough, the title of this collection was set months before most of the world had ever heard of my hometown. Not long after I was laid off from my column, George Floyd was killed at the hands of the Minneapolis police a few miles from where I live, and every country across the globe erupted in protests. I spent the next month covering (for *MinnPost*) the protests, the scenes at Thirty-eighth Street and Chicago Avenue and on Lake Street near the burned-to-the-ground Third Precinct, white racism, black power, prisons, Juneteenth, Minneapolis politics, Minneapolis police, and more. As Lake Street burned that first night, I was also moved to write a song, "Folk Song for George Floyd (Minneapolis Weeps)," because I wanted to forever remember the sadness and outrage of those first few days of the last week of May 2020.

MinnPost allows for long quotations, in-depth reporting, and lots of photographs. Over the past couple of years for *MinnPost*, I've talked to hundreds of people about their lives and covered dozens of stories about all sorts of topics, including climate grief, poverty, housing, environmental activism, anti-Semitism; gun violence and gun control; toxic masculinity and sexist male behavior; the Hiawatha Avenue homeless encampment; immigrant and refugee rights; Somali Independence Day; Frederick Douglass's "What to the Slave Is the Fourth of July?"; the Minneapolis GLBT Pride and May Day parades; the inaugural Indigenous Women's March and Indigenous People's Day in Minneapolis; the Women's Marches; the systemic racism behind evictions in North Minneapolis; the hip-hop architecture movement; the Humanize My Hoodie movement; the Black Lives Matter movement (interviews with the so-called Mall of America 11, a profile of KMOJ-FM, interviews with Black women business owners, and Black Lives Matter leader/activist/ attorney Nekima Levy Armstrong); the opening of the Minnesota African American Heritage Museum and Gallery; the Facing Race antiracism and activism awards; the Liberian immigration movement; and a truly heinous Trump rally at Target Center that left me slightly pepper-sprayed and severely humanity-disillusioned.

For the most part, I've focused much of my recent journalism work on communities and causes whose stories too often don't get told due to the media's omnipresent "white gaze," as Toni Morrison so perfectly put it. Me, I love disappearing into myself and walking up to a stranger who might not look anything like me, making solid eye contact ("Here's my card; I'm a journalist, not a creep"), and asking him, her, or them about their lives and what they want people to know about their story.

As always, I'm working on being a better writer, thinker, and person. I'm happy to have had people tell me my words have meant something to them over the years, fulfilling a dream come true that was probably hatched during the nun poem production party:

a dream of becoming a local writer who writes local stories about local humans for local human publications.

These days I continue to write, and to write it out. I still try to write from a primary place of raw wonder and love, and as I've been going through the stories that make up this collection, it's easy to see that I've written to keep my chin up, to make sense of the world, to feel less alone, to put it down for history, and to stay curious.

"We are [creation] machines," said Andy Warhol. "My favorite place to visit is inside me," said Yoko Ono. Both are artistic and humanistic tenets to which I adhere, too, and about which I preach constantly, but the outside world is rich with people and their stories. Which is to say that I've worked as a newspaper columnist and a trained journalist, but I'm also a good wallflower and observer, and I was born with a calling to try to go as deep as the songwriters, poets, writers, and great columnists I've listened to, read, and written about, and with a passion to write and report about spirituality, seekers, religion, human growth, human behavior, and the soul.

More than anything, I've tried to be a good listener and observer, with a penchant for making mountains out of minutiae.

1

. . .

STAY WARM

ON THE COLDEST NIGHT OF THE MINNESOTA WINTER SO FAR IN 2015, as some God-avenging assassins 4,300 miles away in Paris were about to kill the bodies if not spirits of a bunch of alternative journalists, the likes of which all over the world have always been counted on to comfort the afflicted and afflict the comfortable and champion weird people, ideas, art, music, books, politics, spirituality, and lives, I waited in line at the counter of a gas station on Forty-sixth and Nicollet in South Minneapolis, when I heard the pretty blonde Lutheran-looking female customer and handsome brunette Middle Eastern–looking male clerk exchange a parting shot that, hear ye hear ye, is all the rage here in frozen tundraville.

"Stay warm."

"You guys," I said, as the woman turned for the door, and I let it be known that I'd been counting the times I've heard strangers and loved ones use "Stay warm" in place of "Goodbye" or "Take care" over the past few weeks, and no, I said, it's nothing new, but it's worth pointing out that it's happening, and I am encouraged by any trend where random people are randomly kind to one another.

Ice broken, the customer and the clerk asked what my "Stay warm" count was. I said I'd lost track, it was so damn many times.

We all had a laugh, the woman and I exchanged "Stay warms," I paid for my Mountain Dew, and the clerk and I exchanged bright

9

eyes, big smiles, and "Stay warms." As I walked away, a tiny Ethiopian-looking woman who'd been standing silently behind me in line approached the counter, chuckled, and said, whimsically and in a voice just above a whisper, "And now you have to count two more 'Stay warms.'"

We all had another laugh, and I told her, yes, so I did and so I would, and we all had another laugh and another round of "Stay warms" as I hit the door.

It was a silly sitcom, I swear: a big beautiful bunch of coincidences as far as I or even the most metaphysically trained could tell, not exactly anything to write home much less a column about—until I got back in my car and turned on the ignition in the dark frigid night and, yes, out of the dashboard comes the sound of The Current's Mary Lucia telling everybody how brutally cold it is and signing off with the message for the mess age:

"Stay warm."

The day after the shootings in Paris, the *New York Times*'s Nicholas Kristof used the word *otherize* in describing how we treat one another nowadays, that is, our practice of making enemies and boxing in strangers based on snap judgments, skin color, politics, religion, sports, etc. The same day, *The Onion* succinctly summed up the collective soul-suckery that has become our daily bread and news feed: "Mankind Tired of Having to Remind Itself of Good in World."

This just in: "Minneapolis Man's 'Stay Warm' Research Suggests Humanity Not Quite on Ropes."

True story. Time and again I've heard the, yes, warmth in people's voices, and with every exchange on display has been the sort of kindness, caring, and connection that proves that there's another side of humanity, another way to go, and that people instinctively desire to feel the oneness and love that come with being part of the human race.

"Stay warm" is a concrete participation in that simple communion.

Since just before Christmas, I've heard it repeated over and over, from the mouths of babes and grumpy old men alike: from the barista at Studio 2, from the dude holding the door for me at the

331 Club, from the doorman at First Avenue, from the guy who gladly accepted my "Stay warm" and volleyed back his own "That's the spirit," to any number of the rest of the cold, huddled masses of Minnesotans yearning to be free of another six months of subzero solitude.

Now trending, with a bullet and the hashtag #staywarm, because the world is cold and because telling a stranger to stay warm not only suggests you feel their pain and encourages both outer and inner warmth, it promotes a decided "We're all in this together" pioneer spirit. "I got you, I got this, hang in there," we're saying to one another and, with a bellows of the soul, poking encouraging pokes at the very embers of our hearts.

It's beautiful, really, and maybe even necessary to the survival of the species—because if last winter is any measure, we'll need "Stay warm" and all the variations of same we can muster this winter, including "Stay thirsty," "Stay hungry," "Stay curious," "Stay safe," "Stay free," and my friend Nic's favorite, "Stay hard." Me, I'm sticking with "Stay warm"—left up to personal interpretation for all, as we and we alone get to decide what or who best keeps us warm—and the good news is that the "Stay warm" tsunami is spreading.

I write this from the gorgeous desolation of Lutsen Mountain, one of the coldest places on the planet, where my "Stay warm" sources include the resort reservations clerk, who reports that he exchanges the mighty mantra with "two out of every five" guests checking in, and the owner of the Lockport General Store, who confirms that her customers coming off Highway 61 employ "Stay warm" the "majority of the time" and that it's special because it only happens for a short window, a "seasonal" salutation that in a few months will once again be displaced by "Take care," "Later," and "Stay cool."

I knew it! People are good! Random acts of kindness rule!

"Stay warm," she said with a wink, as icy Lake Superior howled outside her window, and so I did.

2015

Twenty-five Years of the Good Craic

"Dad, I feel dumb," I said, meekly. "I'm not smart. I don't know what's going on."

I was ten years old, the summer between fourth and fifth grade. I had my head down, standing before my father in the shag-carpeted living room of our house on Colfax Avenue in South Minneapolis.

My old man brightened, put his book down, and, come to think of it, this was the first of many good conversations I would come to have with him over the next five decades, which thankfully continue to this day.

"Read the newspaper," he said, instantly, generously, perfectly, in that encouraging lilt of his—the same lilt he used to say, with genuine wonder, "How'd you do that?" when one of his kids did something cool in school or life, followed by, "I'll be darned."

I was a kid, I was overwhelmed. I loved comic books and the Hardy Boys, and I was swimming my way through *Moby Dick* that summer, but all those real-world real-time stories felt out of reach, and I was in no hurry to join the ranks of worried adults. I wanted to be a kid; newspapers were serious business.

"It's too much. Where do I start?"

He picked up the paper and pointed at the front page. "You don't have to read every story," he said, leaning forward, keys and coins jangling in his pocket. "Just read the headline and maybe the first couple paragraphs."

So I did. Then over the years as a twice-daily newspaper reader I read all the great Minneapolis sportswriters, then started reading the rest of the paper, and was drawn to columnists like Larry Batson, Al Sicherman, Jim Klobuchar, and the syndicated Ellen Goodman, because they talked about life, themselves, their friends, families, and neighbors. I grew up reading the *Minneapolis Star* and the *Minneapolis Tribune,* and it was in the 1970s that I got addicted to the feeling of picking up a newspaper off the front step and unwrapping my daily dose of what the Irish call "the craic," or as the Urban

Dictionary has it, "the news of the day, often delivered loudly and with music and alcohol."

I cut out photos and stories from both papers and put them in scrapbooks I own to this day. Somewhere along the line, as I devoured the Minneapolis alt-weekly writers of the '80s, I figured out that writing columns about myself, my family, and neighbors might be a good way to connect and cure loneliness. I was right.

I wrote my first story for the *Southwest Journal* in the summer of 2001, a fantasy about a creature I invented, Ollie the Octopus, who lives to this day in Lake Harriet. Linda Picone, the editor at the time, said she loved the story and ran it, barely touching a word. No wonder neighborhood newspapers like the *Journal* continue to thrive amidst massive print casualties, the digital revolution, and widespread timidity and lack of creativity at the top of legacy newsrooms everywhere.

For many years now, I've poured my guts out in this space, and from time to time I've told you of my life's ups and downs. More to come. The job of a columnist, as I've always understood it, is to reveal something of yourself, to be newsy and openhearted and open-minded as a foundation, but to also have guts enough to risk putting yourself out there, laying bare your hopes and dreams and confessions, and warts and all. It requires both a sensitive nature and thick skin, and I try to balance both with my reporter's chops.

Thank you for reading all these years, and for allowing me to be a small part of your life. For a kid who still romanticizes the tactile magic of newspapers and doorstep delivery, it remains an honor I do not take for granted.

2015

"It Feels Like a Brighter Day"

There was a palpable hum on the West Bank of Minneapolis on August 9, 2016, with the largely East African neighborhood bustling with smiling walkers and shopkeepers, many of whom were undoubtedly beaming about the news that Ilhan Omar was a step closer to becoming America's first Somali American state lawmaker after winning Tuesday's three-way DFL primary race in House District 60B.

Did Omar feel the love?

"Yes, definitely. It feels like a brighter day," Omar told me the next day, sitting in her Cedar-Riverside campaign office surrounded by members of her campaign team. Secretary of State Steve Simon reports that Omar received 2,404 votes, while her opponents Mohamud Noor received 1,738 and Rep. Phyllis Kahn 1,726. Omar will be the DFL candidate on the ballot for the general election on November 8.

After one of the most talked-about races in recent Minnesota politics, a weary but excited Omar talked with the *Journal* about her historic win.

WALSH: You've been going hard for months, all coming to a head last night. How does it feel?

OMAR: Last night was a very emotional night. It's been a very long, exhausting campaign. We dealt with a lot, and it's really hard to be the candidate and to hold it all together and to be the person who continues to say that things are possible, and that we need to stay above all of this, and that we're not going to engage in this and we're not going to engage in that, we're just going to keep working. So last night, to be able to feel emotions was wonderful and I think therapeutic and freeing.

WALSH: Your phone died because you were getting so many texts and voicemail messages. Where have they been coming from?

OMAR: All over. I did radio interviews over the phone from Somalia and the UK and South Africa. It was really late at night for them when the results came in, and many people I found out stayed up the whole night waiting for the results. They were ecstatic when the results came in, and there was a big celebration in Mogadishu, the capital city where I was born. There were a lot of people who followed the campaign and didn't want to miss the opportunity to be the first to know. Everybody wanted to have that memory of "Where were you when the results came in?" so they just showed up.

WALSH: When you got the news that you'd won, did you think of strong women whose footsteps you may have followed in?

OMAR: It was really hard, because except for my sister, none of the women in my family who would appreciate this was able to come and witness this day with me, so that was hard. I grew up without a mother, so there were women who invested a lot of time in raising me and who enabled me to be the woman I am today, and they were not there, so that was hard.

WALSH: As your campaign has gone on, Donald Trump's campaign has been marching on in polar opposite fashion. Have you drawn any extra inspiration from that as you've gone on, and have you ruminated on the fact that he'd hate it that you won?

OMAR: I think we put hope in the people of our district and our state and the America we all came to seek refuge in. I'm not only Muslim Somali East African, but I'm visibly Muslim Somali East African, and our goal has been to get people to not only tolerate that or overlook that but to celebrate that. Everybody who has joined in and pushed us to victory has actually believed in what it could mean to elect someone who [offers] a more visible diversity at our capitol that could instill hope and be an inspiration for a lot of young girls and young women who are being tormented for looking like me. I think in the era of Donald Trump, that sends a clear message that that's not what we're about. We are much better, and greater.

WALSH: You've talked about unity and how you want to be a voice for everyone. That's the immigrant story in this country when it comes to leadership. What do you want to do with your position and what are your main goals going forward?

OMAR: I think with my position I want to help build power for communities that are often powerless and voiceless in our state. I want to be able to push forth our progressive agenda and I want to create a more collaborative environment where people see themselves in politics and see themselves as part of the solution.

WALSH: Thanks to the example set by her mom, your daughter is going to have a completely different life and experience as an American from the one you've had. What do you hope for her and kids her age?

OMAR: My hope is that the road and path to a future success isn't as challenging for her as it has been for me. I think that when you're the first, there's a lot of pressure in regards to the way you would serve the community. For me, the pressure I've put on myself is to run a campaign that is not only paving the way but also contributing to shattering any challenge that could ever exist and leaving enough of a trail that can be followed.

So for my daughter and other daughters and my sisters and other young women, what I hope is that they are proud that we have run a campaign that is built with integrity and grace. It's been about positivity. It's been about allowing people to step into leadership positions that they didn't think they were able to do.

When we started the campaign, it was really important for me to have young women in leadership positions within the campaign, and to be in those roles and have the pleasure of succeeding in those roles. And I think we're all the better for that, because I think they have enriched and inspired other young women who've watched them step into leadership roles and take politics seriously, and that it is possible to do things that people think you shouldn't, and that there isn't a perfect timing for being a leader.

WALSH: Since last night, have you ruminated at all on how far you've come? You spent four years in a refugee camp in Kenya, and I'm wondering if you've had a second to step back and think about your beginnings and about where you are now.

OMAR: I think of my life as chapters. I think about the chapter about prewar [in Somalia] and the lessons I learned in that chapter, and my life in the refugee camp and the lessons I learned in that chapter, and my life as a young person growing up in this country and the lessons I learned in that chapter. And I think it sort of feels like it's all been a training—a training to take on politics that isn't so kind, that isn't so "Minnesota Nice" in our district with people who are very much invested in staying the course and using dirty political tactics to continue to win and hold positions.

So I feel like after last night, a lot of people feel liberated and like they don't have to fear political backlash for believing in change, and that they don't have to be beholden to relationships, and they can actually invest in progress and a better future.

I think a lot about the people who have financially invested in our campaign. My dad was our biggest fundraiser. He's retired now, but he moved back from East Africa to help us, and because of his relationships we were able to raise money. It's interesting because these are not normally people who would invest in a campaign. But they believed, and they maxed out because they believed it was a worthy cause, and I think that's especially inspiring and uplifting, especially for our community.

WALSH: As a Muslim woman, do you have concerns about working in an arena and with a community that is historically and typically male-centered? And where did you first get the idea that such a thing could be possible?

OMAR: I don't think I've ever fit into a mold. My whole family has never fit into a mold. I come from generations of women and men who have not fit into molds. So I don't think I myself considered a lot about my gender and what that would mean. It was more about other people having the concerns, and [how] walking through that might not be much of a concern.

Everything we imagine to be challenging about being a Muslim woman running for the first time has not been much of a challenge. The things that were foreseen to be challenging, we figured out a way to overcome before big challenges arose. I knew there would be a problem with negotiating with elders, because they don't negotiate with women. So having my dad here very early on and having my male cousins coached on the need for them to step up and mediate a lot of the conflicts before they became conflicts was sort of a strategy for us. We examined the risks early on and spent lots of time trying to come up with every scenario that was bad, everything that could go wrong, and tried to come up with a plan about who could be surrogates and influencers for us.

WALSH: How does it feel to know that women and girls woke up this morning to the news that the first Somali American was about to be elected to office and are inspired by you?

OMAR: Scary. And great. I feel the weight of the responsibility and of what that means. I want to work hard to make sure that I am setting a good example for them, and I will continue to do that and make sure that their first doesn't become like a lot of other firsts, who have caused disappointments for others.

2016

Citizen Berquist: The Man with the Van

Many of the stories I've written over the years have been inspired by someone at a bar, playground, gym, restaurant, bus, or ball game saying, "You should hear this," or "You should meet my friend," or "You should write about. . . ." Monika Bauerlein, my former editor at *City Pages* and now the award-winning and conversation-changing editor of *Mother Jones* magazine, was fond of encouraging reporters to hit the streets by saying, "News doesn't happen in a newsroom." I've thought of Monika's words every time I've written about someone like Gjerry Berquist, whom I'd seen driving around town and finally got his phone number from a bartender at the Loon.

• • •

In *Plan B: Further Thoughts on Faith*, Anne Lamott states that "loving your enemies [is] nonnegotiable" and recounts the story of A. J. Muste, a Vietnam War protester who spent night after night holding a candle outside the White House. When a reporter asked Muste if he believed his action would change the government's foreign policy, the candle-holder replied, "Oh, I don't do it to change the country; I do it so the country won't change me."

Another man, another time, another war: in August 2004, Gjerry Berquist went to the Total Tool hardware store near his home in West St. Paul. He was on a mission for grease pencils and hoped to score the fluorescent multicolored kind that the highway patrol uses on crash sites. He settled for four white Markal Quick Stiks, which construction workers use to draw on metal beams. After making his purchase, he uncorked one of the pencils, walked out to his

1986 Volkswagen van, and wrote on the back window, "U.S. Troops Dead In Iraq: 1,425."

"It works pretty good," he says, a peace button affixed to his shirt, another one and an Elizabeth Dickinson for Mayor badge stuck to his backpack. "It writes nicely on the window. It's durable, but a scraper does take it off. You don't want to put it on the finish of your car, though, and you don't want to keep it on your dash, because it'll melt." As of last week, the number on Berquist's van was 1,823. The number that night on www.antiwar.com/casualties was 1,871, but who's counting? The number works out to a sold-out show at First Avenue, a capacity crowd at St. Joan of Arc church, a half-full Midway Stadium, a slow day at the Mall of America, a crowded plot at Fort Snelling, but . . . who's counting? Berquist is. But even he isn't keeping an exact tally.

"Since last fall, I might have changed the numbers maybe ten times," says Berquist, a fifty-six-year-old self-described "public policy participant" and peace activist. "At first, taking in leaps of twenties and thirties and forties, and then realizing that you've got to take a razor blade and scrape off all this. . . . After a while, I realized the exact number doesn't matter. The number is over a thousand. In fact, it's approaching two thousand." Give or take a hundred. Whatever. It's more than the get-in-and-out scenario that was promulgated in March 2003, and a couple of thousand more than when the president promised religious leaders on the eve of the invasion, "There will be no casualties."

"It's a number, and most people just shrug their shoulders," says Berquist, a native of the Iron Range. "That's disappointing. Unless we have a personal connection, somebody who has actually died in this war, I think we generally are distracted by all the other things that are going on in this world. The headlines seem to have more to do with things like Michael Jackson, when our children are over dying in Iraq.

"Nobody's talking about it. Or if they do talk about it, it's just a few moments and then it's what movie they saw, or some rock and roll band, or what really irritates me is what the Twins are doing. For the amount of time that the male population sits around talking about sports, and the thickness of the sports pages, I mean, my God. I'm not denying it fulfills something, but the time and energy and money that gets devoted to sports is unbelievable."

Who does this guy think he is? Telling us there are more important things than Michael Jackson and sports? We are at war, for God's sake. Of course we know our children are dying. Of course we know that the estimated Iraqi civilian deaths in our name is twenty-six thousand. We know, we know, we know, Citizen Berquist. How could we not?

"I don't think we do know," he says. "I don't get any indication from the headlines from any of the papers that I see that they want our population to know how many of our kids have died. I mean, during the Vietnam War on the nightly news Walter Cronkite gave a nightly count of how many Viet Cong were killed and how many Americans were killed. As it came out later, those numbers were just picked out of a hat—they didn't know how many casualties there actually were—but it tried to show by sheer numbers as to how the war was going.

"We don't want to do that now. We can't even take photographs of the caskets that are coming into the United States. We're just trying to keep it quiet, and I suspect it's for the government to try to keep everybody's enthusiasm level high. But I think sooner or later people are going to say, 'Enough. We've had enough. We've lost too many of our children. It's time to reassess why we're in Iraq, and to talk about the lies that got us into Iraq.'"

Berquist is calm, good-humored, and practical. He is no nut or truth-telling village idiot—he simply considers himself "kind of a mosquito, buzzing around the town, trying to remind people not to forget these kids." He is also an amateur radio operator, construction worker, and handyman. In the past year, he has been flipped off, called names, and thumbs-downed. He has also been given plenty of thumbs-ups, "Right on's" and "Keep it up's."

In the past two weeks, with the president's approval rating and support for the war at all-time lows, and the sudden and decided dip in ratings for conservative talk radio shows, Berquist has noticed the same signposts on a street level: the reaction to his van-o-gram has been slightly more positive, even though there are those who still want to kill the messenger.

"I've had a few encounters at gas stations with younger males that want to pick a fight with me about the fact that they have one of their relatives in Iraq right now, and I have no right to put anything on there that could be deemed as being antipatriotic," he says. "And I basically say, 'Hey, this is public knowledge. That number is out there. We all need to know this, so we can make decisions.' That usually doesn't get anywhere. They're usually shouting right away that I'm a traitor or I'm an idiot and all that other stuff. So it really doesn't matter what I say, because they've already made their mind up."

Berquist believes the war will go on for five or six more years. He's concerned about the vets who are returning home with missing limbs and shattered psyches, and the impact that will have on society. Until they're all home, though, he vows to support the troops by putting up big numbers, scraping them off, and putting bigger ones up again. Not to mention handing out spare grease pencils to anyone who might want to start a mobile riot of their own.

"I'm encouraging everyone to do this," he says. "I do some community work in St. Paul, and other things, but it hasn't been enough. This has been out of frustration. I don't watch television; I don't own a television, haven't for fifteen years. I kind of keep away from the newspapers. The companies that are funding the newspapers have a vested interest in making sure that everybody thinks everything is okay, and I just don't think that everything is okay."

2005

Misanthropes for $500, Alex

One of the most impactful books of my life was *Working* by Studs Terkel, which I read on break at my first job, as a sixteen-year-old fry cook and counter person at Red Barn, now the McDonald's on Twenty-sixth and Nicollet. My father was an employment counselor at the time, so I heard weekly stories about workers and working, and Terkel's interviews with people about what they did for a living, how they did it, and what they felt about it, all told in their own voices, pretty much hardwired me for a life of storytelling and listening. The truth is, I'd go crazy if I had to interview politicians or any other rote-talking subjects for a living, which is why I've always been drawn to talking to musicians and artists like Curtiss A.

• • •

Curtiss A hates you, but probably not as much as he hates, say, Dr. Phil, and for sure not as much as he hates Republicans—as demonstrated by the fifty-three-year-old rocker/artist/local legend's latest creation, a T-shirt emblazoned with "Kill Republicans, Not Mourning Doves" on the front, and "Start with Norm" on the back.

This is a column about Curt's obsession with *Jeopardy!* and he'll get to that, but first: "Have we forgotten that all Republicans are criminals?" he rants. "Reagan? Iran-Contra? I don't care how much everybody likes him and thinks he looks like Superman. Fuck him. Fuck Nancy. Fuck Laura [Bush], Nancy, the Bush twins; they should all be eviscerated. And Norm Coleman is spawn of the devil. If more people in Minnesota like Norm Coleman than Al Franken, then we have stopped being Minnesota Nice and we are Minnesota Satan-Worshipper. I . . . hate . . . him . . . more than life itself."

He bows his head and cackles, perhaps knowing how his words will look in print, but more likely because he doesn't give a shit. As usual, Curt is in his own world, standing in his basement playhouse amid thousands of superhero action figures, found-art works, and items of rock memorabilia that would be the supreme envy of any pop-art museum curator. But you can't go see it, because he hates you and because he doesn't want anyone but his family to know where he lives.

"I'm not a *Jeopardy!* expert, I'm just a person that likes it," he says. "In fact, I hate liking the same things that every other person likes. I don't really like having anything in common with anybody except, I guess, breathing. I don't mean I'm not a joiner. It's just that I'm not. I just hate fucking people, but I bend over backwards to be nice to 'em. It's horrible. I can't even tell you.

"I just feel total disdain for the human race. I don't like 'em. I like animals. The slice of the pie of people that I will tolerate is so small of a sliver that I don't think there's a place remote enough where I can go and be not irritated beyond belief by 'em." His hate knows a few exceptions. The front door of his house boasts a Kerry/ Edwards sign. He loves Franken ("except he said UFOs are stupid; wait'l he gets abducted") and Michael Moore ("I wish he was my brother"), and his myriad heroes (and villains) are enshrined in the basement. Photographs of the Beatles, Elvis, and '50s and '60s soul singers overwhelm the walls and ceiling, all of them guarded by a figurine army whose members include Superman, Batman, Vampirella, Green Lantern, Freud, Shakespeare, Frank Sinatra, George Burns, and the monster movie hostess Elvira. And over there, next to two mic stands, a drum kit, and a gaggle of Jesse Ventura action figures, sit autographed photos of G. Gordon Liddy and *Jeopardy!* host Alex Trebek.

"When I was a kid, I really wanted to be a game-show host," says Curt. "In later years, David Lee Roth said it, so it's really not the coolest thing to say, but it's true." Instead, he became the Dean o' Scream, the soul-shouter whose annual John Lennon tribute remains one of the most anticipated club shows of the year, the Minneapolis treasure whose 1981 album *Courtesy* received four stars from *Rolling Stone* ("same as *Rubber Soul*") and whose latest, *Make It Big*, proves that, yes, somewhere along the line, Curt should have made it big.

He has recorded every episode of *Jeopardy!* since 1983, the VCR archive of which is stored in various boxes in various rooms, along with his complete collection of David Letterman tapes, unlabeled and unwatched. He has his pet peeves: he can't stand the kids' tournament, the college tournament, *Celebrity Jeopardy!* or *Rock 'n' Roll Jeopardy!* ("Rock 'n' roll is supposed to be dumb. If you want smart guys, you should have *Jazz Jeopardy!* or *Classical Jeopardy!*"). His favorite categories are comic books, rock 'n' roll, and science fiction, but watch a show or two with him and it becomes clear that he's equally adept at sports, Shakespeare, history, geography, politics, and philosophy. He doesn't watch any other game shows, because he believes they are all a derivation of *Jeopardy!* or, as he calls it, "Jep."

Jep?

"Yeah," he says. "It's like Led Zep, and Def Lep: Jep."

These are heady days for Jep fans. Ken Jennings, a software engineer from Salt Lake City, is in the midst of an unprecedented run. As of this week, Jennings has won upward of fifty consecutive days, a feat that has brought sky-high afternoon ratings and a new viewership to the show. Jennings's expertise and poise bring to mind the 1950s game-show scandals that Robert Redford based *Quiz Show* on, and his unflappability and growing cult already evoke a certain headcase-in-the-making empathy, à la Stanley the whiz kid from *Magnolia*. (Wire stories a couple of weeks back indicated that Jennings had finally lost, albeit in an episode that has not yet aired.)

"He's a Mormon, and like all religion it's either based on alien intervention or lies," says Curt. "And yet, I kinda like him. He looks to be quite diminutive. I find him personable, and I love that he's gotten so comfortable that he's able to trade quips with Alex. And of course, he's got Alex outclassed, because I remember Alex said he only gets about 50 percent right. Alex is actually pretty irritating.

"[Jennings] is so quick on the button, and he's so practiced at it that everybody that gets on there is so intimidated by his prowess. I've read everything you can read about *Jeopardy!* and it's more popular now, and it's sad that we know that supposedly he loses on the seventy-fifth show and makes two-and-a-half million dollars or so."

Still, Curt will watch.

"TV remains, if not my best friend, one of my very, very most loyal acquaintances," he says. "I'm gonna tell you something super mental: someday, if all my plans go correctly, I would like to wind up on a desert island with all of my possessions. And a generator. Someday *Jeopardy!* will go off the air, and Dave will go off the air, and *The Sopranos* will be off, and I won't have anything to watch. I've already decided to not get into anything new. Like, this new season. I limit myself to one show, and this year it's gonna be *Desperate Housewives*.

"For a couple seconds there, I thought I was going to make some money at [music]. Thank God I didn't. I'm so irritated at show biz, but big fuckin' deal. If I had to go out now like poor Roger McGuinn

or anybody who has to go out there and play casinos or whatever. . . .
Thank God. Thank. You. God. I get to watch Jep. It's the top point
of my day. It never disappoints.

"Unless," he adds ruefully, "it's *Celebrity Jeopardy!*"

2004

Confessions of a Commodore

I think about her every year around this time, so last week, a few
decades after we parted ways, I decided to find out if she was still
alive. I thought I might get a whatever-happened-to column out of
it, but when I finally heard her voice, I realized I wanted to talk to
her about something I never talk to anyone about, because who else
on Earth would understand?

Her name was Anne Marie Harvanko. I was six years old, she
was seven, ours was an arranged romance. Don't ask how or why,
but we ended up as junior royalty in the Minneapolis Aquatennial,
representing the Boulevard Center Business Association. I wore a
commodore cap and suit, she a queen's gown and crown, and for
three weeks we sweated through daily events we got dragged to by
our moms—hers an Aquatennial-loving mother of two living vicar-
iously through her daughter, mine an Aquatennial-loving mother of
six wondering, *What the hell was I thinking when I signed up for this?*

Our job was to look royally cute at luncheons, rehearsals, nursing homes, coronations. We were crash-taught etiquette: "The boy
always escorts his queen," read the parents' handbook. "They will
be shown how to hold their queen's hand and should be instructed
that they never leave her side. Help him by teaching him to assist
his queen up and down stairs and the common courtesy of being a
gentleman. The first thing you know, it'll be automatic."

Arm in arm, we visited all the local television stations, including
the old KMSP studio in the Foshay Tower and the WTCN studio
in the Calhoun Beach Club, which at the time was hallowed home
to local legends *Lunch with Casey* and *All-Star Wrestling*. We rode
in parades and waved like we'd been taught at crowds in Hopkins

(Raspberry Festival), North Minneapolis (North Side Parade), Northeast Minneapolis (East Side Parade), and downtown Minneapolis, where our pony-theme float tooled down Hennepin Avenue and beyond, past Dayton's, Donaldson's, and the weather ball. The city was at our feet. I'm pretty sure my brothers and sisters hated my guts.

We were young. Special. Royalty. And then, after the torchlight parade—about as romantic as anything gets for a couple still fending off boy and girl germs—it was over. We never said goodbye, our parents never got us together for old times' sake, and because we played it down throughout and since, it was no big deal that we didn't stay in touch. But when I got her on the line after looking up her father in the phone book the other day ("It's kind of been downhill for you two ever since then," he cracked, before giving me her number), she gasped at the mention of my name and said she had goose bumps.

The next morning, I drove out to her home in Apple Valley. We hugged at the door. She put out Rice Krispie bars, brownies, and coffee. We sat at her dining room table, on top of which rested a yellowed article about six- and seven-year-old us from the *Minneapolis Star* and a black-and-white photograph of us in full junior royalty regalia, wearing expressions that suggested we could break into a medley of "Anywhere's Better Than Here," "You Get Paid to Smile," and "The Ballad of JonBenét" at the drop of a corsage.

"We were special, but we weren't quite sure why," she said, her auburn eyes and hair still beautiful, neither one of us able to fully get our minds around the adult us now before us. "I hated it, and yet I liked being special. Getting that hair permed—I can still smell it. And I had to wear white gloves all the time . . . . I remember the Queen of the Lakes, and how beautiful she was, and I always wanted to be Queen of the Lakes. My mother always wanted to be Queen of the Lakes, but her mother—strict Catholic upbringing—didn't believe in beauty pageants."

She's on her third marriage; I'm on my first. She's got three kids; I've got two. She'll be a grandmother for the first time next week and her youngest just graduated from high school; my youngest would kill for the gown and tiara she wore during our Aquatennial heyday.

She works as a CPA, takes night classes, and, frankly, unlike the recovering suburban beauty queen I might have expected, she's got soul, the kind that's readily evident upon (re)meeting her. "I've always done what I've had to do," she said, jutting her jaw out slightly. "Whatever it's taken."

We compared notes on what it all meant. She talked about how her dad used to embarrass her by telling potential boyfriends, "You know, she was a princess." I told her how I distinctly remember at the end of the three weeks, standing on a stage with the rest of the commodores and princesses, waiting to be crowned to go on to the next round of junior fabulousness. When they put the white hat and crown on some other couple, I felt like I'd let everybody down, because by the end I didn't try to hide that I wasn't into it, that I wasn't trying my hardest to be a perfect little gentleman. I felt like the judges had looked into my soul and seen what I'd known all along: I wasn't special and I didn't do anything to deserve any of this.

We asked each other the unanswerable: did three weeks of adults fussing over us and other kids looking at us with awe/confusion/ jealousy hardwire us for a life of insatiable attention-getting? Did it make us restless? Did it lead to a life of viewing all pomp and circumstance with skepticism? Did it spark my love affair with the city, and her appetite for skating and theater? Did I truly help her up and down the stairs? Did it ever become automatic?

Mercifully, the Aquatennial powers that be discontinued the junior royalty part of the Aquatennial a couple of years ago. So when I go to the parades now with my wife and kids, there are no scenes of uncomfortable kids in monkey suits between the clowns and bands. But every July for as long as I live, I'll remember her smile, and how she looked next to me on that float. And now, since last week, I've got another memory, of her sitting in an easy chair in her living room, knitting and asking me to tell her something, anything, about myself, as if it might provide a clue to what makes her tick and this odd little moment we shared.

After a couple of hours we said goodbye. We hugged at the door. Neither one of us suggested a follow-up date, but I held her face in my hand for a second, just in case I lost touch with my queen again.

2004

The Santa Claus Diaries

There's this game I play with Matty, my four-year-old nephew. He grabs me by the scruff of my shirt, just like Michael Keaton does in the television commercial from the film Matty hasn't been able to bring himself to see yet ("too scary"), and we stand nose to nose until I say "Wh-wh-who are you?" in my most terrified tone. For a few thousand seconds, Matty stares me down, timing impeccable, intensity unyielding, and finally whispers:

"I'm Batman."

Matty loves his superheroes—Superman, Aquaman, Spiderman —but his fave these days is (who else?) Santa Claus. Faster than a Ghostbusters trap, more powerful than a Ninja Turtle, Matty can't read yet, and his psyche would probably be shattered if he knew his uncle was Santa Claus, so I'm trusting you with the following: by sheer luck, I scored one of the most prestigious gigs an inexperienced but thoroughly willing Santa could hope for—the day shift at Dayton's eighth floor auditorium in downtown Minneapolis.

Deep down, I've always been fascinated by department store Santas. I've always wanted to know what life is like in their big black boots, and now, for the next three weeks, I'm the man. If anyone asks, just grab 'em by the shirt and tell 'em wh-wh-who I am.

I'm Santa Claus.

Monday

I got on the bus this morning and studied my set of suggested clauses, given to me by Trixie, the young woman who runs the show at Dayton's. The rules are pretty meticulous: "Never allow the child

to think or feel you aren't real; remember, once the costume is on—
you are Santa Claus. Keep in character at all times: you never know
who may be near. Drinking alcoholic beverages before or during
your shift is cause for immediate termination . . . . Use good judg-
ment if you're out the night before, also. Never promise a child anything. Be aware of your hand positions as you lift or hold a child.
Try to remind children, 'Santa loves you.'"

I was a little nervous. Years ago, I played Kris Kringle in a grade
school play (I got to kiss Patti Larkin on the cheek and I decorated
my red Kris Kringle corduroys with cotton balls for a truly elfin
effect), but until today that was it. As I changed into my gear—
padding, beard, wig, hat, suit, spats, and belt) and rubbed rouge on
my cheeks and white greasepaint on my eyebrows, I got tips from
Bob, a veteran Santa. Bob addressed me as "Santa Jim" at one point;
he said it in the way you might call someone "father" or "padre" or
"sister." Apparently this is a pretty sacred fraternity I've hitched up
with. Bob and Trixie told me not to worry, that I was going to be
great. Then they threw me to the wolves.

For the first hour, a whole series of kids cried, screamed, kicked,
and clawed to get away from Santa Jim. Trixie, who acts as photographer and cashier as well as Queen of Santa's Helpers, said I was
doing fine. But she admitted it was weird—she'd never seen such a
long string of frightened kids.

These kids weren't just scared; they were freaked. I started taking it personally. I thought they were on to me—they sensed I was
a fake, a paper Santa. One kid said I was only dressed like Santa. I
choked. I asked him old he was.

The breakthrough came when a five-year-old girl climbed up
on my lap, huge eyes lit up so bright they looked almost artificial.
I asked her what she wanted for Christmas and she said sweetly,
"Nothing—I have everything I want." When I asked her if she was
sure, she reconsidered and said modestly, "Weeeelll . . . some new
mittens."

That was it? Nothing else? She scrunched up her face, thought
for a second. "A notebook," she finally added. I gave her a Cinderella

coloring book. She hugged me and waved goodbye, and the next bunch of kids jumped on my lap asking for Teenage Mutant Nintendo Super Mario Barbies, there was still a lump in Santa Jim's throat.

Tuesday

Hung around after my shift tonight to watch Bud, who along with Bob and Howard is one of the kings of Dayton's Santas. Bud was interviewed by WCCO-AM on Thanksgiving night, and *Life* magazine is planning a spread on him for December 1990, titled "A Day in the Life of Santa Claus." Bud's a pro, a Santa's Santa. He's been doing it for eight years, and as I sat talking with him in the dressing area tonight, he actually became Santa Claus upon donning the wig and beard. (Me, I became a guy in a Santa suit.) I'm getting pretty good at making the kids feel comfortable, but I haven't really found my groove yet. At least I'm calm. Late today, I mustered my first respectable "Ho-Ho-Ho," but it was lame compared to Bud's naturally jolly laugh.

It's a little hard to believe, but every Santa I work with seems genuinely to want to impart a certain amount of magic. Sitting for four hours a day in the Clan of the Santa Bear (mercifully the little rodent has been shelved this year), I thought I'd be sickened by the commercialization of Christmas. I expected a "herd 'em in and herd 'em out" ethic, but I've been pleasantly surprised.

For example, there are two working Santas per shift at Dayton's, but you'll never see them in the same room together because of the two sets of curtains, two aisles, and two separate rooms where the kids come to visit. (It's an experience not unlike Catholic confession.) And when Santa goes on lunch break in the middle of his five-hour shift (I'm told the mall Santas work four hours straight, which no doubt makes for some pretty cranky Santas), everyone makes a big deal about how "Santa's going to feed the reindeer now."

I blew the reindeer thing today. A seriously dubious kid asked me how many reindeer I had, and I blanked. "Twelve, of course," said Santa Fake, whose dog had obviously eaten his notes on reindeer lore. The kid looked at me suspiciously, so I quickly added, "But I use eighteen on Christmas Eve, because I have so many toys." That seemed to genuinely intrigue him. I know it's eight; I had a weak moment followed by panic, that's all. Anyway, I think he bought it. Which brings up the credibility thing. Most babies are just there—they have a great time tugging at your beard, and they'll gladly sit still for the picture, because they have no clue about what's going on. One- and two-year-olds are absolutely terrified: even if they make it up on to your lap, there's no guarantee that they'll stay there long enough for a picture or chitchat. Three-year-olds straddle the line between terror and wonder, and four- and five-year-olds are the most fun: they believe in you with all their hearts, they're fairly bold, and they know exactly what they want for Christmas. With kids six, seven, and beyond, you run into growing skepticism.

Wednesday

Sheer chaos greeted me as I got off the elevator on this, the morning of the Feast of St. Nicholas. One of Dayton's heinous thirteen-hour sales was in its first hour, and the line to see Santa and the Cinderella display was backed up past the elevators and wrapped around the escalator. "Poor sod," I thought of the Santa, who would see 150–200 kids during his four-hour shift. Then I realized that poor sod was me. In I trudged.

Every morning as I put on my costume, I'm struck how this place sounds like a doctor's office. If you close your eyes, you'd swear you were in the waiting room of an infirmary during a mass flu vaccination. Moms' soothing voices go, "It'll only take a second, honey, he won't hurt you," which inevitably is followed by shrieks, wails, and babes' sonic "Noooo's!" All for what? A photo.

The picture is everything. At the expense of all else—the kids' emotional well-being, Santa's thighs, knees, shins, and sanity—everything revolves around getting the picture and preserving the memory of how it really wasn't: "Here, Joey, look over here!" they cry; "Smile, Joey! C'mon, Joey! If you don't sit on Santa's lap, Santa won't bring you anything." (I always stay Silent Santa Jim on that one.)

This morning, one especially idiotic dad tried to get his son to smile by doing a dance that made me want to laugh and puke at the same time. Then, this afternoon, I spent fifteen minutes with four creepy thirtysomething moms and their screaming, petrified kids. To the moms, I was a prop to be folded, spindled, and mutilated any which way they wished. To the kids, I was Freddie Krueger in a red suit. When they're that scared, the advice from the Santa experts is to become neutral and remain passive. Don't reach out for the kids: let the parents run the show.

But obnoxious parents are the exception not the rule. Most of them appreciate it when you're patient and gentle and you try to talk the kid into a picture ("I want to bring a copy of it up to the North Pole to show Rudolph," I sometimes say). The fear probably wouldn't be so intense if the operation wasn't so intimate. The kids stand in line, jumping up and down, rehearsing what they're going to say to Santa, and the anticipation drives them over the edge. Though I haven't yet received the professional Santa's official baptism (no one's wet their pants on me yet), a two-year-old did some serious drooling on my hand yesterday.

Trixie says the event is easier for the kids at malls, where Santa is in full view and they can get a good long look at the big guy as they wait in line. They see other kids sitting and talking with Santa, whereas in the downtown store they're sequestered until the moment of truth. When they turn that corner and come face to face with the almighty and powerful Claus, it's a mindblower.

Another element of the fear factor is the contradictory messages the Santa trip sends out. After Trixie and I weathered a seemingly endless sequence of scared kids today, she pointed out that we confuse our children by telling them to be very afraid of strangers and then insisting they sit on this weird guy's lap and have a picture taken with him. The reality of that paradox is never too far away: I sit in the chair every day with a poster of a smiling Jacob Wetterling positioned just to the left of the camera.

Thursday

One of the most bizarre aspects of this gig is going out on lunch break and moving, ghost-like, amid my "victims." Unseen. Unheard. Uncostumed. Invisible.

Call it Santa paranoia, but today when I was eating lunch in the first-floor deli, I think one of the kids I had just had on my knee (he asked me for a candy cane and I told him I had a house full of 'em at the North Pole) recognized me. He was sitting in a booth facing me, and he gave me the twice-over and looked hard at my semi-white eyebrows and still-rouged cheeks. He started tugging at his mom—I think he was about to blow my cover—but mom was dealing with his crying baby brother, and told the would-be snitch to shut up.

One of the younger Santas told me he enjoys milking this alter ego for all its worth. When young women come up to sit on this guy's lap and ask him for Porsches and men, he'll flirt with them later as they shop. Out of costume, he approaches them with something like "I'm sorry to hear you've not been a good girl this year, but Santa promises to bring you the Porsche you asked for anyway." The surprised women, this propositional Claus contends, love it.

Friday

Finally, today Santa Jim got a little grumpy. Throughout this first week, I've chosen not to think about the real reason why the kids love me—because, truth be told, I'm the Great Buddha of Gimme. Anyway, today I started thinking about it and it got to me, brought Cranky Santa Jim down.

Then, about a half-hour into my shift that feeling evaporated. A group of ten deaf kids came in with their teachers. They pawed at me and hugged me and kissed me and all at once bombarded me with lyrical grunts and indecipherable wishes. They told me what they wanted by way of their teachers' sign language, and I told them what Rudolph and the elves had been up to. As they left, one of the teachers showed me how to sign "I love you" (at first, I did it with just the forefinger and pinky—like the metal "Rock with

Satan"—until the teacher told me to extend my thumb), and they squealed with delight. It was pretty cool.

So I guess it hasn't been all that disillusioning. For every greedy kid who's rattled off a list of expensive wants like a human fax machine, there have been just as many moments when I've looked into some kid's eyes and seen unconditional love. And some of the requests have been downright charming.

There was the steely-nerved five-year-old girl who jumped up on my lap and blurted, "I want a computer that talks back to me when I talk to it and a goat named Sparkley," and dashed away. There was the little boy who stood in front of me trembling violently, held my hand, and despite his trepidation was determined to recite his Christmas list. There was the little girl who wanted only a doll for her sister; the little boy who just wanted cough drops. Then there was the young lady who, after telling me her long list of very specific Christmas needs, told me, "We don't celebrate Christmas too much at my house." When I asked why, she said, "Because I'm Jewish."

There was the three-year-old girl who brought me a picture of herself and some play money to help defray the cost of my trips back and forth from the North Pole. There was the boy with cerebral palsy who slapped me five and just stood in front of me on crutches, saying "Santa Claus," over and over. There was the kid who just wanted a hole puncher; the one who wanted a screwdriver "so I can help my dad." There was the huge group of Hmong kids who didn't understand a word I said but gave me big hugs anyway. There was the little girl who whispered to me that she wanted a real bear, a real cat, a real dog, a real elephant, and a pig that oinks. And this morning an earnest little boy spread his arms as far apart as he could and asked for a cheetah "this big."

Today Howard, a ten-year Santa veteran who learned his craft while attending Santa school at Macy's in New York City, told me that masquerading as Santa "gets in your blood." I know the feeling. Right now, I'm starting to feel like one of those Elvis or Marilyn impersonators who start believing they're the real thing because so many people believe in them and give them that god-like power. Bob, another vet, says he does it because of the healing hugs he gets from the kids. I know what he means, too. I've got a few days left on this job, and I'm not sure, but if you were to ask me wh-wh-who I am at this time next year, the answer might well be the same.

I'm Santa Claus.

1989

2

. . .

NATURE CITY

MY MATERNAL GRANDPARENTS CAME FROM IRELAND/SCOTLAND/ England, my paternal grandfather came from Graceville, Minnesota, and my paternal grandmother came from Lacrosse, Wisconsin. They landed in Minneapolis, and my father was born on May 7, 1928; my mother, on December 6, 1931, both in Minneapolis.

"My mother and dad were very nice people," my father told me in 2014, just as his memory was starting to go. He recalled a time before Minneapolis was infested with traffic and congestion: "I remember playing in the neighborhood . . . running out the back door and my bike was parked right next to the stoop there, and I'd jump on that and go sailing around south of that house in what was then country and go to this old abandoned grain mill. I was with one of my best friends. And we'd play in that place, cops and robbers, with BB guns. This was Sixty-fifth and Lyndale, there were cornfields around there. I wish I was back there."

I often marvel at this place, and the fact that I landed here and have embraced it with so much passion. It's not called the Land of Ten Thousand Lakes for nothing, and, like my father and so many others, I've had an ongoing eternal boyhood romance with the nature, lakes, rivers, creeks, people, and places of my hometown since I was a boy.

Stop and Smell the Rose Gardens

One summer I found myself sitting on one of my favorite benches at the Rose Gardens by Lake Harriet. Full-on rapture mode was the order of the day, and as I savored the feast of natural beauty and sounds, two young women entered the gates. One enthusiastically tried to show her unimpressed companion the breathtaking grace of the blooming buds, but the blank-faced, slack-jawed girl didn't get it, and they left the grounds as fast as they'd come in.

I felt for the woman, who was so clearly on a mission to testify to some soul mate or another about all that useless beauty, because a similar thing happens every day in the world: you can lead a loved one to a head-spinning kaleidoscope of roses, but you can't make them take a whiff.

Which is good news, since that will keep the numbers down at what Lyndale resident Lisa Broek characterizes as "the most beautiful spot in the city." That much was certainly true Tuesday evening, as a glorious sun set into the placid lake, and Broek and her sons Max and Austin traipsed with a family friend amidst the luscious pine trees, screaming white and purple lilacs, and other fawning flora.

"It's my favorite place in the whole city," says Broek, standing under the ten-year-old crab apple tree the family planted for Broek's late husband, Alan Uetz. "I always come when the blossoms come out like this. It's like a treasure that happens once a year. I can't take in enough of the color. And there are always people here, but you can have solitude, and I never feel like we can't find a place to call our own."

In this, the Best Spring Ever, the early orgy of sunshine has provided a chance to both get away and get in touch—with yourself and nature—like few Minnesota seasons before it have. In the past two weeks, I have been accompanied to the Rose Gardens (and her sister chill-out space the Peace Garden) by friends, musical instruments, a tape recorder, a radio for the ball game, books, note pads, and with my own rapt attention to bird watchers moving at the speed of sloth.

Squirrels playing chicken. Fellow sun-worshippers resting and freeing their worried minds.

A group of Japanese tourists lingering over the lilacs and cooing over the roses. Chirping teenage girls at a Somali wedding. A couple of hippie-punk kids setting up hammocks in the pines. Languid semi-games of badminton, soccer, golf, catch. Kids dancing, running, flipping.

Musicians, playing quietly. Listeners, thanking musicians. Strangers, interacting.

A gaggle of party girls who swear they saw gnomes tripping through the pines one day last week. A stranger who walked by, did a double take between me and the sunset and said, "It doesn't get much better than this."

Which is what I've been thinking; so far the only comparison to the Rose Gardens (née, officially, Lyndale Park, off King's Highway between Forty-first and Forty-second Streets) I can come up with is Northern California, which melds a similar burst of water, woods, and majestic colors. And author and journalist Jay Walljasper, who visits the Rose Gardens several times a week, discovered a kindred touchstone last year.

"I had the good fortune to have to go to Rome and write a story about public spaces, urban planning, and the soul of the city," said Walljasper, his family lolling on a food- and drink-strewn picnic blanket across the way. "Of course, Rome is nothing like Minneapolis, but when I got home I started thinking about what the Minneapolis version is of the piazza, which is the great Roman institution where everybody hangs out. And I decided that clearly the Rose Gardens is Minneapolis's piazza. On a beautiful spring day, it's where everybody wants to be."

Not everybody. Thankfully, not everybody.

"The Rose Gardens for me is an urban retreat from this fast life," said musician, writer, and student Pete Christensen, who tries to get to his favorite meditative spot at least once a day. "It's a place where I can go to escape from the trappings of the mind, and just be present with the beauty of the surroundings and the glimmer of the lake through the trees."

2010

Lucky Us

The summer sun came out for a couple of hours Saturday evening, and so I grabbed the dog and headed to my favorite spot on the planet, Lake Harriet, which has been overrun by thousands of skaters, bicyclists, runners, walkers, swimmers, and tourists ever since President Barack Obama stood on the bandshell stage a few weeks ago and told 3,500 people, "I'm here to say don't get cynical. America is making progress," and made this lake all the rage.

"Progress" is why I've been avoiding it during the daylight hours of late, choosing instead to take in all her glories well after midnight, when there are no people anywhere and the lushness, stillness, and sound of wildlife and insect songs make for the most perfect meditative place a city dweller could ever hope to bask in.

"Solitude gives birth to the original in us, to beauty unfamiliar and perilous," wrote Thomas Mann, a truth every kid with a crayon and a couple of hours alone knows by heart, and it was with this mindset that I set out on Saturday.

I had spent much of my week writing about attorneys, the law, and the terrible things people do to one another, so I was in the mood for no interactions, opinions, stories, or egos and embarked on a mission to save my own soul and refuel my inner juices so as to rejoin the rest of the pack in a day or so.

But as I walked closer to the Rose Gardens and the beckoning sunset, it was clear the universe had other ideas. The horde had taken over my normally spacious and people-free park. The surrounding streets were choked with parked cars, and a wedding or some other celebration was underway. I kept going, straight into the maw, when I was gifted with a mini miracle.

There, flitting upon the July grass amid the rose bushes, bunnies, and birds were modern dancers telling the story of the human condition with precise, passionate movement. I stopped, stared, and held my breath. The dancers of all ages and styles were accompanied by live and recorded jazz, classical, rock, and hip-hop, and their sunset-kissed bodies melded with the earth easily, naturally, magnificently.

I later learned they were part of the Christopher Watson Dance Company's thirteenth annual Dances at the Lakes Festival, which featured professional and student dancers from Minnesota and California, culled from modern dance companies such as Anda Flamenco, Ballet Arts Youth Ensemble, Young Dance, Youth Dance Ensemble, Ballare Teatro Performing Arts Center, Brownbody, and Kinetic Evolutions.

As I stood there, eyewitness to a display of timeless human grace straight out of ancient Greece or Stonehenge, I couldn't imagine a more beautiful moment or a more perfect setting, and I had one thought wash over me: how did we get so lucky?

Two nights earlier, ten miles away in North Minneapolis, more shootings. At the very same moment on the very same planet, Israel and Palestine declared war, again. Meanwhile, we here in our perfect little burg known as South Minneapolis regularly walk out the front door of our mansions to not only a cornucopia of nature, but to the embarrassment of riches that is the free music and other performances at outdoor stages all summer long.

We're spoiled and jaded, straight up. Every day we're privy to numerous concerts by talented, innovative, and committed artists (as well as prosaic, safe, and just plain boring, but I'll save my "When Bad Music Happens to Good Sunsets" column for another day), and I for one have been taking it for granted. For sure, those dancers and musicians rekindled something in me that not even silence or a spiritual practice can, and I plan to carry its grace with me always.

To not take a moment and be grateful for it, to not say out loud, "Thank you for the reminder of humanity at its most fiercely optimistic," is the only definition of sin I know of and adhere to, and so I'm doing it here.

Thanks, universe. I needed that.

2014

Summer of the Super Sunsets

Riffing on the idea that happiness and a joyful state of being is a choice, *Star Tribune* business columnist and apparent Zen master Harvey Mackay recently concluded, "So now that you know what finding your bliss could do for your quality of life, why wait? Organize your life so you have time to do the things you love. I am not advocating you abandon all responsibility. Life's pressures are going to prevent you from playing golf seven days a week, and even sunsets start to look alike after a while. However, the more attuned you are to what truly makes you happy, the more your life will align itself with the things you value and treasure."

Wise words from the power-of-positive-thinking-swim-with-the-sharks guru, though I'm here to disagree with his take on sunsets, which I got and remain deeply attuned to this historically glorious Minnesota spring and summer—the most sun-dappled in a decade, according to the experts.

By a conservative estimate, I've borne witness to roughly sixty-five of the most magnificent and memorable sunsets of my life this year, most at Lakes Harriet and Isles, and every one different—due to the mindset I brought to each (meditative, grateful, contemplative, quiet) and the ever-changing mix of the elements (water surface, cloud cover, wind, rain, etc.) on the canvas itself.

The truth is, I made time for them. Hustled down to the lake to catch just slivers of them some evenings and lingered longer for some more than others, but all provided the same focal point of healing and being. That a sunset is a spectacularly beautiful gift to all of us is hardly breaking news (especially to the many fellow sol-gawkers I saw partaking over the past few months), but because they too often get taken for granted or obliterated by the competition (cell phones, HD, life), it says here that celebrating the primal pull of sunsets is an act of faith and subversion.

By early June, my body clock was responding to the daily walk toward the light. It called to me: the end of the day and the break of night came in a feast of oranges, reds, yellows, pinks, and purples, followed by an often ominous fade to black. These days, amidst the encroaching gnats and buzzing crickets, the sun goes down at 7:30 p.m., with a slow descent that feels languid compared to July's 9 p.m. plummets into darkness, not to mention December's looming 4:30 p.m. blackouts.

Most of my sweet sixty-five I saw with my dog, who routinely took my lead, settled down, and basked. Most were viewed in front of a body of water—per the instructions of all the ancient meditation masters—and a few were witnessed with other people. Strangers, mostly.

There was the toddler mesmerized by the sheer awesomeness of the visceral blast happening in front of him, the medicinal magic of which remained oblivious to his harried, preoccupied mom. There was the gobsmacked Japanese family who couldn't take enough photographs of the simmering horizon, and the Harmon Killebrew lookalike perched nightly at South Beach, staring stoically. There were the painters, working hard with their oils and easels to capture shades of glory and shards of light for all time.

There was the sixtysomething woman wearing a teal-colored T-shirt that is given to ovarian cancer survivors who participate in Silent No More, the walk/run sponsored by the Minnesota Ovarian Cancer Alliance. When I came upon her, she was lost in a thousand-yard stare at one of my favorite spots, a concrete deck with a railing near the shoreline off the Rose Gardens.

We took our place at the rail, the dog and I. I grabbed the hot fence and did some yoga stretches. The sun was blazing and going down fast. Shhh . . .

"It's a good one tonight," I said, finally. The woman perked up and agreed enthusiastically. We murmured about the suddenly green hues reflecting off the lake, and about our favorite sunsets of yore. Then we clammed up again.

After about fifteen minutes, with the sun dipped halfway into the lake and looking like a pumpkin cookie in a glass of red wine, I got up to leave.

"Cheers," I said, popping out onto the walking path. "More to come."

The sunset silhouetted her and blinded her face from me, but even so I could see her brilliant smile.

"Yes, yes," she said. "Many more."

2012

Seize the Light

In these dog days of winter, when the great indoors can be both refuge and holding cell, I have to remind myself to get out there and battle/embrace the elements, because you never know what experiential treasures await, like the kind I had in St. Paul the other day, when my dog Zero and I had a city adventure that we still talk about, that we still shoot for.

It was a little after 5 p.m. The sun was going down at the dog park at Lake of the Isles, which is where he goes to get wild, and where the other humans and I go to be joined in the very simple and civilized act of making our animals happy. More often than not, real peace happens there.

As the dogs romped and their owners shuffled, the natural light of the sundown-moonrise made a crystalline canvas of downtown Minneapolis on the lake horizon. The bright blue, silver, and aqua glass panels of the skyscrapers refracted off the white snow, and as darkness descended, I noticed a long row of tiny lights snaking out across the white terrain. From a distance, it looked like fifty of Orion's belts had fallen to earth, or a UFO landing runway was forming on the lake.

Enthralled, I grabbed the dog and we made our way down through the trees, past the shoreline, and onto the lake. I took off his leash and he darted across the ice, a galloping and free black streak that briefly disappeared into the darkness. When he returned, silhouetted by the glowing skyscrapers and framed by a canopy of pine trees jutting out from the middle of the lake, I called his name. He stopped in his tracks, raced back to me, and then made a beeline to a pyramid of candles in the distance.

I followed him and quickly found myself amid a gaggle of

shadowy figures hovering around the pyramid, which was made of hundreds of glass luminaries. The quiet of it all was eerie, moon-like, and broken only by the shush-shush of cross-country skiers, who motored past in the darkness alone or with sled dogs, and only then did I realize that Z and I had found ourselves in the middle of the Luminary Loppet, which has been going strong in the middle of Uptown since 2002.

We were Loppet virgins and came away impressed with the cross-country ski events, and forever changed and awed by the holy stillness of all that candlelight and natural beauty. There was something truly ancient in how reverent and meditative the skiers and nonskiers alike regarded the churchlike scene, which has to be one of the most photographed of all local winter wonders. This year's Loppet has been moved to Theodore Wirth Park due to balmy weather and thin ice, and this week's column is to implore you to get out of your winter funk and go see the lights.

That's what a gang of us did a couple of weeks ago, at the Red Bull Crashed Ice extreme sports event, which basically consisted of a bunch of dudes from all over the world in hockey gear flying and stumbling down an ice ramp that resembled thirty Minnesota State Fair Big Slides stitched together with chicken wire.

The scene that invaded John Ireland Boulevard in St. Paul that weekend was pure *Chronicles of Narnia* meets *Slap Shot-Rollerball,* what with the floodlights, star-studded night sky, capitol dome aglow on the horizon, and a spirit of oneness among the gathered that suggested they knew they were into something good, silly, fleeting, and super-soulful.

The smell of mini donuts and hot chocolate spiked the nostril-pinching air. NBC cameras captured the action and broadcast high-lights on a jumbotron above the starting gate as leather-lunged youths wearing high school hero jackets on their backs and dead furry pelts on their heads pounded the ramp with faux enthusiasm. Saint Peter, Saint Paul, various angels and demons, and God himself lorded over the proceedings from the ornate exterior of the eighty-five-year-old cathedral that looms over the twinkling capitol city.

People were jumping up and down to keep the blood moving.

Inside the church, some folks warmed up in the pews and took in the quiet, away from the Red Bull numbers. Some lit candles. Some toured the stained glass and bronze-encased shrines of the saints. Some knelt in front of the nativity scene, said their prayers to baby Jesus, then bolted out the door in hopes of seeing Igor from Slovenia do another face plant or back flip onto the ice ramp.

2012

Loving Lake Harriet

The muggy night of July 6, 2012, came with stay-inside heat warnings and, no joke, air as thick and oppressive as any rainforest or moss-draped bog you can name. But sailboats and seagulls surfed a nice breeze coming off Lake Harriet, bicyclists and skaters tooled along sluggishly, and holding forth on the bandshell stage was the Snaps, led by sixty-year-young local rocker Robert Wilkinson, who ended the set by getting a gaggle of sweaty kids to dance to David Bowie's 1974 anthem to androgyny, "Rebel Rebel."

I'd like to say it was in that moment that I realized I was falling in love with Lake Harriet all over again, with my dog and bike at my side and Wilkinson and bassist Jenny Case howling, "You got your mother in a whirl / She's not sure if you're a boy or a girl" to a small but hardy heat-braving crowd of all ages and races. The truth is that there have been countless small but memorable miracles like that at Harriet this summer, with more guaranteed to come—as long as you're paying attention.

A few hours after the chiming guitars of "Rebel Rebel" faded with the sunset, a Kingfield man and woman were cited for indecent exposure by Minneapolis police for swimming naked in pitch-black Harriet. More power and Patrick Scully–inspired nudist life-as-art to my fellow nightswimming brother and sister, for it says here that those feral kids were scapegoats at worst and an anomaly at best: while it's still patrolled by too many "On your left" hall monitors and other assorted buzz-killers and anti-fun watchdogs, it's no exaggeration to say that Lake Harriet is currently undergoing a return to freedoms reminiscent of the '70s.

Check it out. The lifeguards, once the enemy of every playful soul in South Minneapolis, are chill or nonexistent. The cops and park police troll Lake Harriet Parkway, but by all accounts they do their job and serve and don't hassle. DIY lemonade stands dot the shoreline, sunsets at South Beach have been hypnotic, medicinal, blazing, worshipful, and dogs and floaties share the water with freaks and families.

The Peace and Rose Gardens are becoming regular go-to havens for bird-watchers, and the past few weeks have seen a spate of urban jungle wildlife sightings, including owls, blue herons, and deer. A beekeeping and pollination fest is happening there this week, for Andy Griffith's sake, and a sign near the bandstand promises, "Coming This Fall! Pumpkin Patch! Inflatables! Hay Rides!"

For the moment, the hibiscus tea at the bandshell is crazy refreshing; the trolley rides are routinely trippy; the Turtle Park renovation looks to be going swimmingly; you never know who you'll run into around the next bend; and there still may be no more erotic taste in the world than sand mixed with Lake Harriet popcorn.

Established in 1883 (as the stone monument on South Beach boasts), the 470 acres of lushness that is Lake Harriet was named for Harriet Lovejoy, wife of Colonel Henry Leavenworth, who founded Fort Snelling. It comes with more than a bit of nostalgia for me these days, especially on a day like the Fourth of July, when we lollygagged with the neighbors in the Rose Gardens, then meandered down to North Beach, where the kids jumped, dove, and wrestled each other off the dock, just like my parents did, and just like I did with my brothers and sisters in summers of yore.

This scorcher is shaping up to be equally special. A couple of nights after the Snaps, I returned to the bandshell and happened on Jazz on the Prairie, a terrific eighteen-piece big band that played swing and jazz tunes by the likes of Benny Goodman, Count Basie, and Duke Ellington. I made a point to call my mom and dad then and there, lingered over the growing collection of sweet, sad, funny, and altogether ruminative bandshell bricks and pavers, then finished the night with time alone at my new favorite bench, located by the Elf Door and just off the walking path near a plaque that reads "Mindful of Family and Friends Who Have Finished the Course."

I looked out on the water, that chameleonic body of water I have thousand yard–stared down countless times, and felt lucky to be alive yet again—so much so that I let the mosquitoes feast on me for a while before heading home.

2012

Harriet Lovejoy Was Here

The ice was finally off Lake Harriet Sunday night, so as I took in the sunset from my favorite sunset-watching bench facing South Beach, I decided to hold a séance and call up the lake's namesake, Harriet Lovejoy Leavenworth. Lo and behold, the lady of the lake rose up from the swimming area and hovered over a freshly shorn tree stump on the beach. I turned on my recorder. . . .

JIM: Whoa and wow! Good evening, Ms. Lovejoy.

HARRIET: Happy sundown, Mr. Jim. Yet another beautiful one. Can you believe they tore down that tree? It hung over this lake for decades, but now the vista of the beach horizon is all the grander, and people have been using the stump as a prop for photographs with the downtown skyline and lake.

JIM: So good to see and hear you! I must say I'm surprised you answered my call. I've tried to contact you in the past, but . . .

HARRIET: That awful John C. Calhoun got so much publicity in the past few years that I felt it was about time I make an appearance. So much has been made about his being a racist and segregationist, but what you might not know is that, like a lot of men then, he made Bill Cosby and Harvey Weinstein look like choirboys.

JIM: I can imagine. I'm glad to finally get a chance to talk to you. You've always haunted this place. Your name is everywhere in Minneapolis, yet the history books barely mention you. You don't even warrant a Wikipedia entry, yet the so-called jewel of the Minneapolis lakes and all her progeny are named for you.

HARRIET: *History* books. You said it. I was a woman and it was a man's world. Times have changed, thank goddess.

JIM: You're a woman of mystery, for sure. All we know is that you were the third wife of Henry Leavenworth, a soldier famous for fighting in the War of 1812 and fighting alongside the Sioux Indians in the Arikara War of 1823 and building Forts Snelling and Leavenworth. By all accounts your love was strong. It survived separation by the wars, and you were widowed in 1834. Everybody called you "Mrs. L." Soldiers described you as a Florence Nightingale figure who helped heal the troops with courage and compassion—a fitting profile of this lake's heroine. But there's no record of why it was named for you.

HARRIET: I have no idea. I'm not sure I ever even visited it. I suppose it was a way to honor . . . my husband? I guess I'm honored, but it's sort of embarrassing. I hear there are streets, bars, beers, and restaurants named after me?

JIM: Dogs, cats, guinea pigs, churches, songs, schools, florists, apartment buildings . . . . You're a freaking cottage industry here.

HARRIET: It's funny, because I only spent a short amount of time in Minnesota. Not even a year. I mean, my grave is in New York, which is where I'm from.

JIM: How do you feel about having this lake named after you?

HARRIET: I thought it was strange then, and I think it's strange now. The original Dakota name was Bde Unma. I had many Indian friends. I was the first white woman to trek the territory from Missouri to Wisconsin, accompanied by fourteen brave and kind Indian warriors on my and my daughter's journey to be by my husband's side. What did the ancestral Native Americans think of these people coming in and changing the name of their lake to honor some white lady? What? I was supposed to be honored? They never even asked me. You should honor me now by mounting a campaign to change it back.

JIM: Hoo boy.

HARRIET: *Bde Maka Ska* and *Bde Unma* sound about right to me. *Harriet* is an old word from the old world. Meaningless. But I do like the idea that people might think it was named for Harriet Tubman.

JIM: It's about time you got your long overdue and righteous due as a pioneer woman, feminist, and healer. We need you in these times! Also, Love. Joy. *Lake Lovejoy* would be sweet.

HARRIET: Dream on, young man. By the way, wish me happy birthday. I just turned 227 years old. I died in 1854, that big rock over there says "Established 1883."

JIM: The only known image of you is a portrait painted in 1815. You've got a bit of Mona Lisa smile.

HARRIET: I was thinking about how much fun it would be to someday come back to this world as a ghost.

JIM: The look on your face is one of kindness, something this world could use more of.

HARRIET: So I hear. I try to impart it whenever I visit, which is often, at all times of the day and night. I eavesdrop on heartbreaking stories of love and loss, told with such passion, pain, and wisdom. . . . All as you the living walk, run, ride, or drive around this medicinal lake. Sometimes I touch people on their shoulder and take their pain away. I learned that from Wim Wenders's *Wings of Desire.*

JIM: Speaking of which, sometimes I linger over the brick pavers in front of the bandshell: lots of life and beautiful times commemorated and celebrated there. But nothing about you. You should at least have a brick, bench, or plaque, for heaven's sakes. Then again, not much is known about who you were . . .

HARRIET: Typical. Let me tell you. I was one of the undocumented founding mothers of Suffragette City. Women didn't win the right to vote until I'd been dead for sixty-six years. The word *feminist* wasn't around until the late 1880s, but the truth is we worked hard to earn our privilege as pioneer women who cared for the sick and dying. We were strong women. Strong leaders. We fought for our rights every day. The segregationists were horrible people, much like the white racists of today. I had slaves who were my friends and slave families I loved like my own, and we were at war and we were all raising our babies. People are people.

JIM: Happy Mother's Day, by the way. I know you had four children, and that you lost your eldest daughter, tragically, not long after the death of your husband. Your life was not easy, but you persevered and after those deaths and after the war you became a teacher at what would become the Delaware Academy in New York. Go ahead and think yourself unworthy, but a lake named for a wife, mother, nurse, teacher, and lover who gave so much of herself to others seems just about perfect to me.

HARRIET: Well, thank you, but I hardly need your approval or certification. Not your ghost story to tell. Now it's time for me to get out of here: you're starting to creep me out with all your flowery accolades. Ahoy! It's been lovely chatting with you. Maybe I'll go put on my long flowing Lady of the Lake sheets, hang in the pines, and scare some 'mockers and crows.

JIM: I'll look for you hovering in all the same old haunts around here. Please come again! When will I see you next? What should I tell your fans?

HARRIET: Tell them not to forget me. Tell them I'll be here. Tell them to look and listen for me. Let them know that I was more than somebody's husband and that the Ghost of Harriet is real.

2018

Nightswimming

On a Monday afternoon at Shady Oak Beach in Minnetonka, a lad of about eight scaled the high dive ladder. When he got to the top, he had second and third thoughts (it's a long way down), the same that go through any first-time adventurer's head when faced with a test of courage that, if all goes wrong, could end up in a painful belly flop in front of all your friends and a growing audience on the beach.

WTF am I doing up here? said the kid's body language as he hesitantly took the last step up to the platform. A long line of teens and preteens waited patiently behind him. Kids can smell fear in other kids, but they're also wired to encourage fellow tribe members to experience the thrill of flying, so as the eight-year-old stumbled to and fro, gingerly holding on to the guard rails, a chant rose up: "Do it, do it, do it."

According to one report, Minneapolis and the Amazon jungle were the two hottest places on the planet that Monday, with more to come this week. In Minnetonka, the hot kids were getting cranky. The chant took on more gusto. The eight-year-old sat down. Groans. He looked around, considered the ladder, and perhaps thought about the most popular young male role model of the summer, a brave young wizard who knows something about life, death, risk, and rebirth.

C'mon, dude.

Jump.

He stood up, wobbly knees covered by long trunks, and made his way to the end of the board. With no fanfare but the entire beach watching, he lurched and fell feet first to a splashdown as memorable as any of NASA's. When he came to the surface, the kid led with his fist thrusting through the water in what one observer deemed "a total *Rocky* moment", and the beach and dock erupted in cheers and applause.

A couple of hours later, a middle-aged man ignored the "Guard Only" sign on the lifeguard stand at Lake Harriet's main beach, climbed the ladder, and sat down to watch the long sundown. The newly installed diving dock was the picture of summer, crammed with flesh and rocking with laughter and shrieks. The man grew up swimming etcetera in and around Harriet, and survived the Lake No Floaties or Fun years, so it did his heart good to see dogs, balls, people, and no lifeguards 'til the weekend sharing the water.

The man admits to having been a little melancholy about youth and summers past, wistful for those times before adult wisdom and worries when you would go hard all day without a care in the world. As the sun went down, an almost Coney Island–worthy color scheme peppered the beach, and an old friend joined the man on the lifeguard stand. The woman talked about the importance of kids and adults being given permission to go skinny-dipping, so as to feel the wildness of nature on the body, unencumbered by clothes. The man made a note.

C'mon, dude.

Jump.

The man moved on to South Beach, where he again climbed the lifeguard stand, watched a bunch of rowdy teens throw friends into the water, and caught a screensaver sunset. 'Round midnight, he returned to the beach, took off his clothes, tucked them in a tree, and waded slowly into the still black water. He held out his hands baptism-style and eased into the mystical canopy of stars on the lake, whose glistening sheen suggested a freshly dusted black vinyl record.

The still of the night and cool water bathed the man's sunburned skin. He became a turtle, a fish, a dragonfly. He partied with Ollie the Octopus, the Little Elf Door Guy, and the Lake Creature. He became part of the milfoil, part of the wild brush and weeds sprouting up all around him, part of the great frothing carp spawn of the morning sunrise, part of the lake itself. At times he may have been the only human being in the lake-slash-universe, and his naked ass was awed and humbled.

The man let his head bob on the water and felt the kindred spirits of the Ojibwe, the original water people and first lovers of this lake. The night before, as he tossed and turned in the heat, the man had prayed for a moment of understanding, a sign of clarity about why he is here, and hell if he didn't find it in the middle of the night in the lake of his youth, and hell if he isn't going back for more every hot night this summer and for the rest of his life.

2011

3

. . .

FAMILY TIES

FOR A 1996 FATHER'S DAY STORY ON MUSICIAN DADS, I ASKED
the great Slim Dunlap if he had any advice for the great Prince, who
was expecting a baby at the time. I was also asking for myself, as I'd
become a father for the first time the year before.

"Watch *The Simpsons*. Homer Simpson is the best dad on TV,"
said Slim. "All the other sitcom dads are actors; Homer is a real dad.
But really, I don't like giving anyone parenting advice, because you
don't have to try to be a parent, you already are one. It's the purest
thing there is. To your wife, you're this sheltering person; to your
boss, you're this capable, confident other thing; to everyone else, you
project this image of what they want you to be. But for your kids,
you just have to be you. And you don't ever want to put on an act to
your kid. You have to let them see that you're human."

Slim's advice echoes *The Parent's Tao Te Ching*, which I return to
often: "Parents who hide failure, deny loss, and berate themselves
for weakness have nothing to teach their children. But parents who
reveal themselves, in all of their humanness, become heroes."

I don't need to be a hero to my kids; just "Dad" is fine. A few
years ago I asked Daphne Webb, a wise woman and perfectly de-
tached divorce attorney, to tell me what she has learned from dealing with love and uncoupling. "There is one piece of advice I would

give everybody," she said, certainly, leaning forward in her chair behind her desk in her law office in downtown Madison, Wisconsin. "In fact, I'd put it across their forehead backward so that when they look in the mirror they'd see it every day. And that piece of advice is: *Don't take things so personally.*"

Good advice. My kids know I'm all too human and they know I love them. As a divorced dad now, I'm starting to see (hope) that I might be better at divorce than marriage, and I'm looking forward to navigating the future with my former wife and now dear friend, Jean.

"You still have your family," said my buddy Ike Reilly soon after it all happened and I was lamenting to him the pain of being out of my home, and he's right. The foundation is surprisingly strong, built as it has been on mutual respect and love for the beautiful thing that is and always has been my family.

"Each divorce is the death of a small civilization," wrote the late, great Pat Conroy, and I've found that to be true. But I'm happy to report that life remains in my civilization, and I'm happy to have put down so much of how I felt about it all as a young father. These feelings and truths all remain, and for me the happy ending to this story remains a very happy one, indeed.

From Colombia, with Love

The call came on the second Friday in May, at 4:20 in the afternoon. Voice mail never sounded so warm: "This is Patty Reynolds from Lutheran Social Services of Minnesota. I have some information for you."

My heart leapt. Nine months had crawled by since my wife, Jean, and I had started adoption procedures with LSS. In the previous two weeks, we had been waiting—not so patiently—for a referral to be sent from Ayúdame, the orphanage in Bogotá, Colombia, that we had been working with.

Since LSS had warned us that the process could still take another few weeks, I dialed Patty's number with guarded optimism. She answered and after fifteen excruciating seconds found our file and gave me the information.

In the movie trailer of my life, I'd always imagined that the information, the moment, would come in a hospital, and that it would bring only joy. But I admit that on the pie chart of emotions, the Joy slice was only slightly bigger than Trepidation, Exhilaration, Love, and Confusion.

Knowing that Jean wouldn't be home from work for another hour, I paced the house alone. Finally, I alighted on the front steps and waited for her. To give her the information.

During some momentous occasions, I have a tendency to shut down and not recognize the enormity of the situation. But because Carl Jung said that "the biggest crime is to go through life unconscious," I forced myself to watch the world go up and down our street and consider the past two years of my life.

I thought about the money, the dreams, the disappointment. I thought about the day we went to the infertility clinic, and about how the doctor, abruptly breaking from his clinical demeanor, patted me on the back with a wordless gesture of sympathy.

I thought about our brief, hesitant dance with infertility drugs, of those tragic-comic nights (how on earth did we get here?) standing in the kitchen and pushing a needle into my wife. Hoping it wouldn't hurt—then later, hoping she wouldn't get her period. I thought about the dull ache and eggshell embraces that came with each one. A man and a woman pushing a stroller passed by. I thought about Jean. Her strength. Her worldview. Then I remembered something else: a holiday was coming up on Sunday, and considering the information I had just received, flowers were in order. At the neighborhood florist, when the woman behind the counter asked what the occasion was, I stayed vague. After all we had been through, I wanted the information to be ours alone—sacred, if you will.

I thought about what words I would use, and I came up blank. I thought about what a rare opportunity this was, and what a fortunate man I was, to be able to give this information to my wife.

I got back to the house and opened the porch door. As I was

digging out my key, I saw Jean through the window. She'd come in the back door, looking beautiful, frozen in time, wearing one of my favorite flower-print spring dresses, gold-leaf earrings, and a smile as radiant as the weather. She opened the door obliviously and asked how my day was. Pretty great, thanks. I laid the roses down on the table.

"Happy Mother's Day," I said, but I don't think she heard me. Then I took her in my arms, tucked my chin in the crook of her neck, and whispered the information. "It's a boy."

Throughout it all, I only cried twice. Both times came one night in October 1993, when I called my older brother and then my mom to tell them it looked like Jean and I wouldn't be able to have biological children. Until then, I'd been soldiering along fairly well with the news, telling myself that it didn't matter, that I could rise above the vanity of procreation, that there were options.

But the cold reality was that I had always wanted to have kids, and hearing the voices of my own flesh and blood triggered all the sentimental land mines I thought I was big enough, smart enough, whatever enough, to dodge. So there I was, thirty-five years old and crying like a baby, with my big brother Jay saying to me, softly, steadily, "Listen to me. This is important. It's not fair, and I know it's bad right now. But remember: there will be a day a few months, a year, two years from now, when we're talking and you're going to be happy as hell."

There will be a day when you're happy as hell.

For months, that's what I hung my hopes on. That one piece of advice. It allowed me to get through my day-to-day life; I carried it with me one morning on the bus going to work, as I watched the world gallivant merrily by from the window. Fathers, sons. Mothers, daughters. The lucky ones.

And I forgot it one morning while playing basketball with, yes, a group of fathers and sons, when out of nowhere a wave of sadness sucker punched me and left me so weak that I could barely get back down court.

Now maybe that sounds like whining; in the grand scheme of things, a heterosexual white male's wrestle with infertility is hardly a cause célèbre. But the fact is, as my sister-in-law Kim comforted us, we were grieving the "death of a dream." So the dream . . . changed. Because we wanted an infant and didn't want to wait two to four years, we never even considered domestic adoption. Jean's grandmother came from Guatemala, so we decided to adopt from there. But when our LSS social worker, Mary Ellen Olson, discouraged us from going through Guatemala because of recent problems, we went with Colombia, which she said has one of the most efficient adoption programs in the world, having hooked up more than one hundred Minnesota families with children.

But even after we decided to adopt, we weren't exactly home free. In going through the process, I had to learn that there were feelings I needed to talk to Jean about, feelings I needed to work through myself, and things I should have just shut up about. My biggest mistake came one night after we attended an especially intense panel at LSS. I wondered aloud if I could truly bond with an adopted child, and I regretted it the instant it came out of my mouth—not only because I saw the way it deflated Jean, hardened her, but because I knew myself better than that, and how easily I had fallen in love with my nieces and nephews and our friends' children.

Still, there was doubt. What if we went through all of this, only to be forever haunted by a dead dream? What if there was . . . distance? Reluctance? Resentment? What if part of my heart would never fully let this child in, and vice versa?

Of course, that was a very long time ago. Before Patty Reynolds gave us the information (and I quote, "How does a two-month-old baby boy sound?"). Before that magical weekend in May, which we spent telling family and friends the news. Before we saw his picture.

It was a mug shot basically, affixed to the referral form that had been sent from Ayúdame, which also contained his medical history, birth name, and information about the birth mother. He was beautiful: dark brown hair akimbo; big, freaked-out eyes; chubby cheeks; and a sense of humor/spirit that cut across three thousand miles. The connection was instant; he was, from that moment on, our son. Henry Jerome.

That's when it became real. The bond was cemented. The

afternoon I picked up the picture at LSS, I put it on the passenger seat of the car and had a chat with him on the drive back. Introduced myself. When Jean got home from work, we stared at him with love and disbelief. My mom and dad raced over to see him that evening, and I took him with me to the bar that night and showed him to friends, acquaintances, even a few strangers.

"Proud papa," someone said. Damn straight.

Five days later, on the plane from Minneapolis to Chicago, we showed the photograph to the flight attendant, who had adopted two children from Korea sixteen years ago. It nestled in the back pocket of my jeans as we flew from Chicago to Miami, and as we taxied down the runway in Bogotá, dazedly drinking in the sights and sounds of the stunning, vivacious Colombian people bustling in the seats around us.

I propped up the photograph on the armrest and wondered what our baby would look like as a little boy, a teenager, a young man. In less than seventeen hours, his picture would become flesh—a concept that prompted Jean to speak exactly what I felt: "This feels like a dream." (How in the world did we get here?)

When we arrived at the hostel from the airport, we were greeted by Keith and Ann, a couple in their midtwenties from Woodbury who had gone through the LSS program with us. They were one of a dozen couples who took part in our first meeting in September 1994. We had all come from different backgrounds—city dwellers, suburbanites, farm folks—but then our faces shared a common, silent, expression of loss. There was no formal discussion about our bond, but the creased brows and skeptical eyes spoke loudly about the inertia of infertility, and the uncertainty of adoption.

Throughout those early meetings, Ann's face stuck with me. In comparison to the rest of our decidedly tight-lipped group, she was blunt about her vulnerability and anxiety. She asked questions: What if it's not . . . the same? Will people at the mall or grocery store know the child is adopted? What do I say to them? Will the child be the target of bigots?

She was brutally honest, and honestly hurting. Which is why it was so amazing to see her and Keith beaming over their baby girl when we arrived at the hostel. Their stay had only taken two weeks (an Ayúdame record), and they were leaving for Minnesota the next morning. They invited us into their smallish room, where I interviewed them on videotape. Her face was a peach. The doubt and hurt had vanished, replaced by the ebullient glow of a doting mother. She summed up her experience like this: "It's a miracle." The next morning, our social worker in Bogotá, Piedad Agudelo Del Corral, picked us up in a taxi and took us to Ayúdame, where we met with the director of the orphanage. Through Piedad's translation, the director answered our questions about Henry's birth, his medical history, how we came to be chosen for him, and alleviated most, if not all, of the pangs we'd been feeling for the birth mother we'd never met.

We gave the nurse an outfit we had picked out for him to wear. She went upstairs to the second floor, where a dozen or so infants had resided in their cribs since birth, and she dressed him in it. Per Ayúdame's instruction, I wore a suit and tie and Jean wore a dress. We waited in a small conference room, holding hands calmly, more thrilled than nervous. I kept hearing the voice of Don, a big and big-hearted guy from Eagan, who was in Bogotá with his wife, Jolyn, to adopt their third child, a baby girl.

"Your life," he said when we met him in the hostel that morning, "is about to change forever."

Then they brought him in.

He was smiling. His eyes were sparkling. In the updated movie trailer of my life, I'd imagined that the moment would bring tears and that the script would call for astonishment. But when they placed him in Jean's arms, and we started talking to him, it felt like the most natural thing in the world. No tears or astonishment, just a sense of peace. From there, we took Henry out into the world. For eleven weeks he had known only the walls of Ayúdame, and now here he was flying through the chaotic streets of Bogotá in a cab. We arrived at the office of the *defensor de minores,* where we had to sign some papers. As we sat on the wooden bench in the hallway waiting for our lawyer, Henry lay in my lap with his eyes fixed on mine, wisely, uncannily. "I think he knows," Jean said.

Knows what, exactly? That the wait, for all of us, was over. That we were finally together. That we were his parents, he our son. That once upon a time, God dealt the three of us some pretty foul-looking hands but then reshuffled the deck and dealt a beauty.

Over the next few days in our hostel room (bed, crib, bathroom, TV), the wonder of it all slowly sunk in. At various moments, as we got to know Henry and became familiar with the rhythm of parenthood, Jean would simply look at me and roll her eyes in silent amazement, because words failed.

After he'd go to sleep at night, we'd lay in bed and whisper-babble about how this was the most incredible, most incomparable thing that had ever happened to us, and *happened* is the right word here, because it is not something that we did or accomplished or willed. Plain and simple, this was a stroke of fate.

And as for my doubts about bonding, that worry was certainly, poetically, put to rest when Jean and I got violently ill from food poisoning our third night in Colombia. The doctor instructed one of the maids to take Henry away to look after him, and for the next eighteen hours, we were as inconsolable as any parents could be.

Sickness aside, our first three weeks in Colombia were nothing short of a honeymoon. Our room was a cocoon, the pace of our lives perfect. We often said that everyone should have a baby this way, because our main responsibility was to get to know our child and each other, all over again, and figure out the new dynamics of our family. At the hostel, the maids cooked and cleaned. Our only day-to-day activity was to feed, change, and play with Henry. Only later would the walls start closing in around us. But before they did, we traveled in Colombia, in order to someday have something to tell Henry about his native country. We went to a tiny village four hours outside Bogotá, walked the cobblestone streets, shopped at the flea market, and talked with the people. We flew to Cartagena, a resort town on the Caribbean coast, and we took Henry swimming for the first time.

All the while, my misgivings about taking him from his native land faded as my confidence in our ability to assimilate Colombia's rich culture into our lives grew. And it was in Cartagena, while swinging on a hammock with my little boy (he in his diapers, me in my shorts), his beautiful coffee-with-cream-colored little bod resting on my pasty, freckled chest—that I felt more connected to human-kind than I ever had before. I told him a story about the walled city of Cartagena, how its citizens had built the giant embankment hundreds of years ago to keep out pirates and foreigners.

I gently swung him to sleep as the sun sank into the Caribbean Sea. There were no pirate ships on the horizon, but in the hammock, a couple of foreigners-turned-family were making promises to each other. Compared to that moment, everything in my past, and everything that is usually ascribed important to a person's life, can be summed up in one word.

Nonsense.

Meanwhile, the cocoon had become a compound. At the hostel, we met several adopting couples from Europe, Denmark, and the United States. And because LSS and Children's Home Society of St. Paul are by reputation two of the better adoption organizations in the country, the largest contingent of adoptive families came from Minnesota. Forced though it was, the camaraderie between all the families helped relieve everyone's hurry-up-and-wait plight.

Kris and John from Lakeville and their son Mitchell became our closest friends, while another Minnesota couple gave us an unintentionally grim lesson in adoption. They came to Bogotá to adopt a four-and-a-half-year-old boy and his three-and-a-half-year-old sister, but because the kids proved to be something of a handful, the couple, already in their early forties and in the process of raising two older biological children, decided it would be too difficult. In the history of Ayúdame, it was only the second time a child had been rejected after being placed. Because they lived in the hostel with us, we'd grown fairly close to both the kids and the couple. Which is why the day the children went back to the orphanage was like, as the would-be adoptive mother said, "a wake." To be sure, all eleven rooms were eerily still; the only people in the place who weren't crying were the two kids, who were too young to know what was going on. Jean helped pack their suitcase. I lugged it out to the driveway, then went up to our room and stood at the window to watch the car pull away.

All the while Henry slept in his crib.

The pall of that experience put a damper on our bliss. It was a totally unforeseen reality check, as was the boredom that soon set in. Memorial Day came and went. Father's Day. The Fourth of July. We had expected our stay to last four weeks. It stretched to seven.

We started to go stir-crazy sitting in our room, making up errands, playing Ping-Pong and waiting for the word that the papers had been signed. Every breakfast, lunch, and dinner we drove Kris and John crazy with the latest details of our emotional roller coaster. In her June 17 journal entry, Jean wrote: "On Thursday morning, Piedad told us some disappointing news—our papers are in a slow court and we have a bad lawyer. It will probably be two more weeks until we can go home. I cried. Piedad cried. It's not the end of the world, but we are tired of our room, the food, the language barrier. We want everyone at home to meet Henry."

Then finally it was time to go home. The last two days were a whirlwind of activity—we had to visit the doctor, check out of Ayúdame and the hostel, and get Henry's passport and visa at the U.S. Embassy—so the morning we left Bogotá, while Jean was filling out the immigration and customs forms, Henry and I stole a quiet moment in the airport chapel.

In Spanish, Ayúdame means "Help me." No one ever explained who the "me" is, since the adoptive parents or adoptive child could be either helper or helpee. But sitting in the front pew of the chapel that morning with my son, who would be introduced to the rest of his family in fourteen hours, there was no question who was helping whom.

On my way out, I put three fifty-peso coins in three electronic candle slots and said a short prayer: "Muchas gracias."

The plane touched down in Minneapolis on the second Saturday in July, at 9:35 in the evening. At the Chicago airport, we had been hurriedly met by my sister, Jean's sister, and their families. Now it was time for the main event.

We walked off the plane and carried our sleeping boy up the long carpeted runway tunnel—a scenario that one astute friend compared to Henry's exiting the birth canal.

As we emerged, a small, ecstatic group greeted us with cheers, balloons, signs, flowers, cameras, a tiny Twins cap. And waiting in the front yard of our home in South Minneapolis, within a five-block radius of the homes of five other babies recently adopted from Colombia, there hung a giant banner: "Casa de Hank."

At the airport, the house's new proprietor was introduced to his two grandmothers, his grandfather, uncles, aunts, cousins, and friends. But after a few minutes of euphoric hugs and tears, I recognized someone was missing. In the movie trailer of my life, there was one scene I wanted to be sure got played out. I needed my big brother for it, but he was nowhere to be found. At some point during the lovefest, he strolled up to the gate with his wife and two boys, fashionably late. Since I'd been gone, he'd gotten a vasectomy, and I'd gotten a son. I suppose we could have talked about the irony of life's big crap shoot, but at that moment I had a line to deliver, something I had waited almost two years to say.

He made his way through the crowd. With my right arm, I held Henry. With my left, I reached out and hugged Jay. "Remember that day way back when?" I said, barely able to remember that day way back when. He knew what I meant immediately. Fact is, the day had actually come seven weeks earlier, but I'd saved my line for now.

"This is it," I said. Which would make a pretty good ending to a story like this, if it wasn't such a good beginning.

1995

Thanks Given

This is a thank-you note, on Thanksgiving, from an adoptive father to the women who gave me and my wife our children, Henry and Helen. Because of the way adoption works in Colombia, we never got a chance to say it face to face, so here goes:

Dear Birth Mother,

That's not your name, I know. And frankly, using it here feels very formal, considering what we share. But it's all I've got. Besides, I'm tired. It's midnight, my kids are upstairs asleep with colds, and I finally have a chance to sit down and write the letter I've been trying to write since we got back from adopting Helen in February.

This isn't the first Thanksgiving I've had a one-sided conversation with you. The other time was in 1995, after my wife, Jean, and I returned from adopting Henry, also from Colombia. I was supposed to have bought potatoes and corn for the big feast, but I screwed up the night before and spent Thanksgiving morning driving around looking for a grocery store.

Everything was closed, so it gave us plenty of time together. What I told you that morning amounted to little more than a string of thank-yous, and, "He's doing great." But now I want to say more. Because I've learned a lot in the past five years, and because whenever I see a story like this one, or TV news footage from a homecoming at the airport, I know there is another story—your story.

Yours doesn't come with any balloons, or signs, or celebrations. It doesn't get told very often. But it should, because in a lot of ways, what you (and by *you* I mean two different birth mothers) did for us is the most extraordinary part of any adoption story. I've been reading a book, *I Wish for You a Beautiful Life,* a collection of letters from Korean birth mothers to their children. The numbed pain in those letters, written shortly after the women gave birth, is nothing short of suffocating.

Some women talk about their lives, their unexpected pregnancies, and the stigma of unwed motherhood in their country. Some try to explain the circumstances that led to their decision to give up their child. Many ask their children for forgiveness, or say, "This was the best way for you and me to be happy." All talk about their hopes and dreams for a baby they will never know. Some conclude with "I love you"; most with "Goodbye."

If you are like those women, you sent your child out into the world on a prayer. In Henry and Helen's case, we caught it. "A leap of faith" is how Jean described it when we first decided to adopt, and she wasn't just talking about how we came to make our family. She was talking about the ties that bind the lot of us.

Let me tell you about the day we got Helen. (Some of us adoptive parents call it Gotcha Day and recount the details of meeting the same way biological parents tell labor stories.) The afternoon we picked her up, at the home of the adoption agency's director in Bogotá, Henry was dressed in a suit and tie and looking very much like a man on a mission. He told the directors, "I need to bring Baby Helen to my mom and dad now." Which is just what he did.

"Sweetheart." That's what I instinctively called Helen when I first laid eyes on her, even though I can't remember ever using the word before. Her dress was red, her face chubby (*gordita,* all the Colombian women said, pinching her cheeks), her expression that of a wise, shined deer.

"We finally got Baby Helen!" said Henry, holding her in his lap in the taxi on the way back to the hostel, where we spent most of our six-week stay in Colombia. As we drove the streets of Bogotá, I saw women walking arm in arm in that warm, nurturing, non–North American way, and thought of you.

There's a saying that goes something like, "Having kids is like having your heart walk around outside your body." I know what that means, and I know you do, too, except for one big difference: your heart walks around outside my body. I try not to think about that too much, but I also make sure I don't forget it.

I wrote a story about Henry after we got back from Colombia the first time, and I'm glad I did, because I read it the other day, and I had forgotten how much pain we went through with the infertility and all. All I remember now is my unflappable dad telling my weeping mom, "There will be children in that house." Turns out the old man was right. Not a child, but children.

Thanks to you. And this is what I want you to know about those children: they are loved. They are safe. They are beautiful. We take good care of them. We wipe their noses and mouths and bottoms. We talk to them about God. We bust their chops. We are vegetable, manners, television, and two-minute tidy terrorists. They have grandparents, cousins, aunts, uncles, and lots of friends, many from Colombia.

Henry loves swimming, basketball, baseball, peanut butter, his little sister, Pokémon (don't ask), and the other night he told me he wants to learn how to play the violin. Helen loves peas, baths, peek-a-boo, gymnastics (I swear), her big brother, and throwing food on the floor to see how/if her mom/dad will pick it up.

Like you, we have dreams and hopes for them. Above all, we want them to be passionate, curious, and kind. We want them to speak Spanish and English. We want them to be proud that they are Colombian. Colombia is a big part of our lives now, just as you are.

We aim to do you proud, even though we don't know much about you. What we do know, we don't tell even our closest relatives, because one of the first and most important lessons we learned about adoption is that all of that information belongs to the kids, first and foremost. Not that the information is necessarily indelicate or clandestine, but it's up to them to decide what to tell people about their birth parents. What I think I know about you doesn't come from an adoption file, but from my gut. I believe that you are smart and brave, not only for what you did but for living with it. I believe you think about my kids, and I pray that you can still feel them, somewhere. Somehow. Whenever I hear people say that life isn't fair, or that people are weak, I laugh and think about you. Do I have heroes? Plenty. You're at the top of the list. You helped make our dream come true.

So, God bless you. I hope we can meet one day, so I can thank you in person. It would be an honor. Right now, I should go; I think I hear one of the kids coughing. Happy Thanksgiving, to you and yours,

An Adoptive Father

1999

Finding Henry

It's hard for a boy to say "I love you" to his father. I tried for years in different ways, like the Father's Day when I was seventeen and my dad was around the age I am now, and I wrote him a letter that he said made him think all day. I gave up trying to tell him for a while, then went through a thing a couple of years ago where I told him for about a month straight that I was afraid he was going to die soon and did he know I loved him and I thanked him for all the good schooling and the gift of the curious mind and then I shut up about it, but at least now I know he knows.

It's a lot easier to tell your dad you hate him, partially because if it works out the way it's supposed to work out, when you tell your dad you hate him you both know what you really mean is you love him. All dads know this, because all dads were sons who hated their fathers in some fashion, because the only thing sons can see for the longest time in their vast and wild future is their fathers' failure and lameness. Me, I never hated my dad. I just didn't want to be him. Now I do. Now I'm Steve Goodman singing, "I'd give all I own / To know what he said / When I wasn't listening / To my old man."

My son, who is eight years old, told me he hates me last week.

It's not the first time, though I can count on one hand how many times he's said it. We've been locking horns lately, butting heads over homework and chores and the air that we breathe in what feels like a preliminary bout to a pretty spectacular teenage–middle-age main event. We're trying not to yell at each other. He's been sassing my wife and me and asking questions about absolutely everything. He's in third grade. He's got a lot on his mind. He went on a field trip to Orchestra Hall the other day and during "Fanfare for the Common Man" they showed a slide of a gravestone with the word *Father* on it, and when he got home from school he told me it made him cry.

I'm sure some of his gravestone tears sprang from the fact that he's heard me talk about some of my friends' fathers who have died recently. They're all handling their grief in their own way: silence, bitterness, red wine, songwriting, work. I don't know what to say to them, other than "Thanks": I'm pretty sure that they and their fathers had something to do with why I plopped down $21.99 last Tuesday for the first DVD I have ever bought, *Finding Nemo,* which is sort of like Hamlet with cartoon fish. My wife thought we should splurge on it, because last year in California, my son and I toured Pixar Animation Studios in Emeryville and saw the crude models and other beginnings of Nemo. That's what she gave as her reason, anyway, but I'm thinking that maybe she remembered something about the movie that I didn't. Maybe she knew it had something I needed to hear.

We saw the movie in a California cineplex when it was released, so when my wife and kids settled in to watch the DVD the other night, I stole away to my office to write. I had the headphones on and I was happy enough to be in my cave, and then my daughter pounded on the door and insisted that I come watch with the rest of them. I stored my column and opened the door, and they had all the lights turned off, "just like a movie theater." My son, who I think was still feeling chilly toward me about an afterschool altercation we'd had that afternoon, made room for me on the couch.

I lay down and he gave up a piece of the afghan that my grandmother made for my kids before she died. We were at opposite ends of the couch, hard knees touching. I draped my hand on his back and was relieved when he didn't flinch. His foot, which I used to tickle with my hair when he was a baby, and which I'm certain he'd like to use to kick me sometimes now, rested in my lap. As the screen filled with the dreamy-vivid colors of underwater aqua life, he said, "I just love this movie."

Me, too. Nemo's mother is killed at the beginning, leaving just him and his timid and overprotective dad, Marlin. When Marlin embarrasses Nemo in front of his friends, Nemo calls his dad "scared" and mutters "I hate you." Marlin looks wounded, then Nemo gets fishnapped, and father and son spend the rest of the film fighting sharks, beautiful but deadly jellyfish, their own fears, and the ocean's endless currents and detours to get back together.

I dozed off but awoke for the good parts, like when Marlin tells a group of fish about how Nemo rebelled, and "maybe he wouldn't have done it if I hadn't been so tough on him. You gotta be tough on 'em . . . ." And when Dory, the absentminded blue tang fish, tells Marlin, "Hey, Mr. Grumpy Gills. When life gets you down, you know what you've got to do? Just keep swimming."

Nemo and Marlin almost die; in fact they almost kill each other, but by the end they find each other and are happy to be together. Nemo goes back to school and Marlin seems less afraid of life because his son has taught him how to weather the storm. As the end credits and bedtime started to roll, my son kept his eyes on the screen and said what Nemo says near the end of the movie: "Love you, Dad."

He yelled the same thing to me from his bedroom that night, three times. I yelled it back, three times, even though we're trying hard not to yell at each other these days.

2003

Police Off My Kid's Back

After he gets done working at his restaurant job or playing *League of Legends,* our nineteen-year-old son, Henry, likes to take a walk down to the lake or around our neighborhood to clear his head, listen to music, and enjoy the still of the night.

That's what he was doing on Forty-eighth Street a few blocks from our house on a recent Tuesday night around midnight when a cop car bolted in front of him, jumped the curb, and up on the sidewalk, forcing my boy, a Colombian American and lifelong citizen of Minneapolis who was wearing jeans, a baseball cap, backpack, and earbuds, to stop in his tracks.

"They almost hit me," he said. "I was like, 'Whoa, WTF?' I didn't know it was a cop car at first. I thought I was getting jumped by somebody. I had nothing on me, just a bottle of water."

Out of the souped-up, tinted-windowed crime-fighting vehicle jumped two amped-up Minneapolis cops, who threw him against the hood of the car and handcuffed him under the streetlights of Harriet Avenue South. After Henry repeatedly asked what was going on, the cops finally told him he was a suspect in "an attempted burglary" that had happened on Forty-eighth and Pleasant.

"I told them I was walking from my house [the other way] from Bryant, and they didn't really care."

What you need to know about my lad is that he can handle himself. Last month when he was coming home from work on the bus, another passenger had a seizure in front of him, and Henry blew by the flummoxed bus driver, helped the guy off the bus, dashed up the street to the firehouse, and got the paramedics to the scene, hopefully in time.

When the cops moved to search his backpack, Henry calmly told them that they had handcuffed his arms behind his back over the backpack and that they were going to have to take off the cuffs in order to get to the backpack. The cops didn't believe him and repeatedly attempted to yank it off my son until they finally uncuffed him and searched the empty backpack to their satisfaction.

To a backdrop of new and wholly warranted scrutiny of the Minneapolis Police Department, from Al Flowers's police brutality case to Chief Janeé Harteau's signature moment thus far, of skipping a community meeting in the wake of the Flowers incident and the Ferguson riots, to weekly stories about racial profiling and questionable police tactics, to an increasingly encroaching and annoying police presence ("Show us your papers," as one oft-stopped pal puts it) on the traffic-heavy but altogether big-city safe and civilized streets of South Minneapolis, Henry—who is a legal adult and has no curfew and as an American citizen has every right to take a walk at any time of day or night that he chooses—picks up the story of one kid and one otherwise quiet night in his well-to-do lily-white neighborhood:

"They put me in the back of the car without even telling me anything. I had to ask them a few times before they said where we were going, to Forty-eighth and Pleasant. They weren't treating me bad, but they were treating me like I did something. We got to the house that was supposedly robbed. I was sitting in the back of the car, and there were like ten cops and six squad cars around that block. Then I heard on the radio they had another guy on Forty-fifth and Pleasant, and the cops got back in the car and let me out and gave me my stuff back without a 'Sorry' or anything. They didn't even drive me home after that. They did technically arrest me, but they didn't say I was under arrest, and I didn't want to make it seem like I was trying to get away from them. . . . It was ridiculous. I didn't even know what to do, so I just played it like a guy who hasn't seen all the crap cops pull. I just let them do their job. People want to antagonize the cops, but if they want to check you out for a burglary, you have to let them.

When they let me out, I wasn't really sarcastic about it, but I said to them, 'Thanks for protecting the neighborhood, guys. You're great.'"

Will he still go out? Does he feel safe in his own neighborhood—from the cops?

"I'll still go out, but just tell them next time that they should know me, like, 'Oh, that's Henry.' I'm in this neighborhood. What is community, man, if you're just going to be arresting people left and right and not asking questions? Maybe you should get to know the people. That's the thing: do cops alternate [locations]? I really don't feel like they are consistent neighborhood cops: I feel like they're just people who get called to do their job somewhere."

This summer, when coming out of a show at First Avenue, I saw eight cops on foot, bike, and squad cars aggressively descend on a scared Black kid walking down Hennepin Avenue in a scene straight out of 1958 Birmingham. No report of it appeared anywhere, proving yet again that scenes and stories like that are commonplace; I still wonder what happened to that kid, who looked about as dangerous as a mouse, and how many of his civil rights were broken that night.

In the summer of 2014 the *Star Tribune* reported that of ninety-five payouts totaling $14 million for police misconduct since 2006, only eight of the cases resulted in discipline for cops. Which is to say that the police do not police their own, so it's up to the citizenry, weary from the cumulative claustrophobia that comes with constant surveillance and cop cars buzzing around, harassing, and filling quotas, to remind all concerned that, as one post-Ferguson community activist put it, "We're watching."

2014

We're still watching, and wondering about all the Black and Brown kids who've been harassed and worse as a matter of policing practice in Minneapolis. In the wake of George Floyd's murder, calls for reform and defunding of the Minneapolis Police Department are currently under way. "People are getting that there are broader systemic reasons that allow this to go on," Michelle Gross, founder of Communities United Against Police Brutality told me the week

Floyd died. "It's not just about this one person or this one case, as egregious as it is and outrageous as it is. I love that so many people are getting it—that there were George Floyds before George Floyd, and they don't want any George Floyds in the future."

Fire Alarm Fluffy

She started kindergarten last week. They'd been waiting for her. Had been since that morning four years ago, when she and I were dropping off her brother at his classroom and she got away from me, ten paces out in front was all, but more than enough for her to pirouette and pull down on the little red box on the wall marked "Fire Alarm" and fill the halls with a great clang that emptied the school.

I wrote a column (confession) about it then, and she has heard the story so many times by now that when the "emptied the school" part comes, she grins and scrunches up her face on cue—as if she relishes the telling, but also as if she enjoys adding fresh hues to her bad reputation.

I saw her in the sunlight the other day, playing out in front of the house with a stick and a plastic school bus she had duct-taped together, while her brother and mother and I played Scrabble inside. All at once, the three of us looked up from the board and watched her through the window. We laughed at her ingenuity and beauty and solitary spirit, and I knew then that I wanted to write about her, as a way of holding her, I suppose, because she started kindergarten last week.

"I hope you have pictures," said the smiling old woman on the bike path the other day. She had never seen my daughter before, but when she got a load of the dress, cape, sunglasses, helmet, and red ruby slippers connected to the chugging, churning legs, she could see it was something that needed capturing, just as it is now.

Her older brother, who started fourth grade last week, thinks this is a dumb idea for a column. He took a break from standing on his head in the other room, came into my office, saw the words on my screen and the pictures of her strewn across my desk, and said,

"People will just go, 'So what? What's so great about your kid? My kid's great, too.'" And he might be right. Or jealous. For the most part, he's good at not showing it—and good at being the person who makes her laugh harder than anyone else, especially since she takes such pleasure in torturing him.

She was quiet the first two years. Slept. Barely said a thing. Then she pulled the fire alarm and announced her arrival to the world. Now she is the unofficial toastmaster of our neighborhood, making her several-times-daily unbidden rounds to visit the neighbors and the neighbors' dogs, children, grandchildren, cats, and kitchens, and in doing so somehow showing us all how to live by believing that no door is ever closed to her, and by bringing us all together with her brazen belief that it is her inalienable right to do whatever she wants to do right now.

The other night, our neighbors Gene and Marion hollered from across the street. They recently sold the family hardware store at the end of the block and are getting ready to retire and sell the house they raised their kids in. They came out with a homemade purple and green genie costume they'd found during their cleaning and gave it to her. She put it on, and I stood on the sidewalk watching as she went from door to door, showing off, spreading the love, furthering her legend, and living out what Julie Miller sang in one of the best deadpan intros to a guitar solo ever recorded: "One, two, three, four, tell the people what you are."

She is going to break hearts. I see it whenever she sits in my lap long enough to let me brush her hair and put it in a ponytail, and her eyes go from warm and needy to steely and independent in a blink. She loves people but doesn't need them; she is happy just being, and all the adults who think she's going to be a great artist, astronaut, singer, actress, or dancer don't understand that the secret to her success is her oft-incanted phrase, "You get what you get and you don't have a fit," and that she already knows she's made her mark.

In those moments I see that boys, and girls, all those poor future saps, will write poems and songs and articles about and for her—boys like a friend of mine, Craig Wright, who, after seeing her Olympian little four-year-old body swim and do ripple-less cannonballs for the first time in California, called me up with a new song on his lips:

"Splash"
by Craig Wright and Peter Lawton
The Tropicals

You're gonna splash
Wherever you go
You're gonna crash
Like a wave
People will run
Run from the fun
But let 'em all run
Run to their graves
'Cause you're a party getting started
Everywhere you go
Bound to be brokenhearted and make angels
In the snow
Bound to love, bound to hate, bound to give and bound to take
Bound to make a Splash
You're such a beautiful tornado
You could blow the century down
And still deserve a standing 'O'
For any beauty you had found
You're bound to be Someone who
People promise big things to
You're bound to cry
Bound to crash
Bound to make a Splash

Maybe my son is right. Maybe this is a dumb idea for a column. What I told him is that sometimes you write about something that's close to your heart, a blessing you're trying to count, and if you do it well enough, maybe it will make people think about what's close to their hearts, and that's the most you can hope for. If he had stuck around long enough, I would have also told him that you can't really care what anybody thinks about what you do, and that you don't write because people will think it's dumb or smart; sometimes you write because you need to be close to, or restore your faith in, something beautiful and true.

Besides, I had to write about her today. It's my responsibility as a journalist. I am sworn to report that last Wednesday around midday, a great clang filled the city. Local history tells us that the clang was merely a test of the emergency weather sirens, but canny citizens now know there is no coincidence. She started kindergarten last week.

2004

An Ambulance Chaser Is Born

I come from a long line of ambulance chasers.

My paternal grandmother, Norine Walsh, lived most of her adult life at 509 West Fifty-third Street behind the Boulevard Theater and was known to drop everything at the sound of a siren.

"She used to say, 'If there's a fire, we should go,'" said my dad, Jerry Walsh. "One day she was sick with a cold, so she begged off going shopping at SuperValu, which was where the O. I. Borton car dealership is now on Lyndale. But when SuperValu went up in flames later that day, she jumped up and shot out the door."

Norine's gawker impulse spread to her children. When my dad was seventeen, he heard the siren call and snuck out his bedroom window to go have a look at a house fire near the Washburn water tower. When he arrived, three bodies were covered on the lawn, and he, the fire crew, and some photographers waited for relatives to return to what he recalls as "an awful scene."

Two years later in 1948, a plane crashed on Minnehaha Parkway off Dupont Avenue, and my dad jumped in his car and helped firefighters dig for bodies.

In 1966, a small plane went down at the intersection of I-35W South and West Highway 62, and my dad's sister, Eileen Osterbauer, took off with my nine-month-pregnant mom, Ann Walsh. When they arrived at the scene, Aunt Eileen got her skirt hung up on the freeway fence, trying as she was to climb it to get a closer look. Unbeknownst to them at the time, my mom's brother, Joey Holzinger, was driving on the freeway and came upon the plane wreck and the sight of a beheaded pilot.

Call it morbid curiosity. All of which has been passed down to my cousins and sisters and brothers and me, who have spent a lifetime gawking at fires—from the great Donaldson's blaze on Thanksgiving 1982 in downtown Minneapolis to a huge barn and brush fire in southern Minnesota a few Labor Days ago, which I forced the entire station wagon to sit and watch with me.

So when I heard about the fire that was engulfing the Fiftieth and Bryant businesses on the afternoon of February 18, it was in my DNA to run down the street and check out the damage. It was a spectacularly sunny day, and once I'd sussed out that there were no injuries, it felt okay to mingle with neighbors and strangers and do whatever I could do to console the business owners I ran into.

"Nice day," I said to one of the firefighters, whose calm smirk suggested he'd seen much worse.

"Nice day for a fire," he cracked.

Crass, perhaps, but true. There was something ancient in that gathering that afternoon, something the technology of the day didn't capture, because you had to be there: a spontaneous gathering of community, and a primal ritual of watching and wondering about how, in a flash, everything can fall apart. If you squinted, you could see generations of Americans in the faces of the couple of hundred rubberneckers who, en masse, resembled daguerreotypes from storied fires in Chicago or New York or beyond. After an hour, I jumped in the family van to pick up my eleven-year-old daughter, Helen, from school at Burroughs, which sits at the bottom of the hill on Fiftieth Street. When I arrived in the car pool lane, kids and teachers were lolling about and watching the smoke rise in the distance. I hollered at my kid to jump in the car fast and told her she was going to see something she'd never forget.

In no time, she was standing in front of the fire. She saw a couple of friends there. She asked questions. She was quiet and, I think, a little reverent. Then she started bugging me. She wanted to skip chorus practice. I said no. She kept bugging me. I said I'd think about it. When I asked why, she said she wanted to watch the fire. I said okay. First we went home, and when we did, our home looked very different to both of us from when we'd left it earlier that day. It was intact. Cozy. Warm. There were no flames licking at the beams, no charred personal effects, no carnage. My daughter got on the phone immediately, called a couple of friends, and told them what she'd seen. They weren't impressed, so she grabbed her coat and bolted out the door, but returned a minute later. "I forgot my camera and notebook," she said. "I'm going to write something about this."

2010

Letter to a Young Soccer Parent

I saw a harried young dad the other day, scrolling and talking on his phone and pacing the sidelines of a Fuller Park soccer game, whose six-year-old participants looked more concerned with running around and not running into each other than winning or losing. Meanwhile, Dad looked like a caged rat.

I had stopped with my dog to sit on the bench and take in the sight of the young families and their kids tearing up the Fuller turf, just like my family and thousands of others have done in Tangletown since the Fuller Park Soccer Club launched in 1985 with four teams (the Wave, the Bouncers, the Lightning, and the Zaggers). It has now grown to a league of twenty-two teams and 250 kids annually.

Luckily, I didn't see much of myself in the dude. I can't say I was 100 percent present all those spring and fall mornings, but sixteen years after I first found myself standing on the sidelines of my kids' soccer games, and now that it's coming to a (gulp, sigh) close, I'm wishing I could get it all back and hold it tight. So here I am, the weird old guy on the park bench reminding distracted dads and moms everywhere to be present and to volunteer, coach, bring treats, learn the game, get to know your neighbors, and, more than anything, savor it while you can, because it's as sweet as life gets.

Of course, "You never stop standing on the sidelines," as one former soccer-mom-turned-college-student-mom put it to me when I was lamenting this graduation to the next phase of parent–kid love the other day. That is, you never stop rooting for your kids or trying to keep them safe and healthy and active, but the ritual of carting them around, talking about games, and meeting their friends and friends' families happens in a rare and relatively short moment—one that's not to be tolerated but cherished.

Our family knew nothing about soccer when we signed up for Fuller and then Lynnhurst soccer when our son Henry was five years old. Little league baseball, football, and hockey dominated my youth, but like much of America over the past two decades, in short order we came to learn and love the game and its global reach.

These days the Fuller Park Soccer Club acts as a pipeline to Southwest, South, DeLaSalle, Holy Angels, and many other high school programs, especially Washburn, which hosts the annual Fuller Soccer Jamboree, an all-day bash at which veteran high school players mentor the up-and-comers.

More than anything, we came to learn that soccer has been a natural, if largely unacknowledged, community builder for South Minneapolis, right up there with schools, churches, bars, and libraries. There is a thirty-year tradition in this neighborhood of standing or sitting on the sidelines with neighbors, acquaintances, and complete strangers and of getting to know them and their kids a little bit and in turn making big bad Minneapolis feel a lot like a small town.

It's a wave you get caught up in naturally, and the truth is I'm feeling extremely wistful about my last sideline-standing duties on these last first days of October as Helen concludes four wonderful years of playing soccer for Washburn. We've got a couple more games left, then it's on to the end-of-season banquet and the fall fundraiser October 15 at Whiskey Junction starring Helen's uncle's band, the Belfast Cowboys (email me if you want to buy a ticket, as my soccer dad duties still include hawking for the cause), and then it's a wrap.

Hard to believe.

Over the years, every once in a while, one of our kids would ask me why I rearranged my work schedule and drove and biked all over hill and dale to catch their games. My answer was always the same, and simple: "I love watching you play."

I always will. I love watching Henry play pickup basketball, and I love watching Helen play soccer and hearing her sing, because I've always known that the act of play is a testament to the human spirit itself and to ongoing budding growth, and in a world where too much adult focus is on competition and achievement, I've heeded the words of George Bernard Shaw ("We don't stop playing because we grow old; we grow old because we stop playing"), Diane Ackerman ("Play is our brain's favorite way of learning"), and Carl Jung ("The creation of something new is not accomplished by the intellect but by the play instinct").

Sure, true play doesn't come with coaches and parents helicoptering over every move and juice box, but I know from repeated experience that there is absolutely nothing like seeing your kid fly up and down a field or court. We want our kids to be eternally free and to soar along in life, and even if that is an impossible request of them and the universe, I have felt my heart leap time and again at the sight of my child churning across the horizon and, while I'm grateful for every last delicious memory, I know in my bones that I will miss it profoundly.

2016

4

. . .

I'M ONLY ONE

I'M WRITING THIS FROM A CABIN IN THE MIDDLE OF NOWHERE outside Livingston, Montana. It's just me and all the nature, all the creatures and creation of God's country, and my buddy Pete (speaking of wildlife), my former neighbor in Minneapolis and fellow soul-searcher, tinkering away in the basement.

I landed here two days ago. After driving the fourteen hours from Minnesota to Montana, I got out of the car, unpacked my guitar and gear, and stared for a few minutes at the big sky filled with big stars.

Ahhh, I could breath. Finally. Summer in Minneapolis had done a number on me with all its traffic, people, and noise. I wrote a column pleading with my fellow motorists to calm and slow down during construction season and amidst the madness of car, bus, bike, and airplane traffic in the big little city. I was hugely relieved to see Minneapolis in my rearview mirror.

Slowly the stress melted away as I got into the great wide open, and the brilliant sun and magnificent vistas of North Dakota's Badlands and Montana's lush green snowcapped mountains worked their magic on my frayed city-boy nerves. A few minutes after I pulled into Pete's place, as I was sucking in my first few gulps of brisk mountain air, a big brown bear galloped by the hood of my car, rambled up the long driveway, stopped, stared at us in the dark, and then he was off into the night.

Welcome to Montana.

Helluva greeting.

I found out later that the bear-as-spirit-animal-totem stands for strength, confidence, leadership, healing, strong grounding forces, and "the importance of solitude, quiet time, rest." All of which I took as a good sign as I was desperately trying to find some peace and quiet—a theme I return to time and again, in case you hadn't noticed.

Thanks to Pete, I have found some peace and quiet for a week or so. He's been offering me Montana as a writing refuge for a while now, and I'm glad I took him up on it. He and I met as young dads who were starving for conversation and connection that went deeper than grill talk and neighborhood gossip; now our kids are out on their own, in college and working, and Pete and I continue to riff, and now travel.

He's been here for five years, and he's extolled the virtues of Montana to me on a weekly basis. Now that I'm here I get it. I've long considered Minnesota to be the epitome of urban wildlife living, and it has long met my needs as a mecca of natural beauty, solitude, silence, and dreaming.

Little did I know.

Montana is a dream I never had come true, like being in the bosom of America at her most beautiful. I've only been here a few days, which is all it took John Steinbeck to famously conclude, in 1962, in *Travels with Charley: In Search of America*: "I am in love with Montana. For other states I have admiration, respect, recognition, even some affection, but with Montana it is love, and it's difficult to analyze love when you're in it."

I'm in love. The mountains and the sheer infinitude of the Big Sky on my mind and imagination have been good for my spirit, as have the long soaks in the hot springs and long talks with Pete.

Along with my brothers and father, Pete has been my closest male confidant about matters of the heart and soul over the past decade. Much like my good childhood friends Rick Schreiber and Paul

Kaiser, with whom I spent many nights walking Minnehaha Creek and driving the lakes, talking about life and love and lots of girls, I've always been lucky to have good male friends, and sensitive, kind men whom I can talk to about feelings and matters of the heart.

Pete and I talk about our kids, love, life, sex, music, books, ideas, the power of positive thinking, and the importance of presence, and, more than anything, our main topic of scholarship and conversation: the individual and the free person's place in this world. We're constantly chewing on matters of freedom, and freedom of mind: how to live, work, and play in a society that actively encourages homogenization, competition, and copycatting; how to feel truly alive and original and purposeful; how to honor the inner adventurer, outdoorsman, freak, snowflake, lover, singular spirit.

Of course, all this was going on with me before Pete and I met. My brothers and sisters have long (lovingly?) referred to me as their "spacey" middle brother. It came from my dreamy ways, I guess, and come to think of it now, that reputation may have cemented itself during my freshman year of high school, when the English and speech teacher, God bless her, took an interest in me as a writer and encouraged me to enter a citywide speech competition put on by the Optimists International Club of Minnesota.

Which I did and which I took home first place for, by standing up in a roomful of adults and other teens and preteens and nervously reading aloud my first personal essay, typed as always by my mother, under the assigned title of "I'm Only One."

I was fifteen years old, a squeaky-clean Catholic boy finding his squeaky-clean voice:

I'm Only One

On a night when the neon lights infest the streets and I'm just about sick of the entire fake world, I'll turn to the only sincere part of my evening left: the sky. I study the endless repetition of stars. They seem so free, yet they themselves are caught up in their own rat race. From night to night, the stars never change much. But, in my mind, I'll wait for the one I've never seen before. It'll be different. So different that no one else in this world will recognize it but me. That star will mean identification for me. I feel that I have ideas and thoughts in my mind so different from anyone else's that at times, it scares me.

It always seems like everything happens to me. I guess it's because I'm so intent on what I'm doing that I don't see what happens to other people. Maybe I make too big a thing of my problems. When I'm in a situation that causes me to reflect on it for a long while, this situation seems to grow more and more in the direction that I want it to.

I'm alone most of the time. I like being alone. Because I think so much, I have to be alone. Aloneness is a clean experience. It's the feeling you get when you lie by a river fishing, and sleeping. Complete solitude. Not caring what people do to you or think about you. I love that moment more than any other moment my mind knows.

I think a lot. I think about love, life, the unknown, myself, people, planets, and anything else my mind dishes up. When I think of love, I sometimes think that I love too easily. But then I counter with the thought that there is no way in this confusing world that there can be too much love. There's so much hate in the world— and fear; fear of all the other people. Even though I am only one person, there are others in this world, others that think differently than I, sometimes drastically different. Yet as different as we are, we're all the same. The same in overall thinking, body structure, and in most cases, causes.

There is a part of me that would like to write, another that would like to draw, and part of me wanders into the make-believe world of music. But I have to do just one. Why? Maybe I'll be all three of them—a writer, an artist, and a musician.

Music really captures me. It's better than any form of entertainment I've come to know yet. If you listen to music and apply it to your own life or way of thinking, it's beautiful. And if you can do this, it really means something to you. Then you have something to identify with and music will become part of your life, as it has mine.

I'm considered, by most people who know me, a sports fanatic. Yeah, I really do like sports and competition. In SPORTS. Nowhere else. Sometimes not even in sports. For when I think it starts changing my life over who "wins" and who "loses," I'll quit. If I can. Maybe it's just the athletics I like. Not the game itself, but getting

out and doing it, having fun, sweating, and running. Running un-
til my legs feel rubbery. And laughing. And spitting. And feeling
the cool, harsh iciness of a Coke oozing down my parched throat.
That's my kind of athletics.
I've told you about myself. What I think about and what I do.
You may not like me. You may not like what I've said. You may not
have even been listening. But what I've told you has been an idea
of how I'm only one here in this world. Remember what I've said.
Think about it. And tonight, go out and look for your star. I think
I've found mine.

Fall 1973

I found the carbon copy of that speech in a box of writings that lay at
my feet now. Reading all this, sifting through my old kid scribblings
for what I want to be the last time, it's somewhat strange and weirdly
comforting to recognize that the very same themes in the journals
and diaries I kept during my junior high school, high school, and
first years of college and music-making are similar to the ones I
chew on now, though with not as much angst and teenage blood:
solitude versus socializing, writing, music, girls, love, and figuring
out something to believe in, post–Catholic church and school.

Here I need to raise my arms in praise and hallelujah, for in so
many ways my spiritual life was shaped by the intensity and faith of
my mother, Ann Hanna Walsh, the most avid seeker and spiritualist
I know, and an inspirational font of goodness, optimism, humor,
and wisdom. For years she's been going to St. Leonard of Port Mau-
rice, the tiny church in South Minneapolis that all of her kids and
husband stopped going to regularly years ago, but she kept going,
kept her faith, kept forging her own community, and kept reporting
back to us about what she'd heard or learned on any given Sunday.

To this day I ask her how the sermon at mass was on any given
Sunday, and she's both good at recounting the main points for me
and also probably annoyed I'm not there to hear it firsthand.

Of course, Mom the lone wolf at church isn't how it always was.
There once was a time when all of us would fill an entire pew at
Annunciation, the big corporate parish church in South Minneap-
olis we attended as a good Catholic family in the '60s. I remember

some of it: the spooky-cool ritual of walking the Stations of the Cross on Good Friday; the feel-good folk-music masses; the social justice curriculum; inventing sins and lying about how bad I felt about my sins in the confessional; goofing around as an altar boy; and all the language, imagery, damnation, and promises of heaven and hell that rock my world to this day.

The first to drop out of going to church was our dad. He had been a good Catholic and ended many of his letters home from the Korean War with "God bless you" and talk of prayers. Then, "I read a book about a priest who quit the church, and that got me thinking," he told me a few years ago, when he was eighty-six. "I remember sitting in a back pew of church one day and I just thought, 'This is just another cult.' And I walked out. St. Olaf's, maybe. I was married, it just . . . it was a big relief. You're taught something and taught something and then, 'Oh, I don't have to do this.'"

After that?

"I went to libraries and the bookstore," he said. "I went to the weird stuff. Vernon Howard. I'm still attracted to the weird stuff. There are other worlds, I've always thought, and I'm still trying to find them."

Same. To this day, one of the most unforgettable images of my life is that of my father skipping communion. Occasionally he'd join us for one mandatory church appearance or the other, but he drew the line at communion. As most of us rose and walked up to the altar to eat the body and drink the blood of Christ, Dad got off his knees and sat there in the pew, alone with his thoughts and body language that said, "No thanks, you jive turkeys."

He did that at weddings, funerals, everything, whenever we the wafer-weaned sheep went to the altar. *Riiight,* you could almost hear my dad saying, sitting there reading his book or thinking his thoughts as the pews emptied into single-file lines heading up to the altar, and I've always thought that was a healthy thing for his children and grandchildren to see: by his standing up for himself and by publicly avowing his nonbelief to the congregation, we learned to think critically and question everything.

Ultimately, Annunciation and its reruns of reruns played itself out for all of us. One by one we stopped going; I was fourteen years old when I bailed. When Mom finally got tired of badgering me into going to Sunday mass, she told me, "You don't have to go anymore, but I want you to continue searching."

It was generous and wise advice, and I took it and ran.

Thanks for the Skerch, Dad

My brothers and sisters and I grew up in a big house on Fifty-first and Colfax, when the neighborhood was crawling with baby-boomed Catholic families. My dad had his own upstairs office that was filled with stacks and shelves of books, a tiny TV, and a door that was always wide open. All six of his kids walked through that door countless times, collapsing on his couch to find guidance, warmth, wisdom, laughs, and a few bucks "off the bat."

My dad turns eighty in May. He's had some health problems in the past few years, but he's still up and around and kicking. He grew up in this neighborhood, behind the Boulevard Theater and a block from Annunciation church and grade school, and everywhere I go these days I see signposts from his and our youth. It seems like we're getting ready to say goodbye, but I'm not quite ready for that, so today I want to talk about a lesson my father passed on to me, maybe by mistake, maybe the most important one.

When I was eight or nine, my daughter's age, my dad would come into the bedroom I shared with my brother and lie down on my bed, face down on the pillow, exhausted after a hard day's work as an employment counselor. Outside the window, the stars winked and promised UFO sightings—a potentiality that enthralls us both to this day. As soon as he got comfortable, my dad, still in his work shirt and tie, would gently demand, "Gimme a skerch."

For most of the world, the more common term is *back scratch,* but somewhere along the line Dad morphed it into *skerch.* When he asked, we'd set to it, always more pleasure than chore, under or over the shirt, and never longer than five or ten minutes. As we grew up, the older kids would pay the younger kids a quarter for a skerch as we played Boggle or Scrabble or watched sitcoms, sports, the news, or Leo Buscaglia, the hugging guru of the day who said: "Too often we underestimate the power of a touch, a smile, a kind word, a listening ear, an honest compliment, or the smallest act of caring, all of which have the potential to turn a life around."

Diane Ackerman, in her amazing *A Natural History of the Senses,* said that "touch might be as essential as sunlight," which is likely not news to the thousands of SAD sacks around this burg. To be sure, there are all sorts of studies out there about how touch helps and heals. It connects us to another life form, gets us in touch with each other and our own inner pack dog, and soothes the savage beast. It's why we go to massage therapists, have pets, and crave the warmth of another body.

Personally, I'm convinced that giving each other back scratches all those years is what has kept my family close over the years, passing it on, as we have, to spouses, lovers, and other animals as we go.

Beyond the touch part, the skerch would always lead to a story or a talk. Dad would tell me about his work, I would tell him what I did at school. He would make up a story, I would make up a story. It's part of what set me on a path of seeking and storytelling, which brought me to two bookstores last Sunday, doing what my dad has spent his life doing: browsing.

I picked up five new books, including Anaïs Nin's *Henry and June,* Cormac McCarthy's *The Road,* Jonathan Safran Foer's *Extremely Loud and Incredibly Close,* and Rabbi Irwin Kula's *Yearnings: Embracing the Sacred Messiness of Life,* which states early on: "Jewish wisdom teaches that our yearnings generate life. Desire animates. As the prophet Amos says, 'Seek Me and live.' Jewish wisdom urges us to go for it, to seek answers to our deepest questions, to search for spiritual and personal fulfillment while knowing we will never finally get there—oh, but the discoveries we'll make along the way! We are meant to live, to search with intention. When we can uncover our deepest longings for intimacy, pleasure, creativity, and self-understanding, life yields illumination and happiness. Far from being a burden, our desires themselves become a path to blessing."

I can draw a straight line from bolts of wisdom like that to my boyhood bedroom, and as I make my way now as a man and father, part of my studies will always be linked to the action of my hand gliding over my father's back, his oil and sweat pooling under my fingernails, and knowing even then how special it was.

2008

Father Fantastic

Our dad was a great writer and thinker, and I'm happy to have a few of his unpublished pieces he banged out in the late 1950s in anticipation of, as he wrote, "the soaring sixties." He was in his thirties with a mortgage, a growing family, and a good job as an employment counselor, but he was writing his (unpitched?) stories because his mind was curious about the consciousness explosion that was happening, and he was thrilled about the times he was living through.

This is from a short piece he originally called "Metaphysics: My Hobby Is Lonely," which he finally renamed "Public Awakens to Fantastic." It was written around the time I was born, and it's pretty wild how I can hear my similarly enthusiastic voice in his, the sound of another Irish scribe, testifying:

> Not since this decade of the sixties has man had a chance to know so in-depth what his fellow earthlings are experiencing in their everyday lives. Throughout the ages he has developed the conditioned reflex of turning away as soon as what is called reality took on a fantastic air. But no more.
>
> Through communication channels of magazine, newspaper, worldwide telestar television, personal pocket radios, tape recording, and the amazing ability of publishers to now put a book on sale in your corner drugstore forty-eight hours after the event has taken place, we are rapidly becoming aware of anything unusual occurring anywhere. People are no longer afraid they will be laughed at when they report an unexplained event. This of course is leading to the discovery that more of the fantastic is going on in our lives than we dared suspect in the past.

Commenting on this new flood of information, one old occult book lover lounging in the sun outside the Minneapolis public library said, "When I can go down to the little dairy store next to my rooming house and find Charles Fort's *Book of the Damned* in paperback next to the bread and rolls counter then I know for sure the world is in the middle of a communications explosion. When I was young you had to spend many a Saturday afternoon in a dusty old book shop to dig up literature like that."

In recent months paperback book publishers who are as sensitive to new trends as a department store fashion buyer have discovered the public's thirst for occult, metaphysical, and supernatural literature. Drugstores, supermarkets, and bookstores now devote entire sections of their paperback displays to books on the strange and unknown.

A new breed of reader seems to be arising as a result of this deluge of information on the fantastic. There are now pockets of people across our land who gather regularly to discuss the supernatural. From confirmed scoffers they have done a complete turnabout and become staunch defenders. They do not believe everything they hear or read about, but recognize at least the possibility of its occurring.

Ever since man crawled from the oceans to live in caves millions of years ago there has been a battle between the believer and the nonbeliever. The hard-headed and the wool gatherer. The no-nonsense practical man and the imaginative chap with his eye in the sky or on the horizon. If you have been keeping score over the past few centuries the scoffers have been pushing the dreamers all over the field. But like the Marines landing or the cavalry cresting the hill, this new dawn of information is coming to the rescue of the downtrodden visionary.

A few decades later, Dad's seeker (or "delver," per Krista Tippett) son's search for meaning found him in many ports of faith, including a few music venues fronting as churches.

Why Sylvia? Why Now?

At the park the other day, I noticed a thirtysomething woman on the bench across from me muttering to herself. Open on her lap was a loose-leaf notebook with laminated pages, which she was staring at. On her right was a toddler playing in the sand, a school-age kid going down the slide on her left. She looked psychotic, which isn't unusual for this park, or for parents of a certain age.

At one point, she fixed her eyes on an unseen demon and her muttering got more animated, complete with flailing hands, until she was interrupted by a "Mommy!" The woman half-looked up from her notebook and, as sweetly as she could muster, barked, "Just give me a second, honey. I'm working on my play." I watched her memorize her lines for a little while longer; then when we were leaving the park, I said to her, "I'm in awe of your concentration."

"I've got a deadline," she laughed. "I need to learn this whole thing by Monday." It was Friday.

I never asked her name or what play she was rehearsing, because I didn't want to further interrupt what was obviously precious work time. But in her I saw a lot of people I know, a lot of the moms, especially, who are not only engaged in that most American and most insane of rituals, multitasking, but who are constantly being tugged between their lives and their Lives. A scenario like the one I witnessed—a woman trying, literally and figuratively, to be many things at once—would undoubtedly be met with scorn by the family-values brigade, but there is something heroic about that image, historic and purposeful even, and something that haunts of Sylvia Plath, about whom there is something in the air at the moment.

And I don't just mean the fact that three Plath-related pop culture artifacts have surfaced in the last week: the Gwyneth Paltrow biopic *Sylvia*; Diane Middlebrook's Ted Hughes biography, *Her Husband: Hughes and Plath—A Marriage*; and Paul Westerberg's Plath tribute "Crackle and Drag," which appropriates the last line of the suicidal poet's last poem, "Edge." Rather, like the image of that stressed-out actress-mom-at-the-park, tattooed on the collective American parental psyche for the forty years since her death, is Plath, a creative and ferociously independent mind, who seemingly needed rest from the effort of trying to be too many persons at once.

Plath killed herself at age thirty due to a clinical mental breakdown, but the tragic-romantic snapshot for any sleep-deprived or penned-in young parent is the one of the ultimate freedom that came only when, as Westerberg sings, "While her babies slept, she took a long deep breath / . . . Now they're zipping her up in a bag / Can you hear her blacks crackle and drag?"

"Poets rarely become cultural icons," writes Middlebrook. "But Plath's suicide had occurred just when women's writing was beginning to stimulate the postwar women's movement. The posthumous publication of Plath's poetry, fiction, letters, and journals added her voice to a swelling chorus of resistance to the traditional positions women occupied in social life."

Those positions still exist, if only as archetypes, in almost all the moms I know. Even if their mothers worked, they are constantly being self-measured by the stay-at-home mom of yore who seemingly had it all together in simpler times. And no matter how much genuine joy their children bring them, there is another, darker, side that rarely gets addressed. In "Falling," her superb August 27 *City Pages* cover story on Naomi Gaines, infanticide, suicide, postpartum depression, and young mothers on the verge of nervous breakdowns, Beth Hawkins writes: "Whatever choices we go on to make about raising our kids, assuming we're privileged enough to have choices, all new mothers lose their freedom and wholesale chunks of their identities. And there's no going back." So instead of going back, women, unlike men (whose wrestle with domesticity is still more socially accepted as something of a rakish extension of their wild oats–sowing years), women fall in line. No matter how mundane it feels, no matter how much they may be haunted by past thrills of college or clubland, no matter how perfectly they "balance career and family," women are above all expected to settle down and become the perfect mother.

In *The Secret Life of Dentists*, the mostly awful adaptation of Jane Smiley's riveting novella *The Age of Grief*, Hope Davis stars as Dana, a dentist who marries her dental school sweetheart, has kids, loses a part of herself in family life, then tries to recover it by joining a community opera company and having an affair. At the end of the film, Davis, whose face registers the spooked young mom thing with perfect ambiguity, crawls back into her cage, having learned nothing.

Which is why I guess I find the actress-mom-at-the-park's instinct to be so heroic. Maybe it, and the genesis of this column, is because I see something of my mom in her. She was a homemaker, but the home she made was filled not only with love but with her constant forays into politics, books, board games, decoupage, etc. She loved her family, but she had an inner life, a tough mind, and when things got too kid-crazy around her ankles, she had a tendency to say, "One of these days I'm gonna walk out on all of you."

That sort of declaration—and the fact that she never followed through on it—sticks in a kid's mind, and not necessarily in an unhealthy way. What it said to us was that our mom was more than our mom, that there was more to life than us and dinner and dishes, and that despite her yearnings for more, she was going to fight to fuse her selves into a whole. Plath's and Gaines's and others' stories are tragic, partially because they didn't or couldn't get help, but just as interesting are the ones about the day-to-day thrashings that never quite reach the end of their rope.

Stories like the ones that belong to my wife and her friends, who struggle and juggle and pass out at the end of the day and get up and do it all over again. Or to my sister, a high-powered cardiologist who dreams of chucking it all to wait tables and hang with her kids. Or to Hawkins, a journalist-editor-mother who wrote, "God help me if I live to see the day where my self-esteem is tied to the sheen of my porcelain." Or to my friend Pam, a lawyer–mother of two whose lesbian pal takes her drumming and dancing to "contribute to the delinquency of a mother."

Or to Plath herself, who wrote, "Perhaps I am destined to be classified and qualified. But oh, I cry out against it."

2004

Gold Experience at First Avenue

A couple of months ago I was at First Avenue, feeling pretty good.
I'd seen a few old and new friends, and on my way out the door I ran
into a guy I'd exchanged e-mails with but had never met. He introduced himself as Bryce, and in less than two minutes I knew that
he'd been a seminary student, a basketball player and fan, a music
and beer lover, and that he works with underprivileged kids.

"You wouldn't believe this shit," he told me. "Those kids give me
so much. Every day. I gotta tell you about this one game."

So he did, and I forgot about getting to bed early and leaned in.
He was one of those guys you'd like to hang with all night and be
more like—gregarious, in the moment, passionate, all without really
trying. We were talking some serious barfly philosophy when the
sight of two women stopped him in midsentence. His head bobbled
and he said, "God, I'm so horny tonight. Sorry. I'm pretty drunk."

A few minutes later, I was about to split, but Bryce told me to
hang on. "I want to tell you something," he said. "I've been reading
you for years. I know you go through stuff, and so do I. I know you
struggle with stuff, and I go through a lot of the same stuff, and I
know that you want to do a lot of stuff, and so do I and I just . . . I've
just always wanted to tell you something."

"Yeah?" I said. "Sure. What?"

"I hope you won't think this is weird," he said.

"No, go ahead," I said. "What?"

"Listen, this is important," he said. He took a breath. He was
drunk, but sure of himself and his message. "It doesn't matter what
you do, or how well you do it. It doesn't matter what you've done.
How good or bad you've been. You know why?"

I had no idea.

"Because God loves you," he said.

The band and bar chatter swirled. [Longtime First Avenue stage
manager] Conrad had just pinched my ass. [Musician] Mean Larry
was standing a few feet away from us, with some half-naked ladies
who were giving out free shots of rum and glow-in-the-dark buttons.

My priest, a salty-tongued flake who pulls pastor duty at HCMC, was nowhere to be seen. On my bookshelf at home were books about Zen Buddhism and self-as-God, and titles such as *What Really Matters, Man's Search for Meaning, Sensual Orthodoxy, The Outsider,* and *Music of Silence.* On my CD racks were songs by and about skeptics, saints, and sinners of all stripes. "What do you mean?" I said, and Bryce told me, matter-of-factly, without a shred of judging or preaching, like he was turning me on to his favorite CD.

"Look, life's a bitch. But no matter what, God loves you, so no matter how hard you are on yourself, no matter what anyone says, you're . . ."

". . . golden," I finished.

"Golden," he said, nodding.

I thanked him, walked out of the bar, and I haven't seen him since. But whenever I've had a heartache that feels too big to handle alone, or a case of cabin fever that torpedoes my spirit, or whenever I get sick of the sound of my own self, I've tried to remember not only what he said but how he said it, where we were standing when he said it, and how it made me feel like Bill Murray in *Caddyshack* when he received "total consciousness" from the Dalai Lama.

So I got that going for me. Which is good.

2004

The Tao of Spring Forest Qigong

Every weekend, Normandale Community College in West Bloomington transforms into an unlikely epicenter of alternative health and spirituality, with classes and workshops in everything from yoga and tai chi to sound therapy, hypnosis, homeopathy, herbalism, and feng shui.

One of the continuing education program's most popular courses is in Spring Forest Qigong, taught by founder Chunyi Lin, a fifty-five-year-old wise man and healer who operates out of a humble but good energy–steeped healing center in an Eden Prairie strip mall.

"You have to go deep into the heart to find the peace," said Lin, sitting in one of the six-year-old center's meeting rooms last week, as the nine full- and part-time employees quietly tended to the business of healing. "I think that with the more technology that's developed, and people focusing more and more on the material side and gradually coming to find that 'the more you gain and the more you have, the happier you will be' is not the case. Actually, if you want to find the true happiness, the true happiness is in the heart. When peace is found, then you're able to activate the love energy from the heart to help you to heal. Lots of people have critical challenges, and by going deeper into the heart they're able to find that energy, find that place, to help themselves make a balance. And when that happens, they usually call that 'miracles.'"

The miracles happen as a result of qigong, a five-thousand-year-old Chinese meditation, breathing, and energy flow practice that Lin discovered when he was a young man struggling with arthritis brought on by playing basketball and working on the family farm in China. The practice healed his knees and joints completely, and in the early '90s he began refining the "too time-consuming and complicated" version of qigong he'd studied in China into Spring Forest Qigong (named for spring's restorative powers and the connective qualities of trees) as "something simple, that takes less time, and gives more benefit."

"Everything is energy," said Lin. "*Qigong* means *chi,* or energy, and *gong,* or work. Over thousands of years, these masters and doctors discovered so many different ways to cultivate this chi in our body. They have Daoist qigong, Buddhist qigong, but actually qigong has nothing to do with any of the religions. What they do have in common is that the power of chi, of the healing, is through love, and all these beautiful religions talk about love. So you combine all this beautiful love with the energy, and the energy is even more powerful."

Testimonials abound, and Lin is respected worldwide by traditional and nontraditional medical experts alike, yet given the New Age nature of the subject, the most extensive media coverage he and his work have received is a Gary Rebstock–produced KMSP-TV piece from 1997. Rebstock, a former news anchor, is now a communications consultant who co-penned Lin's biography and has assisted Lin in the creation of his instructional DVDs, CDs, and manuals. "There are now some three hundred thousand Spring Forest Qigong students worldwide," said Rebstock, who points to a recent Fox 9 update as a sign of qigong's growing mainstream acceptance.

"Thousands of people each year come to see Chunyi at his center in Eden Prairie," said Rebstock. "He has taught classes all over the United States, in Canada, in the Netherlands, and he's been invited to teach in numerous other countries. This year, in association with his longtime partner, the Learning Strategies Corporation, he'll be teaching in England and Australia.

"There are hundreds of Spring Forest Qigong [SFQ] practice groups now across the United States, and in nearly a dozen countries overseas. This is a grassroots effort. People who have found Spring Forest Qigong so beneficial in their own lives hold these practice groups. They invite people into their homes to share SFQ with them. That alone, to me, speaks volumes about the benefits of Spring Forest Qigong."

To be sure, were Lin afforded a media audience the size the Pope recently drew, the Chanhassen-based anti-guru might have taken his moment at the worldwide pulpit to impart his life mission ("A healer in every family and a world without pain") and his simple philosophy of inner peace through unconditional love, which translates into the easily remembered mantra of SMILE, or "Start My Internal Love Engine."

"If you believe it, it works; if you don't believe it, it still works," he said, smiling broadly, infectiously. "No matter what, when you put a smile on your face, the body magically produces endorphins, that good-feeling hormone that gets you feeling good. Lots of scientific studies show that once you put a smile on your face, the endorphins can even kill the pain cells."

Lin worked as a college professor and teacher trainer in China and came to Sibley High School in 1992 on an exchange program to observe the American education system. Two years later he set up a sister-school program between a school in China and Anoka

Ramsey Community College, and helped forge a sister-city relationship between Coon Rapids in Minneapolis and Zhao Qing in China. He left China to escape the oppression of the Chinese government, and he continues to work with his former homeland, "because I want to bring peace to China."

These days, Lin rises at 4:30 to meditate, chant, and practice qigong. He has breakfast with his wife and elementary school–age daughter (the couple also have a son at Tufts University), and then it's off to work, where he sees clients in person or via teleconference. The demands on his time are growing, but at a time when self-help experts are a viral cottage industry, Lin is a true wise man who deflects any talk of fame.

"I never consider myself famous, I never considered myself that important," he said. "All this fame that is given to people, you don't own it. The only thing you own yourself is the heart. I know I love people. I know I want to receive more peace in this world. In this life, at the time when I'm going to leave, I want to feel I am proud because I have done something together with so many people to make this place a much better place for others, and for our children, and grandchildren, and many people in the future. That is what I focus on. I don't care how people look at me.

"In all the years I've known him," said Rebstock, "I've never witnessed anything self-aggrandizing about him. He doesn't hold himself out as some sort of guru. He doesn't present Spring Forest Qigong as 'the' way, but simply a way. If you have already found a way that works for you, then Chunyi will always encourage you to stick with it. He just wants people to be healthy and happy and to share their love and joy with others."

The weekend of April 19 at the Crown Plaza West in Plymouth, hundreds of Spring Forest Qigong newbies and vets will gather to learn from Lin and other healers at the annual Spring Forest Qigong world conference. This year's topic is "Finding Peace in the Heart," a message Lin believes will resonate long after he and the rest of the conference-goers are gone.

"We're talking to everybody in our team to think about how five hundred or a thousand years from now, Spring Forest Qigong still be out there for people, with the peace, with the healing," he said. "What we're doing now is so meaningful for the future, because we focus on helping people to discover the peace in our hearts. Things outside, you don't have too much control. Just like the weather. Happy or not happy, it's about you. Focus within you and on how much you can do. Purify yourself. My destination is as a healer, and no matter if it's sunny or cloudy outside, my focus is the same: healing. And this time of year, spring, is a healing time, growing time, filled with hope and joy."

2013

Krista Tippett and the Wisdom of *On Being*

"I've always thought I was part Betazoid," cracked Krista Tippett, leaning into the conversation and across the table at her "home away from home," the Birchwood Café in Minneapolis. That self-description—in reference to *Star Trek: The Next Generation* commander Deanna Troi, whose empathic powers are finely tuned to human emotion—is as good as any explanation and description of why Tippett is the most interesting talk radio personality in the Twin Cities.

A 2008 Peabody Award winner for her show on the thirteenth-century Muslim mystic and poet Rumi, Tippett can be heard every weekend by 600,000 listeners on 250 public radio stations, and her podcasts are widely shared among students, seekers, artists, theologians, and scientists of all stripes. But at the moment she remains a blip on her hometown's radio radar, that painfully predictable and imagination-stunted yellathon of sports, politics, and celebrity gossip.

"I'm really proud of the shows we're producing, and I would like more people to hear it, but I don't measure success in numbers," she said. "Every week I get an e-mail from someone who says a show helped them stay alive or keep loving their life, or get through a death, and I feel like if that's the only impact we had all year, that would be enough."

More than enough, and more to come. At a time when talk radio's popularity is on the decline, the smart, funny, mind-blowing,
and soul-engaging *On Being with Krista Tippett* (formerly *Speaking
of Faith*) is gaining new traction. The National Public Radio show
(which airs Saturday and Sunday mornings on MPR) has become a
go-to source of wisdom and inspiration in these tumultuous times,
and if the past two months of Tippett's ten-year radio career is any
indication, 2013 portends great things for her and her growing audience.

To wit: in November, during a historically combative presidential
election, Tippett hosted "The Civil Conversations Project," a four-
part series held at the University of Minnesota's Humphrey School
of Public Affairs that gave voice to ideas, issues, and people otherwise obliterated by the campaign noise. In December she penned
an essay, "Why I Don't Do Christmas," that went viral due to its re-
freshingly frank and thoughtful disgust with the materialism and
shallowness of the season, and she concluded her broadcast year by
introducing listeners to the work of Pierre Teilhard de Chardin, a
Jesuit priest, philosopher, and paleontologist who coined the concept of the noosphere and the next stage of evolution, born of the
sweeping technological connectivity that we the guinea pigs are just
now learning to surf.

"He helped excavate the Peking man fossil, *homo erectus,* which
was definitive proof of prehuman history, and he was this incredible spiritual thinker," said Tippett, nursing a coffee. "He foresaw
that the mind—but not just the mind, but our whole consciousness
and spirituality—would create its own reality and envelop the earth
with this layer of this reality over the biosphere. He predicted the
next stage of evolution would have to be spiritual. And I think that's
where we are—*spiritual*—in a very expansive sense of that word."

In the wake of the Sandy Hook Elementary School massacre,
Tippett's rebroadcast of a show on grief, loss, and meditation in
the world was a real source of sanity amid the media carnage. All
the above doesn't even include Tippett's normal workload in November and December, which included shows on vulnerability,

mindfulness, technology, the poetry of Rainer Maria Rilke, and her ongoing exploration of this unprecedented moment of upheaval the human species is living through.

Or are we?

"There have been other moments, but I think we're in an especially cathartic moment right now," she said, with the same lilt of curiosity that fuels *On Being*. "I say we're 'turn-of-the-century people' a lot: we're living in one of these moments where all the old forms that seemed to work don't work anymore, and we can't yet see what replaces them, and it's true in everything, from how we structure our families to how we structure our workplaces and what government is and what economies are.

"But if you'd been born into this time last century, it would be on the eve of World War I. That'd be pretty cathartic, too, right? But we don't have that total destruction; we have all these fundamental things and basic definitions getting turned inside out. There's no ground beneath our feet. Even though you can look at human history in the past few hundred years and you can say, horses to cars and isolation to trains and all that, I think the digitally driven pace now is so unprecedented. And a lot of it is really exciting—I discovered blogging, and I just got on to Twitter—and the potential of it is thrilling."

To be sure, the sea change is on, which prompted the *San Francisco Chronicle*'s Mark Morford to recently maintain that "the time is more ripe than ever to entertain a certain kind of raw, yelping willingness to become less convinced you think you know what it's all about, to harness the opportunity afforded by this accelerated culture, and to really get it on with our inherent shared humanity."

Yes, please. But are we equipped for seeing all that we see and experience through the wonders of modern technology?

"That's what we're called to do, right? To rise to the occasion," Tippett implored. "We have to shape this, and it's really hard because we're in the middle of it. It's happening in real time. So we're supposed to grow it up and grow ourselves up as it feels like it's taking over our lives. We're in this transformative moment that is stressful and may just, as much as any other point in human history, require us to find the best of ourselves that we don't even know that we're capable of."

Tippett is doing her part—by asking questions and being an engaged listener. Her interviews with such thought leaders as the Irish poet John O'Donohue, Rabbi Abraham Joshua Heschel, author Andrew Solomon, and many more are timeless and edifying, which gives *On Being* legs well beyond its time slot in the here and now. To be sure, the *On Being* archives are a treasure trove of ideas and a very deep rabbit hole to go down.

Their creator is a divorced mother of two and self-described hockey mom who grew up in Shawnee, Oklahoma, amid a fervent Southern Baptist church culture. She studied history at Brown University, was an exchange student in East Germany, and later a Fulbright scholar in West Germany. In 1984, she started work as a stringer for the *New York Times* and the following year became a chief aide in Berlin to the U.S. ambassador to West Germany.

Her stint in politics was short, however, because she realized she wanted more out of life as a *seeker*—a word, as a matter of fact, she doesn't use.

"I don't use the word *seeker* much. Not because it's a bad thing. I'm really careful with words in my show," she said. "I think there's a lot of cliché around a lot of words around this part of life, and then there are things that are ruined by overuse or politicization. I think the best thing often is to use fresh words, and talk about what we're talking about, rather than use labels. So *seeker* to me feels a little unrooted, and to me the most interesting seekers are actually quite grounded and searching at the same time. I once interviewed Robert Coles, who wrote *The Spiritual Life of Children,* and he used the world *delving,* and I like that word."

In 1994, Tippett received a master's of divinity from Yale University, which planted the seeds for the personal and conversational approach that has become the hallmark of *On Being.* She pitched the idea for a spirituality-based radio show to Minnesota Public Radio, and *Speaking of Faith* became a monthly series in 2001 that went weekly in 2003.

"It seemed like a crazy idea, because I'd never done radio before," she said. "I'd been a journalist and I loved public radio, and I knew all these ideas were out there from going to divinity school. I spent about a year talking to people about it: 'I know you can do this conversationally, and the conversations can be listenable, and thrilling, and funny, and warm.' And every time I talked about it, and it was here in this [Twin Cities] community, people said, 'Do it, do it. You have to do it. If you don't do it, someone else will.'"

These days, the budding popularity of *On Being* can be traced to a prevailing distrust of organized religion and, due to the reach of the Web, an increasing appetite for mainstream media content with more meaning and mystery.

"The pattern we have now is people are constantly discovering it," she said. "I hear it every day: 'I can't believe this is happening and I didn't know about it. You make us feel less alone.' To grow the show, we have to find those people, but we're not going to do it by finding more stations. It's a new frontier for us."

For all of us—and it's heartening to have wise souls like Commander Tippett at the helm.

"This deliberation—and it's not just a discussion—it's contemplation: it's inhabiting this reality, and taking up the question of the time: What does it mean to be human?" she said. "So when I think about the future of this, I think it could absolutely evolve into something very different. Bigger than a radio show, and maybe not a radio show in a couple of years. I'm going with this."

2013

Fear and Loving in South Minneapolis

The other day at the dog park at Lake of the Isles, I sat on a bench and listened to the sound of the galloping pack's jangling dog tags harmonizing with the spring birds' songs. It was clear, bright, and beautiful. Perfectly spontaneous. Like no music I'd ever experienced—but also like every other piece of art that connects you with the rest of existence, though I'm pretty sure I'm the only one who heard it.

It lasted all of forty-five seconds, then faded out and gave way to the people chatter, Lake Street traffic, and wind.

I wasn't going to tell you, or anyone, about it, because it sounds slightly insane and because I'm not even sure such moments are pertinent or even communicable anymore, given the fact that so much of our energy of the moment is focused on soapbox bombast, blowhard power, macro- and micro-tumult, and trying to figure out how to deal with headlines such as "The Beached White Male: Can Manhood Survive the Depression?" (*Newsweek,* yawn) and "The Big Disconnect: Our National Discontent Runs Deeper Than Dollars and Cents" (*New York Times,* duh).

Then I went to the Uptown Theater to see *I Am,* a documentary in which filmmaker Tom Shadyac asks, "What's wrong with the world and what can we do about it?" Oprah has an entire television network dedicated to same, though I don't have the stomach for her shark-swim in the shallow end. The same could be said of *I Am,* and several have, but in a culture war where three new poems by Mary Oliver (*Parabola,* exactly) get no play and Donald Trump can flick a booger and be "part of the conversation," if not the next president of the United States, I'll go down casting my vote for a mainstream film that quotes the mystical Sufi poet Rumi (love is the answer, always) and the calm spiritual minds of Desmond Tutu, Noam Chomksy, Howard Zinn, and dozens of others interviewed by Shadyac.

In short order, they get to what makes us tick (love, compassion, connection) and what makes us sick (materialism, competition, and a learned mindset that tells us everything from what "good" weather is to why the stock market is God). The film proffers that the heart, not the brain, is the main source of our intelligence, and that paying attention to it, the moment, and each other holds the truest riches of the human experience.

To that end, one of the film's most impassioned arguments, and there are dozens, for how we should be living our lives comes from a farmer who tells a city slicker that everything around them, all the trees, soil, insects, and animals, is alive. He says it over and over, again and again—"Alive! Alive! Alive!"—like filmdom's Dr. Frankenstein did in 1931 when his creation first gives off a pulse. The farmer's point is that when you don't take for granted the bounty of nature, the world is a miraculous place to be a part of.

(And yes, I am salivating here like my pup, Zero, at the prospects of the kaleidoscope multiple flora orgasm that takes place at the Lake Harriet Rose Gardens for three to four weeks in May and June. Tune in.)

I Am takes pains to avoid the preciousness of, say, *What the Bleep Do We Know?* and gets straight to the questions in a crisp, one-hour-and-eighteen-minute rumination on how we are connected through science, history, and society. Shadyac is a likable narrator and for the most part stays away from self-serving new-guru hype. Plus, his story is pertinent: the son of a doctor turned Hollywood director who has a brush with death and ends up wanting to contribute something more. Pertinent because his trajectory butts up against the so-called American Dream that tells us the brass ring is Hollywood, money, and fame. Shadyac found himself as "the man who had it all" and yet something inside was empty, which admittedly sounds like the plot of every awful Hollywood eat-pray-come-to-Jesus hero's journey torn from the pages of *More* magazine.

Still, I thought a lot about that emptiness, and how people fill it, as I drove home from the theater, where only a few other souls took in the late show the other night. I thought of people I know who have chased wealth and materialism all their lives, did a gut-check on my own financial and personal unease, and came away wanting to recommend it to several seekers, as well as down-in-the-dumps folks I know who it might speak to.

More than anyone, I thought of a woman I encountered in the Edina Lunds parking lot last Friday morning.

For some reason my minivan battery needed a jump, but when I politely asked her for help, she (along with three other women) refused. I suppose because I've spent my life helping stranded motorists, I was stunned. Her face was sixtysomething pinched, and her car—a BMW or Mercedes—was immaculate and black. She went into Starbucks, got her coffee, and when she was safely in her car, she rolled down her window and said, with me standing there with my jumper cables in hand and her driving away, "Don't you have AAA?"

Fair enough. She was either terrified of me, or of life, or in a hurry. But it left me wondering about her. I wondered if she ever hears the harmonies of the dog tags and birds. I wondered about her life. I wondered about how she came to a moment of such clenched living in that crowded suburban parking lot on Good Friday morn.

I wondered about her again as I watched *I Am,* which points out that in Charles Darwin's *The Descent of Man* the word *love* is mentioned ninety-five times and *survival of the fittest* only twice, and that Darwin's most important—if largely unknown—discovery is that the most prominent shared human emotion is sympathy.

2011

Walking the Path

Misery may love company, but William Frost will not be going to that party. He doesn't own a TV. He is rich, free, and in love with his soul mate, Quiana, who just returned with him from a two-week honeymoon in Greece. He has found peace, a peace that allows him to stand in the middle of his thirty-five acres in Northfield and say, "They're having a blast" at the sight of five red-tailed hawks dive-bombing a musky late-summer breeze. The air is tinged with the sweet smell of toasted and sugared grain from the nearby Malt-O-Meal factory.

He walks out his back door and talks about seeing an eagle the other day while driving into town. And you, you wonder how this peace feels, how it translates to the everyday—the drive into town, the bedroom, the solitude, the co-parenting of his and his wife's five boys from previous marriages. He wants to share what he has found. And so he has invited you here, and he has invited you *here*—all you have to do is call him or Quiana, and you will find yourself, as I did, standing over a brick that says, "You are here."

The brick is buried in the earth at the start of the main labyrinth built by Frost. Labyrinths, he will tell you, are meditative ritual tools that date back five thousand years to the Island of Crete and have been walked for centuries by Christians looking to find God at the center. More guy than guru, Frost is a fifty-three-year-old New Jersey–born former professional soccer player, restaurant manager, recovering alcoholic, photographer, entrepreneur, organizer, and author.

Frost's main career, um, path has been that of a landscape architect. But after planting too many trees and flowers next to piped-in waterfalls, he started tapping his lifelong studies of creativity. His master's thesis at Brown University focused on the emotional terrain of creativity, and over the years he became interested in its cognitive elements. That led Frost to become a creativity consultant to some of the biggest companies in the world. It was different from those piped-in waterfalls, but maybe also the same, and so he began to build this labyrinth.

According to Frost, Minnesota is a "hotbed for labyrinths," boasting well over a hundred peaceful paths, including those at hospitals, spas, Como Park, and the campus of the College of St. Catherine in St. Paul. The one at the center of Frost's meadow is 155 feet across and looks not unlike a compacted crop circle, or a vacant lot cut by a drunken push-mower. Nearby are a few Celtic cairns, which he also built, a Zen garden, and Tibetan peace flags that wave on the hawks' wake.

"If people want some coaching, or have a problem or issue they'd like to solve, we can go into coaching mode," he says of the peace-seeking pilgrims who have been showing up, mostly unbidden, at his door. "Otherwise, it's simply an allowing, saying, 'I don't have an agenda for you. The space is here, the beauty is here, go out and talk to a bumblebee as you walk down the path, and you'll get all the answers you could possibly need.' I think of the labyrinth as a truth machine: if you go in with a powerful question, with a sincere intention to listen and to be receptive to whatever comes, in whatever form it comes, you will get an answer. You may not like it, and you can deny it all you want, but you will get it."

He has built it, and they are coming. No charge. Donations accepted. A senior group shuffled around the path the other day, a cable access show shot a piece about it last month, a busload of fifty teachers from St. Paul made the trek, along with "seventy feng shui people," a women's spirituality group, and more. "People come with awe and appreciation," says Quiana. "It's curious; we're not organizing this, but it's starting to become kind of nonstop."

Ask Frost if he thinks there's a reason people are seeking the labyrinths in these times, and he'll snort and say, "What do you think?"

What do I think? Shit, I think I want to move in here, make the world go away, wake up with the hawks, and have tea and languish over the artwork of Brian Andreas. It hangs in Frost's front room and professes, in handwritten scrawl, "I've always liked the time before dawn because there's no one around to remind me who I'm supposed to be, so it's easier to remember who I am."

"We get so top-heavy, especially in the corporate world," Frost says. "We get out of balance, and we discount this whole part of us. Neuroscientists and quantum biologists are all discovering that every cell in your body has the same potential and memory and function as your brain. So you have to allow the brain to create opportunities and exercises that get rid of the noise in the head, the chatter of a thousand monkeys, and let the ego step aside for a moment. Take a walk. Allow for the stillness of the body and mind."

He dabs at his cup of tea, his wife at his elbow. An out-of-tune guitar sits by the fireplace. He picks it up and tries to give it to me as a parting gift, but Quiana intercepts the gesture, rescuing it for one of the kids. Before she does, the creative consultant holds the instrument in his hands like he's never made music, like its function is a mystery. "I've always had the belief that we all come into this world with incredible potentiality of creative force, and that as we go through our lives pieces of that get chopped off," he says. "Another way of thinking about it is layers of defense and protection around that creative nugget and habit. So the question is, how do you peel away those layers, how do you open someone up and access that which is their birthright as a creative being?'

A good start is the labyrinth, where one foot goes in front of the other. The soul meanders, quieter and quieter. A cricket jumps into my hand, grasshoppers dart across my shoes, wings flutter overhead. There's an inner tube on the pond, a trampoline by the barn. My breath is easy and the sun is warm on my shoulders. I'm thinking about how much my dog would love this wide-open space and about what Frost believes: that "everything that attracts our attention in our lives is there for us specifically for a reason. Otherwise we wouldn't notice it."

2005

Being the Buddha at Mile Eight

Last summer, after the late, great Eat Street bar/restaurant Bali went under, the staff of the place gave my neighbor Pete a three-foot-tall statue of Buddha that had been perched in the back lounge. We'd spent several nights there eating, drinking, and listening to great chill-out trance-pop after playing or listening at the Music Box Theater across the street, and I'm sure the Bali kids gave Pete this anti-icon to living in the moment and paying attention as an acknowledgment of their more-than-neighborly business bond.

Soon after, Pete carted Buddha down to last year's Twin Cities Marathon and parked Buddha on the side of the road. After the race, he came by my house with reports of rampant widespread joy and euphoric sights of runners peeling off to rub Buddha's groovy golden glistening belly. The week after the marathon, Pete offered Buddha up to the owners of Kings wine bar, and for the past year the lovable little guy has sat just off the back lounge, keeping silverware-rolling workers and diners alike company in the good karma corner.

So it was with great anticipation that I woke up Sunday morning and met Pete at under-construction Java Jack's. We chatted with stressed-out but amiable owner Jerry Nelson, the pretty girls behind the counter, and a few other neighbors, then headed down to Minnehaha Parkway. Pete carried Buddha, I carried the coffees and my dog Zero's leash, and we found a spot in the shade.

We settled on the immaculately manicured parkway, and I

thought about the conversation Pete and I had had the other night about his cyclist friend who believes that Detroit, bombed-out downtown Detroit, could be the next great crazies haven, on par with Antarctica, Amsterdam, and the City of Lakes. Of course, the parkway is a far cry from Detroit; it is in fact more like pre–Civil War Gettysburg, what with all the mansions and good-life money spilling out onto the sacred shores and hallowed stomping grounds of Lake Harriet.

There was a chill in the air, perfect marathon conditions. We snuggled in at around mile eight of the twenty-six-mile course, having arrived at the same time as the first peloton of the color guard, wheelchair racers, and elite runners—the lot of whom all ignored Buddha, who was partially hidden by a cloister of onlookers, so we moved up the road a bit. Pete wore his pioneer hat pulled down over his ears in defiance of the looming winter and emanated the sort of artist's calm that comes from knowing a perfect id-hits-the-fan storm of love is on its way.

"Watch," said Pete, who served as my play-by-play guru and color commentator for two hours. "The first runners won't even look. Elite runners have one focus. It is not the Buddha. And that can mean enlightenment. They're present to their moment and focused."

He was right. Type A after Type AA after Type AAA blew by with eyes uniformly fixed straight ahead, making for a vista of blank thousand-yard stares and shark's eyes on the prize. No, this group had no time for a statue of Buddha; they were busy being Buddha.

"These are the people who run things," laughed Pete. "The Buddha [statue] won't get any love until the next group."

The brilliant sun rose over the houses of South Minneapolis, a few of which sprouted Emmer for Governor lawn signs. The stunningly sunlit red, yellow, orange, brown, and green leaves blazed down on the sweating, panting athletes, survivors, strivers, mouthbreathers all.

A wonderstruck East Indian man ran by taking pictures of the mansions with a digital camera. A woman in bunny ears ran past three Marines. A woman in a *Colon Cancer Survivor Since 2007*

T-shirt ran alongside people in shirts touting the NYPD, the Green Bay Packers, the Minnesota Twins, Bob Marley, and various hospitals, colleges, dreams, and desires.

"Here we go," said Pete, just as his family joined us, and just before the first wave hit.

It happened in a rush and lasted a total of twenty minutes or so. Runners, feeling the pain, smiled in relief when they saw Buddha. Some said his name out loud, like they'd just seen a long-lost friend. Some cut off others so as to rub Buddha's tummy for "good luck." Infectious smiles radiated from beautiful, beaming, primal people of every color, creed, goal.

A man dressed as Pumpkin Man patted Buddha on the head and cackled off. A woman clasped her hands in front of us as she ran by and bowed a silent namaste to Buddha.

"It makes you want to cry," said Pete, taking the words out of my mouth, a tear running down his cheek a split second later.

The panorama was so magnificent, so rare, and so unmanufactured that I started worrying it would all end too soon. Then I got with the moment and surfed the beauty, knowing it would never end if I truly took the time to take it in and keep it in my heart for good.

We watched the race until the very last stragglers passed. We clapped our guts out for the last runner, then parted ways. I headed home, where my daughter's overnight slumber party was wrapping up. One of the girls, Anushe, whose family hails from India, told us she wants to go to Stanford to study to be a heart surgeon, which reminded me of the group of ten kids I watched spill into the Fresh Wok the night before.

They were all shy sweetness, bright eyes, and curious minds encased in Somali-, Japanese-, Hispanic-, and European-American skins. They moved around the place with great spirits and confidence: the Wayzata high school debate team, post-match and loaded for whatever comes next.

When she came to pick up her daughter, the future Stanford student's mother was thrilled to hear about Buddha's many adventures at the marathon and recounted that a friend of hers from India recently told her that she'd read that Minneapolis was voted the third most spiritual city in the United States, due to all the Zen retreats and meditation centers it supports. And that was before the latest miracle at Mile Eight.

2010

5

. . .

HOOTENANNY

THERE'S A GAME I PLAY WHEN I GO OUT, THOUGH MOST OF THE time I forget about it until the game itself reminds me I was playing all along. The game is "Why did you go out tonight?" Meaning, why did you pull yourself off the couch, leave your warm happy home, your family, your comfort zone, for the crapshoot that is a bar and live music?

Some nights the answer never comes, and you return home from the forage with no more insight than what a trip to the quickie mart might yield. Other nights, you get so many answers you'd need a graphic organizer to keep track of all the lessons and nuggets you stumble upon, so you come home and switch on the dream machine that hums and glows with churchy quiet in the early morning dark and write 'em down.

You shave and shower and leave the house after having had a stupid fight with your teenage son, pick up your neighbor Pete, and talk about how upset you are about what happened. Pete talks you down with the wisdom of another father of another hormone-happy teen, and after you park the car, you call the lad and have a conversation about overreaction and communication, and all's well that ends well until your wife calls you back and disagrees with your parenting style, and all you want to say is that you're "Human," like the great new Killers song, and that you're doing the best you can.

You walk into the Varsity Theater and order a Guinness. You listen to the Mood Swings, Ed Ackerson, Polara, and Janey and Marc and take note of the smallish night-after Thanksgiving crowd, due undoubtedly to the fact that many tryptophan casualties are tired of socializing and stimuli. You run into Samantha Loesch and her sister Molly and get the lowdown on Kings, their new wine-music eatery that is coming to save somnambulant Southwest Minneapolis early in the new year.

You head downtown to Kieran's Irish Pub, where your brother's band, St. Dominic's Trio, is playing to another wrung-out dozen. A couple of old Incarnation kids, Brian Lamb and Mary Stockhaus, are in the house, and you swap notes about the inspiration for your brother's song "Bike Ride on 35W," which talks about freedom and revolution, and whose inspirational break you always take to heart à la Wilco's "What Light."

With plenty of eye-rolls and attitude, the twentysomething tough-girl waitress with the *Real Irish* T-shirt tells you and Pete about the vegan Thanksgiving she got duped into attending. You sit at the bar, taking in the tunes and a pint, and when a gang of post-practice musicians walk in, you say what you and your siblings have taken to saying, proudly, to so many friends and strangers over the past decade: "That's my brother up there."

You tell them about the time when your brother was four years old and he ran around the block wearing nothing but saddle shoes and socks. Then he plasters your hand to your chin with a new one about growing up in South Minneapolis, using all the signposts (Lil' General, Salk's Rexall Drugs) of your youth, and the images of your and his kids meld with all the Irish posters on the wall, and you make note of yet another mystical moment, the likes of which only the truly rich experience.

The next night, you go down to your basement and play "Why do you stay in?" You lift and clean and organize and dig through old boxes of local rock memorabilia for a book you're working on, and listen to your brother's new CDs, the birth of which he and half the town will celebrate this Wednesday at First Avenue.

You're amazed at the bloody sound of his voice, the power of the band, the poetic lyrics about life, love, loss, lust, loyalty. "I Thought We Were Friends" is sure to kick off more than a few kiss-off compilation mixes; "She Loves You Anyway" is a cad-confessional worthy of Westerberg or Zellar; "Out of Bullets" is Crazy Horse good; and, yes, "Bike Ride on 35W" is one for the ages. Duly knocked out, you put on the next CD, by your brother's Van Morrison tribute band, the Belfast Cowboys, and are again amazed at how much better they sound than the washed-up old drama queen Morrison himself.

The music stops and you don't replace it. The silence of the basement suits you. Around midnight, while digging through a box of birthday cards, you find a letter from your brother. The letter is from 1985, written when he was the age that your nephews are now. He wrote it to you after your band Laughing Stock's one and only LP came out. Most of it is too personal to recount here, but a few things you could have written yourself, to him, tonight, and so you'd like to pass them on:

I had to write a letter to be able to say just what I think of the record. Every time I hear it and get a new feeling about it I want to call you up and tell you, but that's kinda hard to do. Still, I think it's important that you know, so this letter's gonna have to do the trick.

It used to be that I would watch you guys play and just itch for the chance to get up there. But now when I see you I can relax and throw myself into your songs and not worry what the people think of me. I'm SO proud of you! When you're singing, it's gotten to the point where I feel like I'm up there with you. When it's your night, it's my night too!

I want you to know I'm behind you 100 percent. No question that it's a personal victory for you, but a record this good has to be looked at as a victory for people who love music. Remember when I said I could never sell anything [if] I didn't completely believe in it? I could sell your music.

I really love you, man. Keep up the fight! Start building the next album in your mind. This is only the beginning. But before you put out number two, I'm going to try to put out my number one somehow. But even if mine is only a pipe dream, yours is real now. Congratulations! There's no one who deserves it more than you! And the rest of the world will benefit from it.

2008

Peace, Love, and Bobby Sherman

It's no secret that kids super-idealize their heroes, and that nostalgia can make even the most indestructible zits vanish with time. But from row 10 at the Minneapolis Auditorium in 1970, my older sister and I, like millions of other teenagers and preteens, were thoroughly convinced that Bobby Sherman was, at the very least, a good guy. Nearly thirty years later, I know this to be a fact. So does my sister. Or at least her answering machine does.

I have a photograph I took from that night, my first rock concert. I dug it up the other day, and its blurry image captures a moment that my memory easily could have recounted more vividly: the frame is dominated by teenage girls in front of us, long hair parted down the middle and hands wildly flashing peace signs. Sherman is wearing black leather pants low on his hips, and a white pirate shirt that would make Seinfeld cringe. He's performing underneath a banner that reads "KDWB/63 The Music People." The only thing the snapshot, and my memory, fails to come up with is the exact song he's singing. It could be the brassy and decidedly not-feminist love song "Little Woman." Or the perky "La La La (If I Had You)." Or "Easy Come, Easy Go," the fluffy hit that more than one cynic has used to describe Sherman's singing career. Or maybe it's "Seattle," the theme to Sherman's short-lived '60s TV series, *Here Come the Brides.* Or it could be the swaggering, sexy (I swear!) "Julie, Do Ya Love Me," the only one that can still conjure dregs of adolescent ache.

The other day, the now grown-up eleven-year-old boy who snapped that picture got a phone call from the fifty-five-year-old Bobby Sherman, and he couldn't have been more thrilled if it had been Bobby Dylan.

"It's pretty much the same show as it was at the Minneapolis Auditorium," Sherman laughed. "You know, the fans want the hits, and that's what we're doing. You were there, so I'm sure you remember—half of the show is the audience. We opened last week in Reno, and they were going crazy like it was back in the '70s."

From 1967 until 1970, Sherman was Leonardo DiCaprio and Hanson rolled into one. He was a short, talented, dishy California boy with a come-hither overbite. Like Pat Boone and Rickie Nelson before him, Sherman exuded a benign sexuality and was inseparable from the character he played on *Brides*—the stuttering, vulnerable, faithful, whipped-on-candy Jeremy Bolt. As older pop stars of the day embroiled themselves in the antiwar movement, Sherman made the same statements palatable for his audience by wearing love beads, paisley, and inspiring the infamous battle cry "Peace, Love, and Bobby Sherman."

"I think I was not offensive to the parents," he said. "They thought I was that proverbial boy-next-door, and that I wouldn't go out on stage and advocate drugs or sex or politics. We had fun. It was the proverbial love-in. And as it was, my life didn't have any skeletons in the closet."

Discovered while singing at a Hollywood party by Jane Fonda, Natalie Wood, and Sal Mineo, Sherman scored a regular job on *Shindig!*—the '60s rock variety show, which led to his role on *Brides*. For three years, he sold millions of records, sold out venues as big as the Houston Astrodome, and became the poster boy for *Flip!*, *Tiger Beat*, and *16* magazines, which he now refers to as "the Internet of the day."

By 1972, it was all over. Sherman starred in an ill-fated *Partridge Family* spin-off called *Getting Together* that was canceled after fourteen episodes. He got married, raised a family, produced records, and wrote scores for TV specials. And unlike so many of his peers who complain about teen stardom, Sherman has fond memories of the chaos. "If I had to do it over again, I'd go right back and do it. I had fun. At first, I was really overwhelmed at how quickly it happened, and how much mail was coming in every week," he said. "It came on so fast and furious, that it didn't really give me much of a chance to digest it, until later. I mean, there was a time when I could have sung 'Auld Lang Syne' with just me and a guitar, and they would have bought anything."

Sherman has made a few charity appearances since his star fell, but when he hits the stage Thursday at Mystic Lake Casino, it will be his first appearance in Minnesota since that 1970 show at the old Minneapolis Auditorium. This is his first tour in more than twenty-five years, as the man who brought a nation to its flower-powered knees has spent the past two decades as an emergency medic, and volunteer, teaching lifesaving techniques with the Los Angeles Police Department.

"I've always had a knack for taking care of others," he said. "There's not a better feeling than helping someone with their lives in the time of stress or trauma. Or bringing new life into the world— I've had five OBs in the field. You can't really compare it. It really outweighs Emmys and Grammys and Oscars and all that, because saving a life makes your day, your month, your year."

After some small talk about Sherman's divorce, his two sons (now musicians themselves), and his home studio, the eleven-year-old kid took over the interview. What came next was thoroughly presumptuous, and unprofessional, but the kid had a request of the guy whose mug used to grin down from his bedroom wall: would he mind giving my sister a call?

Of course, he agreed immediately. He took down her name and phone number, diligently double-checked it, and said he'd call her before his next phone interview. Then he said goodbye, and when he did, he called the kid "Sir."

A few minutes later, the phone rang. "Jim, it's Bobby Sherman again. I called your sister and got an answering machine with a little voice on it, and I just wanted to make sure I had the right number." I assured him that the number was correct, and that the voice belongs to my nephew. I told him my sister was on vacation with her family, and that she'd get the message when she returned home early next week.

Which is today. I have no clue what our hero said on my sister's voice mail, but if you cock your ear to the East, there's a decent chance you'll hear the screams of a fortysomething professional woman coming all the way from Indianapolis.

1998

When in Doubt, Hoot

The tagline on the first poster I ever made for the Mad Ripple Hootenanny was in reaction to the times, which felt GOP cold and lacking in the sort of singer/songwriter/musician community I'd always imagined: "When in doubt, Hoot."

In many ways, the Hoot started in August 2003. My family and I had just landed at Stanford University, where I spent the year taking classes, attending seminars, and bonding with my fellow journalists, who came from India, Israel, Italy, China, North Korea, and all points all over the United States. Early in our sabbatical, one night in Sonoma, a few of us stole away to a bar and picked up some guitars that had been resting by the fireplace and played the few folk tunes from our various countries of origin that we all knew by heart.

It was the first of many warm nights of music I would enjoy playing with my friends from all over the world, and it was there that the dream of well-organized nights of song and spontaneity took root. But I knew that, along with my off-deadline studies, family duties, and relearning what I loved about journalism, I had work to do if I wanted my one-year stay there to feel productive.

So that first week of classes at Stanford, far away from the Minnesota music scene that had enveloped me all those years, I walked into a music store in Palo Alto and timidly asked the clerk behind the counter for a guitar tuner, plus one of those things you put on the fret board that allows you to play chords without bar chording, which I have trouble doing because my fingers are small.

"A capo?" said the guy, who was patient and bald.

"Yeah, man," said me, a tremor of the nonmusician in my voice.

A half an hour later I walked out of the shop with a capo, a tuner, some new guitar strings, and picks. I had spent half of my twenties singing in my original rock-punk-pop bands, REMs and Laughing Stock, and all of my thirties and forties writing about life and music for various publications. But I hadn't sung for twenty years and now here I was aching to be singing, missing it terribly, all the while recalling what Slim Dunlap told me when Laughing Stock broke up in 1986, and I swore I'd never spill my guts on a stage again.

"You'll do it, yes, you will," he said, standing by the soundboard in the 7th Street Entry the night of my band's farewell gig. "It's in you."

I never forgot that, and he was right: the repressed desire to write songs and sing them for people started to burble up in me around 2003 when I would be interviewing musicians for my job as the pop music columnist for the *St. Paul Pioneer Press*. I loved talking music and life with all sorts of artists, but on a professional level it became repetitive. Live reviews were paint-by-numbers writing, and the musicians' egos and their stories started sounding too similar. As a result, music started to feel too much like entertainment and I the entertainment reporter, and so a subtle loneliness would take hold as I found myself yearning, externally, for the natural and unmediafied and down-to-earth camaraderie of musicians and, internally, a deeper relationship with music, singing, and listening.

What's more, I'd always found the "Writing about music is like dancing about architecture" crack to be uninformed, because for me writing about music has always been so much like making music. Still . . .

Rings of Fire (Brothers United)

I gave my brothers their Claddagh rings on St. Patrick's Day weekend almost twenty years ago. We'd spent the previous six months listening out of the corners of our shell- and rock-shocked ears to 9/11 stories about Irish American kids and New York heroes and smartass brothers who'd lost their smartass brothers, so I figured it was now or maybe never.

I wasn't sure what I wanted to say to my smartass brothers, but I wanted to say it once and for all and I wanted to say it with a ring in case something happened to one of us, or in case we found ourselves standing in front of a casket or two having never actually said what we meant to say all these years, through all the jokes and bitch sessions and wise-guy e-mails and quoted song lyrics and phone calls to talk about the game.

I bought my brothers their Claddagh rings on a sun-slushy St. Patrick's Day eve afternoon at Irish on Grand, the groovy little Irish shop in St. Paul that was, at the time, co-owned by my brother's wife's cousin Molly and her husband, Dermot. I lugged my dead-to-the-world-and-drooling three-year-old daughter's carcass out of the car, propped her up on the glass showcase that holds holy cards, rosaries, Ogham stones, Celtic crosses, sun-catchers, and other mystical knickknacks, and told Molly what I needed.

She didn't bat an eye or make a joke. She reached down, cracked open the cabinet behind the counter, and pulled out a small felt case, at the end of which was propped a tiny silver ring with open hands holding a crowned heart. I bought three, for twenty-five bucks each, guessing at the sizes—small for me; small for Jay, my older brother by four years; and medium for Terry, my younger brother by four years.

I gave my brothers their Claddagh rings at bars, to the sound of bands. The Dubliner Pub and Gaelic Storm, Friday. First Avenue and Ike Reilly, Saturday. The Dubliner is a real Irish bar. It's set alone on the corner of University and Vandalia in St. Paul. It's got Christmas lights year-round, the requisite Irish beer and whiskey signs, and a portrait of John and Bobby Kennedy called *Brothers United* that hung in thousands of Catholic American homes in the '70s, including the one my brothers and I grew up in.

At the Dubliner that Friday, a massive white tent had been erected in the parking lot, and portable heaters were set up on the concrete to fend off the March chill. A couple of thousand down-jacketed Friday night lights were dancing and drinking to Gaelic Storm, who raged with a last-night-on-Earth-so-let's-mosh fury, playing fiddle- and bodhran-spiked tunes like "Drink the Night Away,"

"She Was the Prize," and "After Hours at McGann's." My friend Paul and I came late, ran into my friend Theresa and her friend Laura, and the four of us made our way into the front bar and bought shots of Tullamore Dew, the Irish whiskey a musician friend of mine taught me how to drink earlier that winter at the Dubliner.

Straight away, the Dew had me flirting with Theresa, who is my age, and a woman from Galway, who was about my mom's age. Molly and Dermot came by, hand in hand, and the love was ramping up to giddy green levels when we finally saw Jay. He was frazzled, having come over from the Viking Bar, where he and his wife, Kim, had been imbibing in their regular Friday happy hour with the Front Porch Swingin' Liquor Pigs. He had no money, but he had talked the Dubliner doorman into letting him into the bar to find me or an ATM. We scrounged up some cover charge, got him squared away, and got him a shot of Dew. We were both drunk, happy, holding full shot glasses, and the crowd was passing the Gaelic Storm fiddle player overhead when I gave him his ring.

At First Avenue the next night, we were with our adopted brother Ike Reilly, who, yes, we see something of ourselves in—husband, father, friend, worker, rocker, writer, drinker, struggler, Claddagh ring–wearer—so much so that it's more collaboration than listening when he sings stuff like, "Cars and girls and drinks and songs make this world spin around."

This night, Terry was perched on the stairway above us, videotaping the show. After the set finished and the room started to empty, I made my way through the exiting crowd, climbed the stairs, and put my hand on his shoulder. We shook our heads, blown away one more time by the almost naive-for-the-times passion of Reilly and his band. We were both sober and happy and damn near weeping when I gave him his ring.

When I gave my brothers their Claddagh rings, I told them the same thing. "You are my brother. I love you. This ring has super powers. Whenever this world gets you down, remember . . ."

I didn't get to finish, because in both cases we mutually smothered my blabbing with boy hugs. But I want to finish, because I hear stories every day about brothers who don't like each other or don't talk to each other. This isn't that story. This is a story about three brothers who have fought with each other and called each other names, but who still like being with each other. This is a story about three brothers who sit in boardrooms and cadavered client meetings and cold-blooded classrooms, but whose silver rings, worn or not, trump every brass ring they've ever heard of.

This is a story about three brothers who may worry about their kids, money, marriages, parents, careers, and fading jump shots, but not about their stuck-with-each-other love. This is a story about three brothers who keep each other honest by making sure none of them gets too down or cute or self-involved or big for his britches, and who are always there for each other, like the time the middle one needed an ending to a story he was having trouble ending, a story he didn't want to end. He'd written everything he could think to write about the Claddagh rings, but he wondered if they and those nights meant the same thing to his smartass brothers as they did to him. So he e-mailed them and, not for the first or last time, asked for help.

"I remember that band, that friend of yours, the Kennedy pictures on the wall at the Dubliner, and not wanting to go home," wrote the oldest. "I remember saying this ring is too small, I gotta get it sized, still do, means the world to me."

"It's on my right hand now," wrote the youngest. "It won't fit on the left. It's slightly bent upward, and I stopped wearing it for a short time out of fear that it would catch on something and rip my finger from my hand. It means a lot to me; I didn't exchange it for the correct fit because I wanted the original one. You gave it to me at First Avenue after Ike's last show there, told me that you loved me and that this would be a reminder of that (or something). Whenever I get the urge to hang myself, I think about the Claddagh ring until it goes away."

2004

Sing Out!

This one is dedicated to Mr. Janssen's first grade class at John S. Burroughs public school in Minneapolis, most of whom sang with a group for the first time in their lives this week, and all of whom sang a pretty unforgettable song to me one week ago this very beautiful day.

It is also dedicated to the memory of Bob Dylan opening his October 25 concert at the Xcel Energy Center with Hank Williams's anthem to parting clouds and rising energy, "Wait for the Light to Shine," and to the Twin Cities Sacred Harp Singers, along with Neko Case, Slug, Patty Loveless, Baaba Maal, Dave Douglas, Ralph Stanley, Emmylou Harris, the Carpetbaggers, John Hawkins, Aaron Carter, Concrete Blonde, Sean Na Na, Craig David, and many others, all of whom will be singing in your hometown over the next few days.

So should you. Be singing, I mean. God knows we don't need another How to Act During All This message, but Fran Healy is dead right when he sings on Travis's latest, "Don't forget to sing." Nor is Bob Dylan being coy when he sings on his latest, "Everybody get ready and lift up your glasses and sing." Yes, we need to know when to shut up, and when to listen and when to sing backup. But at some point, our job, our reason for being, is to cut loose and let voices carry.

I don't mean to suggest that everybody run out and engage in wanton public singing. I just mean that for the most part, your voice has escaped the Evil Vocal Processing Plant that so many have been sucked into, and to keep it alive, you need to fill your car, shower, closet, or head with the sound of it. Listen to it. Don't try to be someone else, don't try to mimic the guy in the car or shower next to you. Don't try to be older or younger than you are, or something you're not. Sing your song.

The therapeutic benefits to doing so are obvious. Lost your job? Sing. Losing your mind? Sing. Your favorite basketball team lost by thirty? Again? Sing. Warble. Wail. And if you feel a need to be with others while doing so, make your way over to St. Sahag Armenian Church Saturday morning (sign-up at 9 a.m.) for the Third Annual Minnesota State Sacred Harp Winter Singing Convention. Be sure to bring something to add to the potluck, and don't forget your voice. You might discover its true power, if you find yourself like I did a few years ago, standing in the middle of what the shape note singers call the hollow square, singing and gasping and testifying to the mystery of life and music and community.

Those zany shape note singers make the same sound as the four young black women I walked behind on Hennepin Avenue a couple of weeks ago. They were skipping arm in arm under a shaky-looking construction trestle, on their way to a club, singing at the top of their lungs. I couldn't make out the song, but the sound of their time-of-their-lives voices was true.

Speaking of which, I listen carefully to the sound of my kids singing these days. I know the clock is ticking on their innocence and that one of these days, some critic or another will tell them they're doing it wrong. Then someone else will teach them "how" to sing, and the giggling at the sound of their own beautiful mistakes will be replaced by timbre and scales, and they'll be on their way to sounding like everybody else.

It's already starting to happen. Our six-year-old, Henry, loves to sing along to Dream Street, the new boy band whose CD he asked for and got from Santa. He sings that stuff—the first stuff he's claimed as his own—like he means it, like he wrote it, like they're his songs to sing.

Our three-year-old, Helen, especially, loves to sing. And scream. She's three. Her favorite movies are *The Sound of Music, Mary Poppins,* and *The Exorcist.* In church, which I don't go to as often as I might, she holds hands with my mom, whose singing voice is the first I ever heard, glorious and steady and comforting, and she belts out "The Our Father" like a gospel singer who's gotten into the wine.

She sang into a microphone for the first time at a coffee shop a few Fridays ago in front of an audience that included the great bassist and father Johnny Hazlett and the pop music columnist of the *St. Paul Pioneer Press* and the music editor of *City Pages*, who were having lunch with Helen, who got a chocolate chip cookie and two thumbs-up and one Wendy O. Williams comparison for her efforts.

You should have seen her face when she heard her voice—big, loud, undesigning—come out of the tiny P.A. that Johnny switched on for her. She puffed up her cheeks, and her eyes got huge and glassy, and she looked like a completely different person. She sang "Silent Night" and made me do it, too, and the sound of my girl's little big voice and the cold aluminum of the microphone on my lips reminded me of how much fun it is to sing.

Now it's your turn. Get your boss's voice out of your head. Get your parents' voices out of your head. Get your worst critics' and your favorite teachers' and singers' out of your head. Sing your song. Sing your song. Sing your song.

2002

"Possibly the Most Awesome Place on Earth"

The first night I landed in Montana, Pete took me to the Murray Bar and Hotel in Livingston, which, since it was built in 1904, has served the likes of Buffalo Bill, Calamity Jane, and Robert Redford (during the filming of *A River Runs through It*), and which the late, great chef and storyteller Anthony Bourdain championed as one of his favorite spots on the planet.

When he visited Livingston, Bourdain stayed in the Peckinpah Suite, named for "Bloody Sam" Peckinpah, writer of *Gunsmoke* and *The Rifleman* and producer/director of westerns *Ride the High Country*, *The Wild Bunch*, and *Pat Garrett and Billy the Kid*. The hotel manager took us up the elevator ("circa 1904," she said proudly) and showed us around. Pete sat down at the lobby piano and played a tune amidst the taxidermy, and we ended up in the bar talking to the bartender and sitting on what could've been the stool where Bourdain sat when he asked a local Livingston resident, for a segment of CNN's *Anthony Bourdain: Parts Unknown,* "When's the last time you looked out at those mountains and opened your arms and said, 'I live in possibly the most awesome place on Earth'?"

Bourdain had killed himself only a few days earlier, and Pete and I, a couple of middle-aged cowboys ourselves, talked about the whys and why-nots of something so tragic. Bourdain's decision to check out hovered over our trip, from too-soon dark humor to real feeling and understanding, and early on I told Pete that Bourdain would have liked hanging out with us and so many of our crew, that we would have been sympathetic and empathetic soul brothers—just give us a call, dude. Pete nodded and drove along, seriously not giving a fuck about anything that wasn't impacting him in the here and now and in front of us.

But my oh my, Bourdain was so right about Montana. Stunning. Moving. Gorgeous, like nowhere else. Rough country: no country for old men, women, or obsolete anything. People work hard here. People work the land here.

Taking it all in from the back deck of Pete's cabin, the Crazy Mountains in the distance and the Yellowstone River gushing along in front of me as the sun rises and my coffee steams and the birds chirp as loud as any Minneapolis freeway, it occurs to me that I basically drove eight hundred miles up a mountain, up from the super humid swamplands of Minnesota, up, up, up to the clean, crisp, 5,400-foot elevation air of Montana, and hell if all the elements, nature, rivers, hot springs, cattle, rainbows, and glorious countryside aren't proving more than good for my asthma, allergies, and stretched spirit.

I'm taking a break from playing music at the moment. I do it fairly often, to recharge my batteries, to write new songs, to stay offstage, and here is where I need to finally admit I probably have tinnitus—incurred first by my front-row-and-head-in-the-speakers experience of hearing the Suicide Commandos, the Runaways, and the Ramones at the State Theater on July 1, 1975, followed by incalculable times at band practices and gigs, with my head positioned a few feet away from blaring Marshall stacks.

These days the ringing is always there, and although I still think

a good live show and noise hangover are worth it, it helps to take a
few nights off away from the clubs.

The First Dad Rock Column in the History of Rock Criticism

What were the '80s like, Dad?

Well, kid, let me tell you. That was the decade MTV started wa-
tering music down. But your dad, and lots of other folks you know,
regarded music as more special than that. Sure, we watched MTV
out of the corner of our eyes and cocked our ears to commercial
radio for stuff like Prince, Madonna, and Springsteen, but most of
the time we couldn't be bothered. We were snobs basically, and we
listened to stuff like *Real Rock 'n' Roll Radio*.

What was that?

A radio show. I've still got tapes of it in the basement, if you're
really interested. It was on KUOM-AM, which everybody now knows
as Radio K (770 AM). It was on every Saturday morning for a couple of years.

Your mom and I would wake up late after being at the bar the
night before, and we'd tune in to hear Billy Golfus, Peter Jesperson,
Kevin Cole, Dave Ayers, Blake Gumprecht, and others play records
that you'd end up buying because those guys said they were cool.
Some of those guys became friends of ours, because we trusted them
and because—we didn't know this at the time—what we shared was
sacred. Like communion. What were the bars like?

They were like the Clown Lounge at the Turf Club, and the 7th
Street Entry, and the 400 Bar are now. Remember when I took you
to the 400 that one day, and I was interviewing musicians for that
movie they made for that museum in Seattle? Remember when you
met my friend Grant Hart?

Yeah, he was smoking that funny-smelling cigarette that he and
your friend Billy (Sullivan) put out when he heard me coming.

Never mind that. Grant was in a band called Hüsker Dü. And

they were incredible. They did everything themselves: they made their own records, which were incredible on their own, and they drove their van all over the country, booked all their own shows, and sold their records in independent stores like Oar Folkjokeopus, because that was part of the art. Plus, it was fun.

Why didn't they just use the Internet?

It wasn't invented yet. We used something called word of mouth. And fanzines. All sorts of 'em, with names like *Your Flesh* and *Cake* and *Easier Said Than Done* and *Maximum Rock 'n' Roll* and *Matter.* For local music, instead of chat rooms, we had the newspaper *Sweet Potato,* then *City Pages* and the *Twin Cities Reader,* and the critics were in bed with the musicians, sometimes literally, and like the musicians, most of the critics would spill their guts, like Tom Hallett does regularly in *The Pulse* now. What I mean is, people actually wrote stuff. Passionate stuff. Our basement's full of this junk. You should check it out sometime. Actually, I can quote a lot of it to you off the top of my head, if you're interested.

I'll pass. Okay, how 'bout just one?

I'll give you two, about the Replacements. In 1983, Uncle Dave wrote in the *Minnesota Daily,* righteously, "Unprofessional? Sure. Thrilling? You bet. There isn't another band going that you could see twenty nights in a row and be moved every time for a different reason."

Then there was Steve Perry's cover story of the October 1989 issue of *Musician* magazine, which called the 'Mats "The Last Best Band of the '80s." The next month, Jon Bon Jovi wrote a letter to the editor that said something like, "How can the Replacements be the best band of the '80s when I've never even heard of them?"

Hey! I heard on the radio the other day that Bon Jovi's coming to the Target Center in July. Are you going?

No. Sadly, that's the week we'll be attending our family reunion in Colorado.

What was a typical week like for you in the '80s, Dad?

This is gonna sound like science fiction, but it's all true. I grew up at First Avenue, where your mom and I met. It was a haven of *diversity,* before anyone started using that word, where reggae bands and soul singers would share bills with punk bands and new-wave techno outfits.

One night, we'd see Man Sized Action do Naked Raygun's "Bomb Shelter," or Rifle Sport's Chris Johnson doing his contortionist act, or the Morells or the Slickee Boys or the Wallets getting goofy, or the Del Fuegos hollering "To the bar!" like a challenge, a battle cry, then jumping offstage and racing each other and us to see who could get to a beer first.

One night, you'd see Hüsker Dü define *anti-establishment.* The next, the Time would define *off the hook,* ten years B.C. (before cool). One day, you'd go to band practice and the guys would be buzzing about some single, EP, or LP they got at Oar Folk that week.

One night, you'd go see the English Beat, and First Avenue would throb like you've never seen a room throb before or since. The next night, my band would be playing in the Entry, and Prince would just happen to stroll in, listen to a song, then go back out into the mainroom to jam with Sheila E.

Did that really happen?

Yep.

What else?

There was the night at First Avenue we saw the Replacements do a song called "I Will Dare" that was getting airplay on the briefly cool WWTC-AM, and as Paulie played the opening riff, the whole room surged with new fans, faces, and friends.

What was the name of your bands again, Dad?

REMs, and Laughing Stock.

Why don't you sing in a band anymore, Dad?

Partly because I got sick of sound checks and hauling bass amps and kick-drum cases up three flights of stairs to our practice space before and after gigs. Mostly, it was because I wanted to write. I wanted to write down what happened then, and now, so I wouldn't forget it.

Do you miss it?

Some of it. Hanging out with the guys and writing and recording songs was a blast. And now that I think about it, I actually do miss hauling gear and the stop-and-smell-the-stale-smoke tediousness of sound checks. And the hot lights on my face, and the feeling of roaring into a microphone at the top of my lungs, with three guys who could make the sound of a locomotive engine pushing me from behind. I miss that, yeah.

Sounds great.

It was, but it's not dead. The seeds that all those bands planted, and the bands that came before us, took root. There's a terrific scene happening right now in this town, even though it sometimes feels like its participants are too hung up on irony, apathy, and second-guessing.

Back then, regionalism was a big deal. We felt a kinship with all these bands and clubs in Chicago, Athens, New York, Cleveland, Washington, Los Angeles, Seattle, and Akron. In fact, you're starting to see regionalism happening again, as a reaction to all the bad music that's being sold nationally. Look at the Twin Cities, for example. There's a thriving scene here, and lots of great new music that feels, all of a sudden, like it is bursting at the seams, ready for the world.

Like now, there was a community so tightly knit that if some band from Athens, Georgia, came in with the same name as your buddy's band, REMs, you'd automatically side with the hometown team, even though you suspected the Georgia version was the breath of fresh air we'd all been waiting for. It was a community so tight that, to this day, even as we're cocooning with our kids and studies, when we see one another in the co-op or the bar or the movie theater, there is a warm nod of recognition.

I never knew any of this stuff. Where can I find out more?

I suppose you could read or rent *High Fidelity*. That's your dad, and uncles, and most of their best friends. They remember. They were at the Steve Earle show the other night, and plenty of them will be at Jeff Tweedy's show later this month at the Guthrie. They still love songs and the covenant of smart rebellion.

Or you can read Nirvana biographer Michael Azerrad's forthcoming book, which is called, appropriately, *Our Band Could Be Your Life*. It comes out in July, and it documents a lot of this stuff with entire chapters devoted to the stories of thirteen bands, including Hüsker Dü, the Replacements, Black Flag, Sonic Youth, Big Black, Fugazi, and Beat Happening. It's an important book.

When we talk about it, do you miss it?

Not at all. I felt part of something then, and it makes me want to feel part of something, always. The message of that time was, Go forth. And look at what we're all doing now. We're doctors and bums and lawyers and divorcés and parents and songwriters and screenwriters and copywriters and musicheads and out-of-touch-but-fighting-it thirtysomething, fortysomething, fiftysomething couples. So to me and your mom and others, the '80s never ended. We still listen to new music, and we still love bands that have that certain something-something.

Um, Dad?

Yes, son?

Can I have my Eminem CD back?

Sure.

Did you like it?

Sort of. But it's not really my thing.

2001

They Sing 'til They Drop

One of my newest tunes is "Flight of the Dog Day Cicadas," inspired by the insects that, come every swampy August, make this town sound like it's been invaded by a locust. Dog day cicadas live underground for years, then spend the last three months of their lives wailing away their mating call until they shuffle off their mortal exoskeleton. Hear 'em? How's the song go? "Dog day cicadas / They sing 'til they drop."

Same here.

Writing about music focuses my intellect and helps me make sense of all the emotions it conjures, but the truth is, there is no feeling like standing under a hot stage light and singing your song, your raw and to-the-bone and of-the-moment feelings, to an empty or full room; nothing like opening your heart to strangers; nothing like getting over yourself and out of yourself and out of your own head to make a noise, joyful and otherwise. No wonder I take long breaks from it all and yearn for so much quiet in the rest of my life: I'm resting up before the next possession and for the next exorcism. Feel me, fellow singers?

In retrospect, I learned a lot about discipline, writing, journalism, storytelling, and music during my twenty-year break from making music. I don't think too much about it in terms of "music career," because for the most part it was so much fun, but for sure I didn't miss the feelings of failure, or frustration, or all the unbalanced emotions that being in a very urgent punk-pop-noise rock band conjured up in me. But by the end of my hiatus, deep down I suppose I missed the thrill of it all, the sheer terror of it all, the showbiz of it all, the art, the insanity, the freedom, the volume, the creativity . . . . But at that moment I enjoyed writing more, and I followed that feeling.

None of which is on the table for me at the moment here in Montana, where I'm concentrating on just being. The magnificence of it all reminds me of my not-so-latent and repressed John Denver–Henry David Thoreau–Mother Nature's Son side, and all the natural beauty has me hankering again for a simpler, slower pace for my life and work and family.

Then again, the world is as loud as you make it, wherever you are, and Lord knows at the moment I am all about the quiet of my Montana hermitage.

This Week's Best Bet: Shhh . . .

When I was a young music-addicted teenager, one of my favorite summer rituals was to bike over to Lake Harriet with my tape recorder, sit near the edge of the water, and watch the sun set as I listened to my favorite compilation tapes. Pretentious? You bet.

And maybe even a little dangerous, thought my oldest sister, Minnow, who came upon this scene once while walking around the lake with one of her friends. She was probably worried about her weird little brother, who sometimes seemed to prefer music to people, so when we were back home she took me aside and said, "Music is great, but do you need to have it all the time? I mean, silence is good, too."

I've thought about her comment often over the years, especially when there's a pause in the cacophony. Or, rather, when I choose to make a pause in the cacophony. Which is what I do from time to time, most recently last week.

There were lots of things to do and shows I should have been at, but with the exception of listening to a few new CDs I'd been wanting to dig into and going out to a couple of clubs for fun, for the most part I stayed home, spent time alone, and put on the sounds of silence.

Now that admission is not going to go over too well with those who have come to expect nonstop picks and pans from your neighborhood music scribe. Nor will it be popular with the music industry, which is built on nonstop pickers and panners who get you out to pay cover charge, buy drinks, and purchase as much music as you can possibly purchase.

Don't get me wrong: obviously, I believe music to be one of the great paths to community, spirituality, sexuality, peace of mind, inspiration, self-discovery, fun, blah, blah, blah. But listening to music is an intense engagement. It can be emotionally exhausting, all that hearing of others' stories, as well as emotionally recharging, because the best music is, well, *music*. What a perfect word.

But in the end, it can also be somewhat unsatisfying, because no matter how much we're discovering about ourselves, the fact is, we're reading somebody else's Cliff's Notes on the book we're writing. That is, music is part of life, not life itself, so the best bet for this weekend (or next, or sometime soon, anyway) is: you and the sound of your own breath. Try it. Try what I did last week. Turn it all off. Take a moment (or ten) to listen to yourself, your head and your heartbeat, and you might be surprised—at what you hear and at what you hear after that. Silence is not only an essential part of life, but an essential element of music listening, because it provides a spatial relationship to the music itself, a black hole to music's white noise. And nothing sounds richer than music heard by fresh ears. For a long time, I thought of music as my meditation. But I've changed my tune on that, after talking to those who truly use meditation for balance. And they're not the only ones who know the secret of silence: I watch older guys in the barbershop I go to, and they often all just sit there, not talking, looking out the plate-glass window at the world rushing by.

At first, I thought they were sort of sad. Now I think they're wise guys who've found a sanctuary and some kindred spirits who have discovered that sitting on the sidelines is more important than being in the rat race.

The other night, I saw self-help guru Anthony Robbins on TV. He's a fascinating guy, and some of what he says is true, but mostly he makes me nervous. He talked a lot about improving oneself and spouted that old bromide about how human beings reach only 60 or 70 percent of our full potential, and all I could do is think that maybe there's a reason for that. I mean, I wonder if Anthony's 30 percent ever likes to do what mine does: goof off and do nothing.

"Silence is good, too." I've always believed that, ever since my sister suggested as much, and most times these days I recall her words after huge concerts, where the music has been going nonstop for eight or more hours. I get to my car and get in and the sound is . . . nothing. Like a womb.

I was also reminded of her words last summer in Seattle, when I was covering the opening of the Experience Music Project, a shrine to technology and activity. I heard plenty of musicians and dignitaries that weekend, but at the moment the person I remember most was the cabbie who drove me to the museum on opening day. Outside, the city teemed with press people, cameras, cacophony. He and I were sitting in the cab, stuck in traffic, windows rolled up, air conditioning on. I knew I had a long day in front of me, and so did he. I asked him what kind of music he liked.

"Jazz," he responded. "The world is so crazy, you need to have something that lets you get away from it all and think."

He's not alone; witness the popularity of so much ambient

music, zone-out music, background music, techno, Muzak, lo-fi, electronica, New Age, and anything else that stills the waters of the modern world. It may not be an original thing to say that there's too much stimulation, but it might be to say that if our great president was really paying attention to the soul of this country, he'd take a tip from his own work habits and his good friends the Mexicans and declare a national mandatory daily siesta.

Because it seems to me that North Americans are fried. We can't pay attention, we're easily distracted by big oil and bad entertainment, and it's time we got our bearings. There are people on this planet who are more peaceful than our stressed-out, overworked populace, and it seems to me that we could learn something from them.

What I'm saying is that everybody should sign up for the president's new fitness program and take a little quiet time, ten minutes a day or something, and get a grip. I did last week, and this is what I heard: buses, airplanes, cats. A coffee machine burbling, car wheels screeching, a morning dove cooing. The hum of a computer, the buzz of a bee, the laughter of kids. Bullfrogs, dogs, crickets, screech owls, more cats, a dripping faucet. Baseball on a radio, coals spitting through a grill, wind through the pines. Wind chimes.

The far-off echo of the distant memory of John Prine singing, "Stop hollerin' at me"; Whiskeytown singing, "Breathe in, breathe out"; and Mama Cass singing, "You gotta make your own kind of music, sing your own special song / Even when nobody else is around."

2001

Can You Even Still Hear This Song?

Here in Montana, I'm working on some new songs I like, and re-arranging some of the songs from a CD I released last year that was, like so much musical and artistic product in this world, ignored by most of the rest of my fellow human beings.

Onward. My hard lesson learned is that it makes me realize that we do not in fact live in a utopian all-supportive music scene I once believed existed, organically and well-nurtured, and that while community is an important and healthy thing to be part of, it's more important to do your own thing. It also makes me glad and proud that I've been generous with my time, enthusiasm, and ears over the years.

The good news is I'm not going to stop listening to or making music, and I know for sure that my mother, brothers, and lover got something out of several songs on the record. But I won't lie: the lack of feedback and, yes, attention made me, like countless others whose music has fallen on deaf ears, wonder about why I put myself out there and risk so much, when it really feels like nothing matters, like nothing of the heart is of any substance, like nothing of my heart is worth listening to.

The first song on my record *Songs for the Band to Learn* is "Gentle Man." I wrote it as Donald Trump and all the screaming white male faces of the 2016 Republican National Convention filled my muted TV screen, as I thought about all the gentle men I know and love. Ironically enough, the song wonders,

> In a world gone wrong
> Can you even still
> Hear this song
> And the quiet heart of a gentle man?

The joke is, almost no one did. A few friends, some of my fellow songwriters and family members told me they dug it, and deejay Andrea Swensson played it on her local music show, critic Chris Riemenschneider gave it a nice sentence in the *Star Tribune*, and fellow songwriter and author Dylan Hicks wrote me a nice blurb, but that's it, so at the moment I'm sitting here on top of a mountain, thinking about what's next.

Anyway, onward. The entire experience leaves me wiser, hollow, relieved, and I'm left to wonder how much attention is ever enough for any of us, or if that's truly what we want. I know, at long last, I don't. Here in Montana, I'm living out another set of lines from the new record:

> Here I am at the crossroads again
> Wondering if I'll ever find my way back in
> Is this it?
> One and done
> And nothing left to give?

Dan Israel and the Struggle

"The only people for me are the mad ones, the ones who are mad to live, mad to talk, mad to be saved, desirous of everything at the same time, the ones who never yawn or say a commonplace thing, but burn, burn, burn like fabulous yellow roman candles exploding like spiders across the stars, and in the middle you see the blue center light pop, and everybody goes, 'Awwwww.'"

By writing that in 1957, Jack Kerouac launched a few generations of mad ones—freethinkers, musicians, artists, dreamers. It may be the most romantic passage from *On the Road,* one that endorses seizing the day, but what it doesn't address is what fuels those fabulous yellow roman candles, what darkness lies at the blue center. What it doesn't address is the Struggle.

The Struggle bonds us like nothing else. And I don't mean turning points or tragedies; I mean the day-to-day struggle that comes with deciding to continue on, to find our path. We need to hear the sound of the Struggle because it makes us feel less alone and because when we hear it—one person telling another about his or her struggle—we hear hope: we can get up in the morning, put on the coffee, and drag ourselves out into the world, knowing that the Struggle is universal.

At the moment, we are not getting to hear the strugglers so much. What we are getting instead is a lot of fake music, a lot of happy music for fat times that does little but numb and provide escape.

Sting doesn't struggle, nor does Yanni. They have all the answers, which inevitably makes for truly tedious music. But at the core of all great music is some struggle or another, and some of the most rewarding music centers around the Struggle itself. The Chills' "Song for Randy Newman, Etc." is one of the most gut-wrenching, in which songwriter Martin Phillips faces off with his cross of creativity, bleeding his way through a recurring chorus of "Hunger, hunger, hunger."

Slim Dunlap's "Nowheres Near" is the sound of a band discovering that "No one cares, cuz we're no one." American Music Club's "Johnny Mathis' Feet" finds singer Mark Eitzel asking his would-be mentor, "Johnny, Johnny, can you tell me how to live?" Dismissing struggling musicians as narcissistic whiners is an understandable reaction because songs of failure may be the most difficult to hear. But they should be heard because struggling musicians are us—people who struggle.

I never laugh at the old joke that goes, "I'm a waitress, but I really want to direct," because to do so is to trivialize the struggle toward self-expression, which is part of every homo sapiens and has been a springboard to tons of interesting art about the artistic process, from *All About Eve* to *Driver 23* to *A Fan's Notes*.

Over the years, I've heard countless horror stories from struggling musicians about paced hotel rooms in the middle of the night, suicide fantasies, crises of faith, and worse. Most talk about their muse like it's a blessing, yes, but also a curse, and it is a curse that you and I will never quite know.

Because no matter how successful a musician becomes, he or she will always be a struggling musician because the blank canvas always awaits: Talent does what it can, genius does what it must and all that.

Besides, it's irrational to dismiss musicians as whiners when the Struggle (the title of several songs I know of) has been responsible for so much memorable music. Such as, off the top of my head: "Over the Rainbow," "They're Blind," "Trouble in Mind," "Work and Hope," "I Just Wasn't Made for These Times," "Otherness Blues," "Nothing'severgonnastandinmyway (again)," "We Gotta Get Outta

This Place," "Fast Car," "Ballad of the Opening Band," "White Christ-
mas," "Strength," "Fight the Power," "Seven Year Ache," "Police &
Thieves," "Worn Down by the Chase," "I Can't," "Looking Out for
Me," and "Last Words."

Those last four are by Dan Israel, a Minneapolis-based songwriter whose band, the Cultivators, has been kicking around the
local club scene for the past few years. They appear, along with seven
others, on Israel's stunning new solo album *Dan Who?* which comes
to us as the unvarnished work of a desperate man who has spent his
life doing what he was called to do to a chorus of shrugs. And at the
moment, I can't recall a more honest recording.

Over the course of the record, we get to know Israel intimately,
but not only him. *Dan Who?* is about every artist you have ever
known or been: they are difficult to be with because their plight is
so ego-driven, so raw, so naked. They find themselves at family func-
tions trying to explain why they're still broke, trying to justify their
latest vanity projects. When they're with other musicians, they put
on brave faces and commiserate on the nobody-understands-us tip.

But when they get home, alone with their thoughts, they feel
dirty, as if they need to shower off all the B.S. they've been spinning.

Israel's record gets to all of that and more in a way that I've never
heard before. Framed by his lonely voice and lonelier acoustic guitar, he confronts his own envy and bitterness and the fact that while
the rest of the world has moved on to more serious pursuits, he has
been left stranded with his muse, his past, and his future looming
like a dark abyss.

In the wake of his chased dream are failed relationships, lack
of recognition, and an amorphous search for self-worth and sanity.

"Don't tell me that I'm helpless and weak, / unless you've lived
inside my brain," sings Israel. "I don't even want to hear you speak /
I don't think I should have to explain." He doesn't have to explain, of
course, because *Dan Who?* does it for him. Ironically enough, these
songs couldn't have come from a full-time professional musician.
Between Cultivator gigs and his day job as a "glorified secretary" at
the Minnesota Legislature, Israel wrote and recorded about what it

feels like to be a twenty-nine-year-old musician staring at his own obscurity and mortality.

"Nobody wants to play a losing hand, / nobody wants to book a losing band / Too much supply and not enough demand, / and you're out twenty grand," he sings at one point, then, "All my friends have grown older and changed / So have I, it feels a little strange / They look at me and don't know what to say / All my friends have slowly slipped away."

As those passages might suggest, the first half of the record offers not a single moment of levity, just the singer's uncool admission that he's hurting. But *Dan Who?* is a revelation not because it's about Israel's failings but because it's about his feelings—a rare achievement in songwriting these days (the record's best song is "Overloaded," about trying to fit in with the hip crowd and dealing with music industry cliques).

Spending time with Israel's bald-faced tunes over the past couple of weeks has reminded me of so many people I know from so many parts of the country. It has also convinced me that people should go out and buy it, to offer some support. To that end, *Dan Who?* is an enraging work to hear in the context of the Napster debate, because if music should be free, then so should food, wine, books, and everything else that provides us with nourishment, ecstasy, guidance.

That is to say that we should be taking better care of our artists, not getting mealy-mouthed about how they get paid. Because if we invest in them, we get as a reward remarkable gifts, like the end of *Dan Who?*

After all the darkness, there is some hard-won light. There's a love letter to his big brother ("Looking Out for Me"), a semi-apology to his worried parents ("Tears of Joy"), and a sunny love song ("Hang On to Now"), none of which could have existed without the songs of Struggle that came before. All three suggest that *Dan Who?* is a get-it-out-of-his-system steppingstone to bigger things.

Pablo Picasso once famously said, "Every child is an artist. The problem is how to remain an artist once he grows up." Israel infamously sings, "I used to try to please everyone, now it's just people that I shun / You said, 'Work hard,' and that's all that I did, now I'm no longer that nice young kid."

He is singing from a crossroads that every artist eventually comes to. The relatively easy decision to go down the starving-artist path usually happens when you're a teenager sowing your oats, mad at the world and full of yourself. But what happens when a dream too tired to come true leaves a rebel without a clue?

Dan Who? is what happens. The title obviously is in reference to the nonreaction—imaginary or otherwise—of club bookers, critics, and local audiences when confronted with the singer's name. Well, somebody buy a billboard, hire a blimp, and give this guy his due already. His name is Dan Israel, one of the mad ones, one of the strugglers, and he just made the record of his life.

2000

Free and Grateful

Like I said, I feel Dan Israel, and all the independent artists, and I told Pete so.

"I love Dan Israel," he said, a vista of snow-capped mountains, redwood trees, and the deer and the antelope at play filling the windshield of his truck. "Dan Israel's records are great for long-distance driving, and he's been with me through a lot of miles." We popped in Dan's new one *You're Free,* and I reminded myself—in these crazy days when it feels like so much is at stake—to stay focused and practice gratitude and keep my head and heart open to all sorts of learning and love.

Gratitude: I was thrilled to record my last record with Dan Kowalke, guitarist and producer/engineer for the Belfast Cowboys, and I was more than encouraged by the fact that I was able to create and execute a successful Kickstarter campaign. I had a blast at the CD release show for the record. I love the guys in my band, the Dog Day Cicadas, and all the people who know and love and support the Hoot. Just happy to be here and to be part of something, and I'll keep writing and singing songs, if only for me and the birds in my 'hood. Luckily, I do remember the handful of times I've heard my songs on the radio, and I know full well what an electric feeling that is, knowing that your song is being heard by thousands simultaneously at that very moment, and that rush that comes from being heard, validated, and loved—just like the legends. A few of whom I got together with (speaking of good Hoots!) one evening at a Starbucks outside the St. Louis Park movie theater.

Talk about great singers: it was an honor to sit and chat that night with Bobby Vee, who died in 2016 and whom Bob Dylan called "the most meaningful person I've ever been on stage with . . . . I consider him a brother."

That much was evident at a very memorable 2013 Midway Stadium Dylan show in St. Paul, with a late-stage Alzheimer's-stricken Vee in attendance. "I used to live here, and then I left," Dylan said. "I've played with everybody from Mick Jagger to Madonna, but the most beautiful person I've ever been on stage with is Bobby Vee. He used to sing a song called 'Suzie Baby.'"

That Thing You Do!

The Tom Hanks–written-and-produced film *That Thing You Do!* is about a fictional one-hit band (the Wonders) from Erie, Pennsylvania, whose fictional song ("That Thing You Do!") peaks at No. 2 on the *Billboard* charts in the summer of 1964.

In real life, the group was the Trashmen from Minneapolis, whose song "Surfin' Bird" reached No. 4 in 1964.

"This is really the story of the Trashmen. They could have been the model for the Wonders," says Minnesota music historian Tom Tourville, sitting at a coffee shop with singer Bobby Vee and Trashmen guitarists Tony Andreason and Dal Winslow. The foursome has just taken in a preview screening of *That Thing You Do!* Their review of the movie and the music? Four thumbs up.

All four men, now in their fifties, agree that Hanks's depiction of their musical heyday is accurate—sometimes spookily so. The musicians swap war stories that in the film are works of fiction—involving the power that local deejays and label owners wielded, the rigors of touring, the screaming girls, and the too-familiar specter of opportunistic managers like the one played by Hanks, Mr. White. For those who lived through it, *That Thing You Do!* triggers very real memories.

Take, for instance, the film's most electrifying moment: when the heretofore no-hit Wonders hear "That Thing You Do!" on the radio for the first time. According to this Minnesota music panel, the enthusiasm that Hanks captures in the scene is no Hollywood embellishment. "When I heard the 'Bird' for the first time, I was in the driveway, sitting alone in a buddy's '62 Oldsmobile—that's where the best-sounding radio I could find was—with the seat back down, listening to the battle of the bands," Andreason says. "And when it came on, I almost flew right out of the seat. I remember every moment of that. I really do. And I still get that same feeling when I think about it. It was just wonderful."

"My strongest memory of that is when 'Suzie Baby' reached number one [in 1959]," says Vee, whose first band, the Shadows, hailed from Fargo, North Dakota. The group had the dubious distinction of filling in for Buddy Holly at a concert at the Moorhead Armory the night after the rock 'n' roll legend was killed in a plane crash in 1959. Vee, who subsequently scored with hits "Take Good Care of My Baby," "Rubber Ball," and "The Night Has a Thousand Eyes," spent several years in Los Angeles and now lives in St. Cloud.

"I was in Aberdeen, driving along in my '53 Mercury, and I was passing a car. And the deejay came on: 'Here it is. Number one. "Suzie Baby." Bobby Vee and the Shadows.' And they went into the thing, and I was all over the road. It's amazing I didn't roll the car over."

Another instance of film-imitating-life is the first time the Wonders perform "That Thing You Do!" at a talent show. The drummer, bored with the ballad's sluggish tempo, speeds it up and transforms it into a sugary pop song. The joint erupts. That kind of musical spontaneity—and the crowd's reaction—is exactly what happened the first time the Trashmen played "Surfin' Bird."

"It was at Chub's Ballroom in Eagle Lake," Andreason says.

Deejay, promoter, and former *Pioneer Press* staff writer Bill Diehl "was there. We didn't know when we were gonna change chords, so [drummer] Steve said, 'This is what we're gonna do. When I'm gonna go from B to E, I'll just nod my head.'" (Steve Wahrer died of cancer in 1989.) "And so he did, and when he did, the kids went crazy. And Bill came up to us and said, 'Where did you find that song? That's a hit record. You've got to record that.' And that's how it started."

Which is how it started for the Wonders. (And if this "Thing" makes its way onto pop radio in 1996, look for it to take on a life of its own, in the same way that "I'll Be There for You (Theme from *Friends*)" did last year.)

In the movie, as the song climbs the charts, the band members eagerly check its progress with every issue of *Billboard*. Was that type of career-study the case with the Trashmen and Vee, or did they adopt a more laid-back approach to keeping tabs on their success?

"I still have 'em," Andreason says.

"I can show you every copy," Vee says.

"You followed that religiously," Winslow says. By the end of the night, talk turns to staging a double bill of Vee and the Trashmen. The enthusiasm isn't the "Let's make a hit record" temperature of teenagers, but the restrained "Let's get together and have some fun" outlook of adults. And that, after all, is what it's all about. Like *That Thing You Do!* these guys cut their teeth in a more innocent time, when rock 'n' roll meant one thing: fun.

"The movie captures that feeling about rock 'n' roll," Vee says. "And that's one of the things that's so attractive about rock 'n' roll. It's not about the best singer, best guitar player, best drummer, best anything. It's a feeling. It's fun."

At one point in the movie, one of the band's mentors tells the drummer, "Ain't no way to keep a band together. Bands come and go." True enough. And when the Wonders eventually do split up, Mr. White consoles the drummer. "One-hit wonders," he says. "It's a very common tale."

Maybe so. But don't tell Vee that the tale has an unhappy ending. He performs more than a hundred dates a year at fairs, festivals, and casinos, and this year his touring schedule has taken him to Australia and London twice, and he's considering an invitation to perform on New Year's Eve in Malaysia.

But even though he's not on the top of the charts anymore, Vee says he's on top of the world. "I feel like my life is so much richer now," he says. "I know how to be in relationships now, with myself and my family. And I feel blessed that I can still go out and do this. It might sound corny, but I still like what I'm doing. I really have fun. I get energized by it. And when I think about this movie, I think about people like Paul Molitor and Kirby Puckett and Tom Hanks. And I want more of that in my life. Positivity. And I believe what I do—and what [the Trashmen] do—really enriches people."

The Trashmen still get together to play a handful of gigs every year. And thanks to the New Jersey–based SunDazed label, there has been a flurry of re-releases and new releases, which will culminate in a four-CD Trashmen box set that hits stores this winter. Not bad for Minnesota's most famous one-hit wonder.

"I told Tony the other day, people can call me a one-hit wonder if it's still selling thirty-five years later," cracked Winslow.

Just before the credits roll at the end of *That Thing You Do!* there is a "Whatever happened to the Wonders?" synopsis. With the exception of one of the band members, who ended up as a record producer, all the lads have taken straight jobs and become family men. Not unlike Vee and the Trashmen.

Audiences undoubtedly will come away feeling a certain sense of melancholy for the decidedly unglamorous way their heroes' lives have turned out. But according to Andreason, in real life such eulogies leave out one important fact: "We were so thrilled that we were musicians, and that we got a record that got played on the radio and did sell," he says. "We never looked back when it was all over, and said, 'Gee, this is too bad.' I never looked at it that way, because we had a hit record. And that's what all musicians want. A hit record."

1996

The Magic of the Mad Ripple Hootenanny

My hit record is The Mad Ripple Hootenanny. When I set off for Stanford University as a John S. Knight Fellow in the summer of 2003, I hadn't sung on a stage for twenty years—this, after seven years straight of being in a band that practiced several nights a week and gigged regularly. But working as a rock critic, and knowing what I know from being a lifelong listener, I came to know I wasn't learning enough. I knew I wanted to dive into the snake pit of singing my own songs and see what it felt like to struggle as an artist. I had a vague sense of wanting to experience everything that comes with it, everything I'd been reporting on for two decades—the wonder, discipline, mysticism, highs, lows, discovery, passion, ambition, stress, dreams, failures, and moments of feeling so alive when performing that the only comparison to it is great sex.

Only problem was, I was terrified of singing in front of people. After twenty years, I had happily talked myself out of ever risking like that again. But in the three weeks after I bought the tuner, I wrote my first-ever solo song. I played the tune for our gathered Knight fellows around Christmastime, it went well, and I kept writing songs, some of which I still like and play.

When I got back to Minneapolis that summer, I kept writing songs and started playing out. Gradually I got more comfortable on stage, took a stage/band name—The Mad Ripple, after a project and song I created/wrote for a rigorous and mind-blowing art class taught by David Hannah that I took at Stanford—and made a CD, *Sink and/or Swim.*

In October 2006, I walked into Java Jack's coffee shop near my house in South Minneapolis. I introduced myself to the owner, Jerry Nelson, and asked him if he'd be up for me booking a songwriter/ storyteller round-robin night at his place. The idea was to put four or five songwriters on stage together, in a one-night-only collaboration that, over the course of three hours, could be something special. It was the germ of a germ of an idea. I told him I'd been going to hear songwriters at bars and coffee shops but had routinely been unable to hear, due to loud crowds, unrelenting chatter, or bad sound systems.

Jerry was excited, liked the idea, and took me down to the basement, where it was love at first sight: a quiet room where we could sing without a PA, and maybe make something of a scene. I called it the Mad Ripple Friday Night Hootenanny and started putting lineups together for every Friday night, with the idea being that it would last only that month of November 2006.

People loved it, supported it, and came out. We kept it going, and we did two years straight of Friday nights at Java Jack's before taking a break. People met each other, played with each other, made out with each other. Since then the Hoot has landed in most every joint in the Twin Cities, as well as New York City a couple of times, Palo Alto, Duluth, Minnetonka, Mankato, and more. Two years after my first record came the follow-up, *Her Tattoos Could Sail Ships*, and after a good three-year run at the late, great brew pub Harriet Brewing, these days the Hoot is in mothballs, after wrapping up a three-year residence at Studio 2, the former Java Jack's.

There have been countless magical nights and moments at the Hoot, and every night it lives up to what my friend Dan Wilson, the great Grammy-winning songwriter and leader of Semisonic, once wrote: "I had been reading books about the early days of Bob Dylan like *Positively 4th Street* and *Chronicles,* and feeling like I was missing the more intimate and neighborly part of being a songwriter and performer. It was like I'd been living in the clouds too long. The Hoot was a way back to earth: if it was a performance, then all of us in the room were performers; or maybe all of us, including the ones with the instruments on the stage, were the audience to our own home-brewed show."

The Mad Ripple Hootenanny has given me everything I wanted out of playing music, including, yes, some monetary income, so when I get too down about it and question my own worth, and music's worth in my life, I try to remember all the wonderful smiles, songs, and meaningful nights the Hoot has provided me with, and to soothe the savage beast I'll call someone wiser than me in all this, someone like Willie Murphy, the legendary Minneapolis-based blues musician.

Because along with the quiet, I've also come to know that I've been damn happy when I'm in a groove and regularly playing music and gigging. Musicians are some of the happiest people I know, and playing music, having it flow from the tips of your toes to the top of your head on a regular basis, is a big part of the reason. To wit: a year before he died in 2019, Willie Murphy told me gigging regularly is good for you.

"I feel that, I really do," Murphy said when I suggested to him that playing music keeps your spirits and health up. "It's always been a truism for me and many of my musician friends that you can feel really ill and get on stage and it just goes away while you're performing. Sometimes I'll think I'm too tired to play, and then I remember the music will perk me up, and it always does. It's habitual. It's a good habit to have.

"One of the hard parts about growing older is that your friends die as you get older, and some of your musician friends can't do what they used to do. I've been lucky because I've always taken care of myself. I became a vegetarian in 1969. I had some lapses, but I haven't eaten meat in twenty years, and I attribute good health to that. I haven't bought a drug in years."

Because he was still doing gigs regularly, Murphy didn't have trouble remembering songs or lyrics, and he said his singing range was as strong as ever, save for having to strain for some of the high notes on his register. But the music has always been "a continuum, and to some extent, the same. The toughest part is the toll it takes on the body.

"You get tired out faster," he said. "As you grow older, you lose muscle mass, so you're not as strong. Hauling equipment is not as fun—of course, it never was much fun, but in the days of Willie and the Bees we always had roadies, but nobody can afford roadies now. I do have friends who come to my gigs, and they do help. One of my drummers is a mad man physically, and he always carries my amp."

Good stuff. I put on some Willie and the Bees as Pete fried up some sausage, potatoes, and eggs for our regular morning feast in Montana, and something about Willie's wailing blues harp reminded me one more time, as a listener and participant, how drawn I am to all sorts of sounds and sonic gatherings, but that I have a big soft spot in my heart for music that feels unprocessed, raw, and as far away from the commercialization of music as possible.

Inside the Hollow Square: Shape Note Singing from the Heart

A fireball sun rises over the Merriam–Lexington Presbyterian Church on the corner of Dayton and Howell in St. Paul. Folks greet each other this Saturday morning with hugs and handshakes, and carry crock-pots and pie tins into the church basement. The marquee on the front lawn advertises the next day's sermon: "Who Needs God." No question mark.

There are about a hundred faces, and everyone wears the same giddy grin of anticipation. They've come to participate in what they all affectionately refer to as a "singing." For outsiders (and there are no outsiders in this music, as I will soon learn) that translates to a day of shape note singing, the source material for which is found in the 150-year-old *Original Sacred Harp* hymnal.

Shape note singing is a traditional folk music that has its origins in the Baptist churches of late eighteenth- and early nineteenth-century New England. That's the official, dusty-as-hell story. But as one newbie put it, "Shape note singing is the rock 'n' roll of church music."

The potluck lunch is stuffed into warming ovens and refrigerators for the time being, while people mill about, recounting previous get-togethers. A theme repeats itself. They use such words as *overwhelming, participatory, awesome, passion, joyful,* and *overcome.* There are tales of mass weeping, told with real wonder, as the singers amble up the wooden stairs to a spacious second-story room.

Acoustically, the room, with its foundation of wood and plaster and its low ceiling, is ideal for singing. But it is also sweltering, even with the windows open wide and hand fans beating a constant breeze.

A quilt hangs on the wall, raffle tickets are sold. Name tags are worn, scrawled with the singers' home states of Alabama, Nebraska, Iowa, Illinois, Missouri, Michigan, Georgia, Wisconsin, New Jersey, Minnesota. Several singers cradle water bottles in their laps. A man with a Tasmanian Devil necktie gets up in front of the group and welcomes everyone to the ninth annual Minnesota State Singing Convention.

The crowd is split into four small sections: alto, tenor, bass, and soprano. Each group faces the center "hollow square," where a different song leader for each song stands in the center, pounding out the song's rhythm with his or her hands. I sit in the tenor row next to Matt Wells, a cherubic fellow who recognizes my inexperience and responds with generosity.

"This is probably as close to a traditional singing as you'll ever find in the North," he says. "One tip: if you can hear your neighbor, you're not singing loud enough." Which is a problem, since I'm lost. My hymnal rests dubiously on my lap, and Matt on my left and another guy on my right do their best to guide me, but the shapes (which denote fa, sol, la, and mi), notes, and lyrics fly by too fast. Occasionally, I catch a melody by ear and ride it like a wave, singing boldly, loudly, ecstatically. Mostly I just screw up, fake it. But from the encouraging glances I get from the other singers, I know that mistakes are welcome.

"In most areas of my life, I'm always worrying about what's happening in five minutes, what's happening in an hour, what I have to do tomorrow, what I have to do next week," says Steven Levine of Minneapolis, one of the group's most enthusiastic singers. "When I am singing, I am absolutely in the moment: I am inside the chord, I am inside the music, I am inside the feeling of the song."

Forty-five minutes go by, and many singers have taken to keeping time with their hands while simultaneously wiping sweat from their brows. I'm sitting with my back set straight, coaxing sounds out of my diaphragm I didn't know I had. I have sung punk rock in bands in bars, at wake-the-dead volumes, but this is connected to something even more primal. There is no audience. We are singing for ourselves and for each other.

"It's overwhelming. It takes over," says Judy Mincey, a round-faced fortyish woman from Calhoun, Georgia. "It takes every bit of your energy, and your mind and your concentration."

She's right. A mess of emotions floods my mind and tear ducts. It's a complicated, and entirely unexpected, reaction—to the songs' spiritual subject matter, yes, but more than anything, it feels like a direct response to being in such close proximity to so many boisterous voices. There is a real feeling of community, togetherness, democracy. In the songs, there is common ground and a refuge from organized religion's petty differences. "You leave your differences at the door when you walk in," says Jim Pfau, one of the convention's organizers. "And that's one of the reasons that you can have people singing this who are Catholic, or Lutheran, or Baptist, or agnostic, or Jewish, and getting meaning out of it. It's very tough to explain, because it's not just that you enjoy the music. The words have meaning for almost everyone who sings them."

During the break, a twentyish, bleary-eyed, unshaven guy in a T-shirt tells me, "I was at Gluek's [bar] last night. We just got hammered. I was thinking, 'What am I doing?! I know I have to sing tomorrow.'"

After ten minutes, the singers return to their seats, but I'm exhausted, so I retreat to the back of the room. A nine-year-old girl takes to the hollow square and leads the group expertly, followed shortly by Syble Adams, a sixty-one-year-old woman who came to shape singing from her family's tradition with the Baptist churches in and around her hometown of Henagar, Alabama.

She chooses the hymn "Gospel Trumpet," and from the moment the voices rise up to sing it, the group feeds off Syble's good-natured, guileless energy, and vice versa. She smiles rapturously, then, astonished, stops singing altogether and drinks it in, repeatedly clutching her arms through her gray silk blouse. It is 100-plus degrees in the room, but Syble looks as if she could use that quilt.

The voices, singing about Jesus and sinning and salvation and forgiveness, reach a crescendo, and the air crackles with electricity and shouts. The hymn concludes with an eruption of applause. Syble collapses into warm embraces, meant to stave off her "cold chill bumps." It is an amazing thing to behold—as unforgettable a musical moment as I have ever been part of.

"At our church, we definitely believe in the spirit of the good Lord taking over sometimes, and filling you so full that you feel like you're just going to go right on into heaven," Syble says later. "I was freezing today. That doesn't happen too often, don't misunderstand me. It did today. It was awesome, beautiful, wonderful. The voices sounded to me like the roof was going to open up."

I'm invited, as anyone always is, to stand in the hollow square, where an easygoing guy named Gordon leads. I twirl slowly, taking in the faces beaming up at me—Syble, Matt, Judy, Steven, Jim the newbie, the hungover guy from Gluek's, and all the rest, singing, smiling, testifying, worshiping. It is dazing, all this unadulterated well-wishing. It feels like the group is a vat of hot spinning cotton candy, and I am the stick. The singing ends upstairs, and lunch begins downstairs. The spread is ridiculous. Pies, cookies, cakes, barbecue, pasta salads, potato salads, beans, coleslaw, watermelon, iced tea, lemonade, and plenty of authentic Southern home cooking. Jokes are made, about how the food is the real attraction, how the singing is actually just an excuse to feast. People are gathered at long lunch tables, making the verbal introductions that their bond in song didn't allow for earlier. As I head out, I vow to come back for another singing soon. I wonder aloud what these voices, raised in praise, must sound like out in the street, in the neighborhood listening below.

The newbie answers, matter-of-factly, "Like something they never hear," he says.

1998

Gather 'Round, Children, and Ye Shall Hear a Tale of Standing in Actual Physical Line for Tickets

It was the night before Bruce Springsteen tickets went on sale, and all through the Twin Cities, not a creature was stirring. I know because I checked.

First, I tooled past the dormant Civic Center. The big crater and motionless construction dinosaurs made it look like a scene from bombed-out Bosnia. It was virtually the same everywhere else I visited late Sunday night—Dayton's in downtown St. Paul, downtown Minneapolis, Rosedale, Southdale. The still of the night was disturbed only by the occasional rustle of a balled-up newspaper rolling, tumbleweed-like, past the stores' glass doors.

Of course, that's what I'd expected to find. But to tell you the truth, part of me hoped that I'd pull up to one of those silent retail giants and find just one person propped up in a lawn chair with a cooler, book, and boom box at their side. Waiting. Instead, everyone was snuggled safely in their beds, alarms set for 8 a.m., and visions of front-row seats dancing in their heads.

And that's sad, because, well, like the song says, the night belongs to lovers. And because, of all the rock rituals that have been slowly eradicated over the years, the one that hasn't been given its proper eulogy is the long-gone ceremony of camping out for tickets.

I did my time in line for three Springsteen tours and can safely say that it was a hell of a lot more fun than dialing a phone number and hitting redial until you get "Thank you for calling Ticketmaster. This is Carol. May I help you? This call may be monitored."

And it wasn't just me. It was hundreds of us who skipped school or called in sick to work for a shift (or two) to secure our place in line. We waited for hours. Ten, fifteen, twenty, more. Crazy, you might say. Foolish. Or, like a friend's mom quipped, "I'd only stand in line for tickets to the pope." (To which we, of course, blasphemed, "Bruce is the pope!") But anyone who has spent a night of blissed-out anticipation under the stars, seduced with a bunch of strangers by lines like, "At the end of every hard-earned day, people find some reason to believe," knows otherwise. Buying a record or T-shirt was one thing, but camping out for concert tickets was another. It separated the fanatics from the fans. It was a sign of commitment, an unequivocal act of passion and proof positive that you were alive. You wanted to work for it. You wanted to be part of the process. Beyond all that, it was a great party.

In the summer of 1984, Springsteen opened his *Born in the U.S.A.* tour at the Civic Center with three concerts—which meant the only way to get good tickets was to get to the Civic Center box office early.

We showed up the afternoon before, and there were already twenty people in front of us. Doubt set in immediately. The two guys at the front of the line took on a mythical quality, and whenever one of them would get up to go to the bathroom, whispers followed in his wake: "There he goes. I know a girl who knows a girl who talked to him, and he said he got here two days ago. The cops came by once last night and asked if he was okay but didn't make him leave. Pretty cool. And now he's set. First row, definitely. Second, at the very least."

The vibe was an easy mix of competition and community. We all wanted the best seats possible, but we were all in it together. Friendships were forged, romances bloomed. We bummed smokes off each other, traded bootlegs, borrowed newspapers, shared blankets and doughnuts and coffee, and huddled with each other when the rain came.

Pearl Jam whines about convenience charges being too high. But for those of us who actually enjoyed the wait, the rush of the doors opening in the morning, and the final payoff, the Ticketmaster monopoly has extracted another price.

The last time I stood in line for concert tickets was that summer of '84. At 6 a.m., as the sun was rising, I took a stroll from the beginning of the two-block-long queue to the end, to fully take in the surrealism. People slept, played cards and talked. Every tape deck was tuned to Springsteen. "Adam Raised a Cain" bled into "Fourth of July, Asbury Park (Sandy)"; "The River" commingled with "I'm On Fire." To this day, I can hear that mishmash medley in my head and still it gives me goose bumps.

To stretch my legs, I walked through downtown St. Paul. The streets were empty except for a rotund fellow—a kindred spirit in the night—walking down Cedar Street. We stopped and swapped war stories, talked about how many Bruce shows we'd seen, boasted about the rows we'd seen them from. Then we said goodbye, wished each other luck, and got back in line.

The next time I saw him was a month later at the concert, when I finally turned around to see who was attached to the hammy, sweaty fist that had been frantically pounding on my back, trying to get my attention, during the encore-baptism "I'm a Rocker."

According to promoter Catherine Swedberg, 75 percent of the people who bought tickets to Springsteen's upcoming concert at Northrop Auditorium did so in person Monday morning. Swedberg was astonished at this data, because her experience has been that most concertgoers these days prefer to take advantage of the phone.

But Springsteen fans are a different animal. Sure, they're older now, so the facts of life forced some to buy their tickets by phone. But most showed up. To work for it. To take part in the process. To feel alive. They got down to their neighborhood Dayton's by 9 a.m., got their wristbands, and lined up according to their randomly se-lected numbers. Then they stood there for an hour, tops, single file.

And rest assured, when they made it to the window and got their tickets, every one of them left feeling a little cheated, and like they cheated to get them.

1996

In Praise of Great Expectations

The weekend is upon us. But before getting busy, I say we take a moment of silence to celebrate silence. And great expectations.

I've been thinking a lot about both since one night earlier this summer, when I sat with a small crowd on the wooden benches in front of the Lake Harriet Bandshell. Conversation was as lazy as the setting sun, until I overheard another concertgoer matter-of-factly murmur, "I love the sound of an orchestra tuning up."

I listened, for what seemed like the first time, and she was right. The orchestra in question was the Minneapolis Police Band, and in a matter of minutes their music proved to be so purposefully bland, it drove me from the lake with the force of a great wind gust. But before that, as the tooting brass section wrestled the squalling strings, the wind cried promise.

And anticipation. Which is a part of the live-music experience that rarely gets talked about, but can be as thrilling as any of the other more traditional high points, be it an unforgettable encore, between-song story, or unexpected cover song. I'm talking about the blink of an eye that occurs at every live gig, that cracked window of time between when the recorded warm-up music fades and the applause swells, and the only sound is silence.

Every time it happens, every time the lights go down, and I turn to devote my full attention to the stage, I listen for it. And every time I hear it, I think the same thing. Sometimes I say it out loud:

This is how it feels to really be alive.

In a movie theater, the feeling is the equivalent of a box of popcorn on the lap and the words on the screen, "The Following Preview Has Been Rated PG by the Motion Picture Industry of America." At sporting events, it is the feeling that comes right after "the land of the free" and before "the home of the brave." What lies ahead could be a classic or a flop. Nothing has happened yet, so anything is possible.

With live music, that feeling is especially acute. And I know I'm not alone in that feeling. Since that night at the bandstand, I've been studying preshow faces. And though they range in age and race, the one thing they share is the exact same expression of wonder.

In all cases, the majority of the crowd is turned toward the stage. Audience members may talk among themselves or absentmindedly tap their toes, but as they do so, their eyes always, inevitably, wander up and alight on the still equipment, like pre-Mass churchgoers gazing at an altar. Sometimes they point at something on stage and say something to their neighbor.

What are they looking at/for? At the Guthrie last month, as a sold-out crowd waited for John Prine and his band to begin, they were looking at a stand-up bass and two guitars. The footlights caught the woodwork, and all three instruments shimmered like polished chestnuts. At the Entry a couple of weeks ago, the stage setup for California pop/ska/punkers Smash Mouth was simple: two amps, drums and a microphone stand that advertised a no-frills garage band. A few weeks earlier, the Target Center stage was adorned with candles and flowing drapes, in honor of her highness-in-the-house, Erykah Badu. And last week at a benefit for Minneapolis Mayor Sharon Sayles Belton at Paisley Park, a life-size cardboard stand-up of the Artist stood in the place that the real one would later occupy.

Different music, different venues. But all had the unmistakable look of a gorgeous gift waiting, teasingly so, to be unwrapped.

Perhaps the most tantalizing and recognizable of all the preconcert icons in the Twin Cities is the giant white screen in front of the stage at First Avenue. A cross between a cloth covering a chalice and a tacked-up curtain at a kids' magic show, it reveals nothing—unless you're sitting upstairs, or you're in front of the stage, lifting and peeking. There have been plenty of nights when that screen starts to rise, and the hair on the back of your neck goes up with it.

Does it ever get any better than that? The cynic in me says no, that it's usually all downhill from there. But of course that's not true—even though concerts, like love, are uniquely exciting at the start. For example, the first time I saw the Rolling Stones was in 1975, and I barely remember the show. But what came first I'll never forget.

The lights went down, and an army of heavenly horns came out of the Civic Center's PA system. Later I learned that the horns belonged to "Fanfare for the Common Man," but to fifteen-year-old me, it was the sound of Roman gods entering the premises. The horns blared on for a good three minutes before anything else happened. By the time they faded and Keith Richards's offstage riff to "Honky Tonk Women" started up, the place was going bonkers. Talk about feeling alive.

Of course, bigger doesn't always mean bigger potential. Great expectations can be had at a VFW hall, a dive bar, or a basement, for there is something intrinsically pulse-quickening about the sight of dormant equipment, a scurrying roadie, the sound of a tuning orchestra.

All of which inspires a delicious sort of mystery, and questions. What will they start with? What does the guitar player look like? What will I feel? And, of course, the most burning question of all: What if . . . ?

1997

6

· · ·

FAMOUS LASTING WORDS

"FUTURE BURGERS OF THE WORLD UNITE!" SAID PETE TO A MAS-sive field full of cattle grazing under an equally massive "Prime Beef Country" sign as we tooled along Highway 12 in Montana. We were on our way to a brewery block party in Helena, where Pete and his Tom Petty tribute band, The Waiting, ripped it up at an early evening gig.

Driving back to Livingston from the gig, the Montana highway stretched deep into the redwood forests, lakes, and streams. During our treks, Pete had instructed me to be on the lookout for wildlife crossing, regaling me time and again with his truck's recent bloody encounter with a deer, so I was very much on the job at my post, hyperalert on the passenger side and staring down any deer, moose, or antelope that might get too close to the side of the road and us.

After a few miles of driving in silence, exhausted from the drive and gig, and getting goofy and bleary from night driving and going sixty-five miles an hour on an otherwise vacant highway, Pete said, "Wanna see something crazy?"

Before I could answer, he turned his headlights off, and I mean OFF, leaving us in complete darkness: dark-side-of-the-moon, middle-of-nowhere darkness; a darkness I had never experienced in my life; a darkness so cold and vast and remote a fear in me rose up like no fear I'd ever feared before. The fear shot through me, and I was shocked by its force and immediacy. Pete cackled and did it again, and one more time. My heart almost blew up.

"Fucker! Stop it!" I laughed/screamed, pretty much involuntarily, as my life flashed before my eyes, my juices flowed furiously, and for all my protestations, I was happy to be alive, if scared shitless.

Over the years I've written plenty about death (and near-death and post-death), and I've also written many obituaries, which it turns out can be an extremely meaningful way to celebrate a life, and Life, because the ending of each life provides an opportunity to talk about how special an individual is, and what gifts they left us with.

For just one example, one summer afternoon in 1997, I sat on the banks of the Mississippi River with the late, great Hüsker Dü singer/songwriter/drummer Grant Hart, and what he told me that day is the first thing I thought of when he passed away on September 13, 2017.

We had spent the afternoon together at an Irish pub in downtown St. Paul, where he took a couple of hours to carefully tell me about his life and heroin addiction. He told me that as a Pisces he loved water and rivers, and that as a kid he would often sit by the Mississippi, chilling and playing guitar. He was thirty-five. He squinted out at the river and told me that his life philosophy is "Leave the campsite cleaner than it was when you found it," and so he did.

Around the same time, I did a long interview with Chris Osgood, the godfather of Minneapolis punk rock, who I talked to just a day or two after his father and several of his family members were tragically killed in an airplane crash. After recounting some of the most horrific details no son should ever have to recount, Chris had the manners and presence of mind to wish me and my family a Happy New Year, and I've never forgotten that lesson in grace.

Ah, death. It's on my mind these days, as I sit with my father in the hospital and walk my wheezing and failing dog around the block and lake, but it's always been there, "a taste of ashes" as the Irish say, ever-present and so often a life-affirming topic of conversation, in that it gives us, we the living, perspective.

Which I suppose is why the Irish love to say, "Who died?" to open the craic proceedings, and there's a reason the obituary page is known as "the Irish sports page," "the Irish comics," and "the Irish racing form." We start our day up with the sun, with breakfast and coffee, and a few on-point summaries of well-lived lives and a couple of tragic tales to boot, then we're off and on our way into the day, living and breathing and considering our lucky lot to be alive.

As an occasional obit writer, I've learned the main lesson that famed obit writer Maureen O'Donnell said she learned from writing hundreds of thousands of stories about the dead ("That life is short, and to be grateful"), which is why I also keep in mind Robert Frost's words whenever I try to do justice to any given life ("No tears in the writer, no tears in the reader; no surprise in the writer, no surprise in the reader").

Tears in the writer? A bottomless well's worth these days, and I've been letting 'em flow, most recently for my friend Norm.

A Lesson before Dying

The Sunday after the Vikings' Minneapolis Miracle playoff victory over the Saints, my brother Jay and I drove down to Sioux Falls, South Dakota, to say goodbye to our old friend Norm Rogers, a true rock 'n' roll believer-warrior-soldier and drummer for Minneapolis music legends the Neglecters, the Jayhawks, and the Cows. Norm passed away last night after fighting cancer for much of this past year, and so through tears I need to tell you what I learned from him during our visit last month.

"I have the wisdom of a dying man," he said, sucking on a cigarette and fondling a crisp red apple. He'd lusted after that apple so much that we'd gone on a mission to the grocery store for it exclusively, now here he was about to bite into it for the first time. "I find pleasure in everything," he said. "I cherish every moment."

And how: I can still see him looking at the red skin of that apple, like it was everything, and he bit into it like it was, because as he reminded us with every word, every shake of the head, and every laugh, being grateful and present is just that—everything.

Norm doled out his wisdom matter-of-factly but seriously. Everything he said, everything we talked about, between the lines, he was telling us: let me be a lesson to you, and for God's sake be grateful for this gift of life.

"Enjoy every sandwich," is how Warren Zevon put it, and so we did, Norm chomping on a late lunch, and my brother and I raising our glasses of Guinness in a toast. Later we retired to Norm's assisted living home, which was festooned with pictures of family and posters of his old bands, where he told us of his love for the Foo Fighters, whom he was thrilled to have caught in Sioux Falls last year.

After four decades spent rocking hard in the bands and bars of Minneapolis, the last part of Norm's story is one of redemption. Two years ago after he got fired from his job at Brit's in downtown Minneapolis, he hit the bottle hard. His family scooped him up, moved him to Sioux Falls, and got him into treatment, where he got sober.

Soon after he suffered a stroke, but as the haze of alcohol wore off, his memory returned and in short order he forged new bonds and deeper connections with many of his newfound family members. During our five-hour hang he was sharp as a tack and clear-eyed with memories of our times meeting at the University of Minnesota and forming bands in the late '70s at the dawn of punk rock.

A former sailor (or "the worst excuse for a sailor the Navy has ever seen," as he put it), Norm's lilting cackle was a song unto itself, and his drumming was bat-out-of-hell furious and as relentless, powerful, and urgent as the punk rock that inspired it. "We were part of something," he said, with the perspective and certitude of a man whose life was flashing before his eyes. "We were part of a movement."

One life can give so many gifts, a sad fact that we realize profoundly when death comes calling. For one example, Norm's terminal illness gave us the chance to tell him what he meant to us, to hug him and say our long goodbyes, and it gave me and my big brother a chance to go on a road trip and talk about Norm, family, friends, and everything under the sun. I'll always cherish that trip, thanks to Norm.

He and Jay were bandmates and fellow philosophy majors at the University of Minnesota, and the hours flew by. We met his niece and visited her home, and a few weeks later Norm's Sioux Falls and Minneapolis families gathered at Brit's. The Irish wake humor was in full effect throughout the night, with many old punks making the joke that we're seeing more friends at funerals than rock shows these days, and the truth is that there is a similar carpe noctem to both.

Tears. So much of our time is spent these chaotic days with our armor up, thick skins getting thicker, numbed by the news of the day, suspicious of humanity itself, wary of love and human connection, all of us all the while trying fruitlessly to come to grips with pain and loss and getting older, and then the news of an old buddy dying pricks your skin and penetrates your heart and leaves you blubbering and opens you up to let life back in, just like Norm said we should.

Last night, my answer to the What Would Norm Do? question was to go see Run Westy Run at Mortimer's. As I headed out from my own funk and hibernation, I was reminded of a tweet my friend Ellen Stanley put out from the Folk Alliance music conference in Kansas City a few days ago: "Mary Chapin Carpenter on the value of live performance: 'There is no substitute for being together . . . . I couldn't live without it.'"

So true. Turns out Monday was the birthday of First Avenue's MVP stage manager Conrad Sverkerson, who attended the festivities in a suit and even took to the stage with his brothers and sisters for a joyous Swedish birthday song sing-a-long. Crammed into the club were many of the Minneapolis rock scene's brightest lights and many of Norm's friends, a group that has been through its share of collective loss—friends, family, innocence—and as Run Westy Run lit up the night with their swampy-Stonesy-sexy-punk-blues, Norm passed away.

I got the news when I got back from the club, but in honor of Norm, for much of the set I fixed on drummer Peter Anderson and that relentless Westies beat. I made my way up close to the stage, where I let Peter's kick drum hit me hard in the chest, feeling Norm's spirit all the while, and hell if it didn't sound like a heartbeat, the one we're all attached to, the one that never stops.

2018

Famous Lasting Words

A few years ago when Muriel, his late beloved wife of sixty years, was in the hospital with a serious condition, one of Jim O'Rourke's eight kids sat in the hospital waiting room and asked him if he wanted to talk about death.

"What's there to talk about?" Mr. O'Rourke asked daughter Anne, the oldest.

"Well, for example, where funeral to be—Our Lady of Grace or St. Joan of Arc?"

"Well, my friends would probably be more comfortable at Our Lady of Mink," said the long-suffering Catholic, "but when I go, I want some good music, so bury me out of St. Joan of Arc and sing along with Mitch." They sang "On the Sunny Side of the Street" a couple of weeks ago at Mr. O'Rourke's funeral. Here's why.

Mr. O'Rourke, which is what I and everyone else called him out of fear and respect while growing up in this burg, was the patriarch of one of the biggest clans to ever play kick-the-can in the alleys of South Minneapolis or baseball at Annunciation Grade School. In the '60s and '70s, most of his eight kids were known all over the neighborhood, and a lot of us tore through their two-story house on Fifty-first and Dupont Avenue like it was our own.

Mr. O'Rourke's health had been good of late, especially for a man in his early nineties. He'd been living with his son Bobby's family, and a checkup in June found him to be in great shape: a tough, fit, old Irishman. The worst pain in the lifelong Minnesota sports fan's heart was the performance of his teams this year, which he endured religiously on the flat screen in his basement bedroom. That hurt, along with the bedsores Bobby would clean every other day.

In mid-October, Mr. O'Rourke had a massive heart attack. Upon arrival at Methodist Hospital in St. Louis Park, he was attached to a ventilator and given painkillers. He made wisecracks with the staff and family members, and after two days the nurses told the family he didn't have long to live. Anne explained to her father that the miracle they'd been waiting for wasn't going to happen, and that the next step was to keep him comfortable until it was time.

As his seventeen grandchildren and eighteen great-grandchildren can attest, Mr. O'Rourke had many sayings, including "And the rest is *H* for history," in describing meeting Muriel and the legacy they left, but no one saw what was coming last.

"A few hours before my dad died, the chaplain gathered us all around," said another daughter, Joanie O'Rourke Oyass. "She asked us to go around and say what we most admired about our dad. So we all did that. Then she read a poem, and we all went up and kissed him goodbye. There were twenty-five people in that room. He had a word of advice for each one of us.

"My dad actually was afraid of death, but he knew this was so hard on the rest of us that he wasn't going to show that side.

"When we were all done giving him a kiss, he took off his oxygen mask and said, 'Well, I don't have a lot to say. But thanks for joining me on the journey, and I'll see ya on the sunny side.'"

2011

Working Stiffs

Every working day, Joe and Sean are surrounded by death. They spit at it, chisel it, live with it, laugh at it, make art out of it. They're good at what they do. Someone comes through the doors of Minneapolis Granite and Marble Company on Chicago Avenue, having just buried their kid, husband, wife, brother, sister, or lover, and Joe Huber and Sean Mooney take their order for a gravestone and promise to make a monument out of their loss.

Then they put on their goggles and put their art school chops to use. They carve an epitaph and the name of the deceased with an X-Acto knife. Maybe they add some artwork. They dig into polished stone that comes cheap from China and India, leaving whatever message or image the family wants: a skateboard, snowboard, flower, angel, saint, Jesus.

Not long ago, for a little levity, Joe made a headstone for himself. It now rests at his parents' home in Bloomington, a smiley face that says, "Joe's Place." Sean hasn't made his yet, but he wants something funny. Not like Sandra Day O'Connor's ("Here Lies a Good Judge," yawn), but something like "Don't Laugh, You're Next." Or the one Bill Murray got at the end of *The Royal Tenenbaums*: "He Saved His Entire Family from a Sinking Battleship."

Joe and Sean, both in their midtwenties, work hard. They have a few dozen monuments going at a time, each in various stages of creation. Some are covered with sandblaster's rubber, paper, and stencils; others are plastered with notes from customers. Some are being sandblasted and flashed with a frosted finish. Some are empty, enormous slabs of stone that cost $5,000; Joe and Sean's work is included in the price.

On a Monday afternoon in the workshop, Joe is wearing fatigues and a tropical bird shirt worthy of Margaritaville. He's stocky with close-cropped hair and has a sprinkler-easy way about him. Sean, who is smaller and moves around the place with economy and worker-bee focus, wears a T-shirt advertising a friend's tattoo shop. They both answered ads in the paper for the gig. Joe graduated from MCAD, Sean from the St. Paul School of Art and Design. The shop has been open since 1906, and there have been other cutters, but Joe and Sean are this generation's design team.

Over the door of the sandblasting room hangs a horseshoe that protects the craftsmen from eternal misspellings. Next to it hangs what Joe deems "one of the most important features of the shop": a small nude Pamela Lee Anderson calendar from 1998. Over by the time clock is a five-year-old cover from *Sports Illustrated*'s swimsuit issue. "'Are You Satisfied, Bob?' is going to be a chapter in Sean's book about this place," says Joe, standing over a row of in-progress tombstones. "Once we were sitting here cutting up markers. And you do think, 'What is this?' This is like the punctuation mark at the end of a person's life. This is the end here. Your last thing. I think the guy's name was Bob."

"Yeah, it was Bob," says Sean. "A white marble marker. Real plain."

"I cut out the lines, looked at it, and said, 'Is this good?' 'Cause you've always got to double-check and make sure everything's going to blow in, and the design works just right, whatever. I just looked at it and said, 'Well, are you satisfied, Bob?' Like, 'That's the end of it. Hope that's good enough.'"

"You either live on in memory, or you don't," says Sean, as he puts the finishing touches on a piece of rock with a small X-Acto. "That's how you beat it. You see the [markers at the cemetery] that are grown over [with weeds], and they're gone. There's nothing left. You look around and you think, 'This is all that's here, and what does everybody know? What's lost to the world?'"

Joe majored in painting, Sean in sculpture. They use the phrases *2D* and *3D* the way car mechanics toss around *tire rotation* or *oil change*. They love their work, which can be seen in cemeteries all over the Twin Cities. But Joe admits that "even though there's this idea that they're sacred objects, the romance and reverence kind of goes out of that when you're doing so many a day."

They enjoy their time in the cemeteries as a break from the nose-to-the-headstone routine. It gets them into the fresh air. For the most part, they crank out their markers to the dead and don't ask why.

"We've had people come in who want a stone for their brother, who died fifty years ago as a stillborn," says Joe. "Sometimes people on their deathbeds request a stone for a sibling that's been dead since they were kids. They just want to tie up loose ends. If it's parents, and it's a young person who's died, they really care. They want something special, so we do a lot of custom stuff. I think some of the coolest things I've made have been for young people. I put some drums on one, pottery on another. I've done some nice portraits of young people from photographs.

"One of the first monuments I ever did was for a young man who got shot. His dad came in and out almost every day while I was working on it, looking at the portrait as it was a drawing, and then looking at the portrait as it was going on the stone, going, 'He had a dimple here,' or whatever.

"He was pretty cool and real lighthearted, and his friends would come in. I met a lot of the people that had been around the kid. And everybody was happy and fun. We had just gotten done cleaning it and were getting ready to put it out. The dad came in and we turned the cart around and he looked at it, and everything changed. It hit him. Choked up. Tears in his eyes. I was like, 'Oh, man. That's what we're doing. That's what this is.'" Joe plays drums in an as-yet-unnamed indie rock band. Sean skateboards and builds furniture. Both men practice martial arts. They are young, strong, and alive.

"I deal with death every day, but it's almost not a reality for me," says Sean, his tattooed arm etching a detail into a small marker as Joe hauls another slab on a forklift. "I'm not afraid of it in any way. Not that you don't care about anything—just live to the fullest every day, because you never know. We've made a lot of stones for people our age and younger."

2006

Tears in Heaven

I can't stop thinking about the guy who left his baby to die in the minivan a week ago. Much in the same way I think about Eric Clapton, who performed Tuesday night at the Xcel Energy Center, whenever I hear his song "Tears in Heaven," which Clapton wrote in 1991 after his four-year-old son, Conor, crawled out of a window and fell to his death. I wonder if this guy's pillow feels different from how it did a week ago. I wonder if he can see the sun. I wonder if he's gotten out of bed. I wonder if he knows where he is. I wonder if he's thought about that dad in Texas who held a press conference the day after his wife killed their five kids.

A press conference.

I stayed in the hospital with my infant daughter and wife, who were both sick, for six days two summers ago. After forty-eight hours, when I walked out the doors and into the sunlight for the first time, everything looked like it was covered in cheesecloth. Nothing tasted good. I felt like I was on drugs. I knew my daughter and wife were going to be okay.

This guy baked his four-month-old. What does that do to you? Can you imagine that? That's what everybody's saying, followed by, "Do you think he should go to jail?" But what about, "I'm sorry. I'm so sorry, man."

Saturday morning, I drove around Lake Harriet in a pickup truck with my neighbor's father, who lost his son-in-law last year. His fatherless grandsons and my two kids were in the back, riding precariously and giddily. We were all waving at people on the walking path, many people were waving back, and halfway around the lake, somewhere between the Rose Gardens and the bandstand, I thought about you.

I'm sorry.

Not only for your loss, but for thinking about you, knowing about you, because all this judge, jury, and executioner crap is straight-up crass, and the main thing I can't get out of my head is how do you tell your wife that you forgot your baby in the car and you better sit down, honey, and I had a lot on my mind and, yes, didn't they tell you? Dead. I'm not joking. Is someone there with you? Dead. That's what I said. Dead.

I'm sorry.

If you're out there, that is, which I wouldn't be. I'd be on Neptune. Have you heard what the pundits are saying? I haven't, because I don't like to think about you and them, frankly, but as long as we are, whatever happened to the old journalism adage, "Comfort the afflicted, and afflict the comfortable?"

And make no mistake, this guy is the afflicted. He burned his child alive by mistake, and there but for the grace of God goes every last one of us.

Would you want to live with that? Timothy McVeigh got off easy, compared to this guy. I would move to Hell. I would be in a rubber room. I would never smile again. Last month, a friend of a friend killed herself after she rolled over and suffocated her one-month-old baby while taking a nap. I think about her husband a lot these days. I'd like to tell him I'm sorry, too, and I'd like to tell both these damaged dads that maybe the nightmare will end for them someday.

Nancy K. Schriefer, a Cottage Grove writer, recently sent me her book *A Message from Sam,* which she says she wrote as a way of dealing with her grief after the death of her daughter. The dedication reads, "For my daughter, Kris, whom I love and miss . . . lots and lots."

My sister Peggy, a psychologist who is struggling with her own first-time motherhood demands, just sent me a piece from the *Philadelphia Inquirer.* It's the story of two Pennsylvania parents, Judi and Kenny Rogers, who adopted a child after their five-year-old biological son Jake drowned in 1998. This is what Judi wrote in her journal last summer, as they started the adoption process: "Jake is irreplaceable. We would never even attempt to replace our bubbly redhead with the pirate grin. He will be part of our family forever."

The story ends at the airport, with Judi and Kenny coming home with their adopted baby boy, Lukas, from Guatemala City: "No one seemed more content than his new father. Kenny seemed whole. Ken Rogers Sr. watched his son rocking the new baby. 'You look good, Ken,' the grandfather said. 'Yes, you look good.'"

Five days later, a young father in Minnesota drove to work, locked his minivan, and now complete strangers are wondering if his pillow feels different. I hope Clapton sang "Tears in Heaven" on Tuesday night, because after the week we just lived through, we can use every lesson we can get in how to make music out of heart shrapnel.

2001

Family Man

A few years ago, Karl Mueller handed out pens stenciled with the words "Your Friend, Karl Mueller." The gesture was inspired by Suicide Commandos founder Chris Osgood, who a few years earlier had passed out guitar picks inscribed with, "Your Pal, Chris Os-good."

Last Friday morning, Karl died in his wife Mary Beth's arms. That night, Osgood found himself at a cabin in the north woods with friends, several who consider Karl to be a dear friend. At din-ner, Osgood lifted a glass of wine to his tribe, present and not, and talked about the gift of friendship and the preciousness of life. Then one of the diners, in an attempt to make sense of the day's events, grilled Osgood for two hours on the history of the Commandos.

"It started when [Commandos drummer] Dave Ahl and I were kids," began Osgood. "We were skateboard buddies." Which is how so many great bands start—friends first. And though it went unsaid, it was the kind of conversation that Karl would have loved, overflow-ing with names of long-lost musicians and clubs, and the kind of secret-code minutia (amps, gear, and guitars) that musicians use to talk about the passion and that forge thicker-than-blood roots.

A few weeks ago, I knew Karl wasn't doing very well. He was my neighbor, and he'd come out of the house to see my puppy and talk to me and my daughter and her friend through his newly installed voice box, the price of his yearlong battle with throat cancer. I asked Mary Beth, who sports an "[eye symbol] [heart symbol] K" tattoo on her right arm, if she wanted me to write anything.

She was optimistic. She said there was a good story about "band as family," which I presumed to mean how the Soul Asylum circle had risen to the occasion and helped care for their mate. But she may have also meant that once in a great while a rock band becomes a really big family.

If you're reading this, if you were one of the girls who crushed out on him when he was a fourteen-year-old punk rock bag boy at the Uptown Lunds, or the owner of Ron's Market down the street from his house who was devastated by the news of his passing, you were part of Karl's family. He wasn't that particular. There wasn't an insider-hipster bone in his body. He just loved rock, and he loved to rock. His dad died when he was young, so it was just Karl and his mom, Mary, and so when he became friends with Dave Pirner and Dan Murphy and unleashed Loud Fast Rules on the bars of the Twin Cities, his family grew. When Soul Asylum got bigger, his family got bigger.

In the fall, Karl drove with my family and me to the funeral for our friend Dave Ayers's father. Ayers was Soul Asylum's first manager. Karl sat next to me on a folding chair as Dave's wife, Ambrosia, sang "Amazing Grace." God knows what he was thinking at the time, but as we drove back from Shoreview to the Cities, he told us much of his life story, but never once mentioned the chemo or radiation or the shitty cards he'd been dealt, probably because he didn't consider them all that shitty.

Up in the north woods last Friday, people talked about the first time they met Karl and the last time they saw him, and took silent comfort in the knowledge that similar spontaneous memorials were going on all over the world. A couple of hours after getting the news, Ayers told a few of us about Dan Corrigan's photo shoot for the cover of *Clam Dip and Other Delights,* the 1988 Twin/Tone EP that spoofed the cover art of Herb Alpert and the Tijuana Brass's *Whipped Cream and Other Delights.*

"He was this silly, funny guy with such a heart. He was such a good sport," said Ayers. "That thing stunk so bad that day. It was a combination of sour cream, paint, and whipped cream, and then there was all this seafood. He sat there for hours. After a while, he got tired, and a little cranky, and just as he was about to climb out, someone put a dollop of the stuff on his head and put a chip in it. He sat back down, and that was the shot."

And that was Karl, who died on June 17, 2005, after a courageous battle with cancer. He is survived by his family.

2005

Notes from Karl's Bench

My friend, neighbor, and Soul Asylum cofounder Karl Mueller died eleven years ago this month.

I think about him every time I go by the house he shared with his wife, Mary Beth, who launched the nonprofit Kill Kancer (*www.*

killkancer.org) after Karl passed away from esophageal cancer at the age of forty-two. I think about the funny punk rock things we talked about, and about his great band, and about how much fun it looked like he was having as he rocked and played his way through life.

I'm lucky to have been in regular conversation with Karl over the years, drawn as I have been to his memorial bench in the Rose Gardens, which I land at with my bike and dog at least a couple of times a week. I always mutter a "Hey, Karl" as I settle in to write, read, and meditate, and without fail his memory and this bench put me in the mood for some peaceful rumination on life and death and all sorts of loss that we the tenderhearted human race endure daily.

It's been a lot lately, but Karl's bench demands gratitude and mindfulness. The plaque reads "In Memory Karl Mueller Loved and Missed," and were I to add anything after all these visits, it'd be something Karl told me not long before he died, after I'd asked him what he'd learned from fighting for his life, and what message he'd like to impart: "I'd say to people just live the best you can. Enjoy the lilacs while you can and slow down."

So I try to do as Karl said, making sure I don't take this rich life for granted, but I also admit it's been tough to stop and smell the roses of late, sitting here as I have, thinking of all my friends and family who have suffered life-altering losses, and of all the losses to come, and of the big mystery it all amounts to. The good news is that, poignantly and hilariously, all that reflection on grief—along with the macro sorrows of the world and the hourly chaos of the newsfeed—gets interrupted by life itself.

To wit: as I write, a Wiffle ball just hit me in the head. The party responsible for the bonk, a bunch of summer-psyched rug rats, is running wild behind me in an exuberant game of Wiffle ball, and they're still laughing at the weird man on the bench they just clocked with a foul ball. My dog is going crazy, barking at the sights and sounds of the game, and now one kid has just taken my pup for a stroll to get a sip of water at the drinking fountain a few feet away.

As careful readers know by now, I bear witness to the quiet magic of the Rose Gardens regularly, and I'll continue to sing its praises from Karl's bench. People come here from all over, to drink in the

4,000 plants and 250 species of flora and to take photos and selfies amid the roses, dozens of strains of which fill the summer breeze with the scent of life itself. All around me these days, summer-vacationing kids hang in hammocks in a canopy made of heritage trees—the cucumber magnolia, river birch, golden larch, mugho pine, white fir, Austrian pine, Japanese yew, and water ash—that will likely outlive every last one of us.

Like a one-stop slice of life from Utopia or Narnia, the view from Karl's bench takes in the Peace Garden, sunset, and a nonstop parade of multi-culti humanity. Today alone I'm sharing the park with Mexican, Jamaican, African American, Caucasian, and Japanese gawkers, and over the years from this perch I've witnessed so many inspiring yoga classes, dance performances, plays, and ridiculously beautiful Hmong and Somali weddings, I've lost count.

What's more, across the way sits the Heffelfinger Fountain, whose top pedestal features a cast of water-spewing harpies and satyrs and a dolphin-surfing cherub. Carved into the base is a progression of human faces, signifying the natural process of growing and growing older. A sundial next to the fountain reminds, "Count only the sunny days," and hell if you can't catch a whiff of those lilacs Karl was talking about.

2016

The Day David Bowie Died

The most oft-repeated mantras on Facebook the day David Bowie died were "David Bowie helped me fly my freak flag," "David Bowie helped me feel less alone," and "David Bowie inspired me." Some fans threw up their hands at the thought of saying anything at all, unable to properly eulogize such a hot creative flame gone, poof, so they clammed up altogether.

His music flew all across the globe Monday, and as post after post flew by it was as if all the glitter and stardust that Bowie had been sprinkling on us all these years had finally landed and actually rubbed off, and so now we all wanted to report in and testify, that we had a ticket stub or a story.

I discovered Bowie in all his androgynous rock 'n' roll star glory when I was a fifteen-year-old Catholic kid looking for adventure, and while I have many life-altering memories of my times spent with his music (starting with dancing to the Suicide Commandos' blistering version of "Suffragette City" at Regina High School), one of my favorites came on his sixty-ninth birthday, last Friday, at Studio 2 Café in South Minneapolis.

The night started out with the former Java Jack's and DevJam owner David Hussman and I toasting Bowie's birthday and talking about "Heroes," an epic and emotionally-wrenching and uplifting song I've had the honor of singing at First Avenue with the Rock for Pussy crew a couple of times, and which I discovered Friday night that David has deep recording knowledge of. Hussman and I have become friends over the past year, as he and his wife, Andrien Thomas, and their family have worked hard to bring live music and the Mad Ripple Hootenanny back to the corner of Forty-sixth and Bryant. And while we share similar community-building and live-music missions, our main conversational bond as rock dudes has been Bowie.

David Bowie has always been shorthand for a particular freedom, and freedom of expression, sexuality, and otherworldly enthralling ROCK, and so as so many have said since Bowie succumbed to cancer Sunday, he was and remains a voice for all sorts of eternal teenagers, aliens, freaks, and space travelers. So it was perfect when, after Friday's live music concluded, Hussman dialed up his iPod and right there in that sleepy little neighborhood a small dance party broke out to Bowie's "Golden Years," "Fame," "Young Americans," and "Let's Dance." I thought of Bowie that night, and his brilliant infectious smile and confident roar, and how tickled he'd have been at the sights and sounds of his music transforming a cozy little family bistro into a mini-disco on his birthday. Sweet.

As the snow fell and people milled about and finally out into the night, the very sounds of those records brought me back to when I first discovered them with my friends Paul Kaiser, Greg Larson, and John Brownson at DeLaSalle High School. We'd been tipped off to Bowie by an upperclassman, John Ennen, and all us young dudes fell hard for all that urgent-sounding pre–punk rock, driving around the lakes and playing poker to endless plays of *Diamond Dogs, Station to Station, Young Americans, Low, Heroes, Changesonebowie,* and rushing to the Southtown Theater for the opening of *The Man Who Fell to Earth.*

I didn't think much about it at the time, but as rocker/author Laurie Lindeen put it when I interviewed her for a story about Rock for Pussy in 2008, "Bowie is everything that appeals to me in one package, which is rare: beauty, fashion, great songwriting, acoustic songs, and rockers, the whole package. I've always gone through androgynous stages—boyish stages and really girly-girl stages—and I realize that guys don't have that freedom at all. So he was probably much more helpful to guys, to say, 'You can have these phases too, and we're all cool.'"

That was me, and my friends. We grew up amid the sexual and political freedoms of the glitter-bombed '70s, and as the Studio 2 Café mini dance party reminded me, I knew in my bones it all stuck with me for good. After high school, I had continued listening to and writing about Bowie, saw him twice in concert, and for a couple of years running, on the morning after Rock for Pussy, I had to explain to the Little League umpires why the coach of the Lynnhurst team was wearing slept-on rouge and lipstick.

These nights my Bowie fix has been sated by John Eller, who mans the Tuesday night piano bar at Nye's Polonaise Room in Northeast Minneapolis with real artistry and generosity. Nye's is now rumored to be shuttering at the end of February, and when it does, gone will be the monster magic sound of Eller expertly ripping through the Bowie catalog and leading people in all those great songs, and the sight of strangers' faces transformed in recognition of all those great songs, and in their own supremely unique connection to all those great songs. Time and again I've seen it happen: they really can't believe what they're hearing, that it's *David-fricking-Bowie* being played so well and with so much heart and grit. They become teens again, or they remember the teen they were, or the time they discovered Bowie amidst all their own ch-ch-ch-changes. It's a beautiful thing to behold, and I'm heartened to know that Johnny will be playing his broken heart out this Tuesday night at Nye's, and that there and all across the known and unknown universe, Bowie's music will never die.

Speaking of which, of loss and love, my friend Mike Wiley buried his twenty-six-year-old daughter Lauren this week. My brother Terry sang Van Morrison's "Into the Mystic" at St. Joan's at the memorial service Wednesday, then he reprised it at Lee's Liquor Lounge Saturday night with the full Belfast Cowboys band as Mike and his wife, Janey, danced.

I will never forget the sight of Mike under that mirror ball, just days after his daughter's funeral, dancing with his love, and Lauren's friends dancing and singing as one hive gang, and it made me feel once again that music has healing powers beyond our understanding and that those who really truly hear it and play it truly never die.

That's all I've got. Ouch. Tears. Good night. David Bowie is dead and I'm freaking sad.

2016

The Funeral Singer

When Curtiss A sings "In My Life" at tonight's John Lennon Tribute at First Avenue, it will conclude an impressive run of the rendition that started for the Dean O' Scream on December 9, 1980, when he sang it on the local entertainment cable staple *Night Times Variety*, just hours after the former Beatle was slain outside his apartment in New York City.

Since then, Curt has sung it every December 8 at his reliably powerful Lennon tribute, and in recent months Curt has sung the Lennon/McCartney–penned tune at the funerals of his friends Bruce Allen, Kevin Folly, Steve Foley, and Buck Hazlett and his children, causing friends to dub Curt the "Funeral Singer."

Tonight, the Minnesota rock legend will dedicate "In My Life," which *Mojo* magazine in 2003 deemed the best song ever written, to a special guest: himself.

"I had a stroke last month, so we're doing it for me because I almost died, and make sure you say, 'He laughed,'" said Curt, who laughed. "Sometimes I sing it at weddings. I don't know if I agree with [*Mojo*'s listing], but I do find it quite poignant. We do it in tandem with 'Here, There, and Everywhere,' and those kinds of songs are devoid of hopelessness. They're the opposite of that. They're like Christmas carols, or something.

"'In My Life' has a beginning and ending, a bridge, and it's pretty and poignant, and usually it makes people cry. I remember doing it years ago for someone's funeral way back when [Suburbs cofounder] Chan [Poling] played the piano for me and I stood out in the audience, or in the congregation, and sang it from there. That was the first time I sang it at a funeral.

"If somebody wants me to do that, it's an honor. So that's what I'm thinking. It's not hard to sing a song, but it's hard to say goodbye to someone you love. It doesn't scare me to sing a song, but afterwards I'm glad it's over. It's not like a gig. At a gig you're trying to entertain people; at a funeral or wedding you're trying to touch a soul.

"It's always a little transcendent. When it's happening, it's somewhat daunting. I think I choked up most at Buck's because you don't want to be doing that because it's your friend. Plus, now I'm old. Just waiting. The terrible thing about surviving all this time is that all your friends are dead, and the countdown for you really begins."

2008

Zero Our Hero

One day when our late, great dog Zero was just a little black fur ball of puppy love, as energetic a mix of black Labrador and Australian shepherd as has ever graced this cruel world, I was talking with a friend who had just put down her beloved pal.

I was on my way to throw sticks and tennis balls and swim in the Mississippi River with my buddy that day, and we were both free and easy and supremely unaware of how very lucky we were—and yet so we were, oh yes, we were—so when my friend Judith, a veteran dog owner and lover, said something about what we owe our dogs, it stuck with me then and every day over the past wonderful thirteen years.

"Wonderful" because that's how long our family was lucky enough to be with Zero, about whom my son Henry so wisely said last Friday around noon, as my daughter Helen and their mother and my dear friend, Jean, sobbed over our going-to-sleep-forever member of the family as he lay on the living room floor that he'd patrolled so valiantly all these years: "Zero knew us all better than we know each other."

Nods among the sobs, hugs on top of those. That he did. Good night, buddy. Such a good boy. Pretty black. Best dog ever. Off to the big dog park in the sky. No worries, my boy. Don't be afraid. Go get it. Run free. Love you so much, ZZ. Love you. Thank you. Thank you. Thank you, Z.

Laughs amid the tears. We ran through his greatest hits, his hilarious highlight reels, his goat-like eating habits, his crazy bark. We reminded each other of the time he waltzed through the Famous Dave's kitchen; of the myriad soccer, baseball, and softball games he loved attending and being part of; and of his constant, glorious, ridiculous, mortifying humping that made us the laughingstocks and pariahs of the Lake of the Isles dog park. We massaged him and kissed him goodbye.

Ouch. Zero was my constant companion, so much so that I can feel him on my hip as I write this, just as I can still feel him attached to my voice and hip from our walks. He loved the snowy late nights when it was just he and I on the streets going down to Lake Harriet, silently moving through the big billowy snowflakes and quiet city.

Our favorite hang was at the Lyndale Park Rose Gardens near Lake Harriet, which we paid our last visit to last Tuesday, on a glorious fall afternoon that brought him all sorts of smells, sniffs, and sunshine. He went downhill fast over the next couple of days. His paw stains are still on the seats of my car.

There's a lesson in dying, one that we learn from the dearly departed over and over again, and anew. From Z in life as in death I learned about presence, gratitude, unconditional love, and the value of simple joys and cheap thrills. Part of my wisdom was inspired by the conversation I had with my friend that sunny day long ago, when I was so carefreely headed to the river with my beast. "I hope I did him right," she said, of her recently departed companion. "I hope he had a good life because of me."

Meaning, of course, did she fulfill the contract, the one we all make with our pets? We take care of their needs and in return they give us love, laughter, warmth, cuddles, and in short order become, yes, my son, our confessors, confidants, best friends, partners in crime. We are the stewards to our dogs' life experience, masters of their universe, and gateway to the world—not to mention playmate, partner-in-goof-off-ery and always-game running buddy.

I kept the spirit of Judith's words in mind all these years, and I made sure Zero knew how much I loved being with him, that I wasn't simply doing my dog-sitting duty. I made sure I always appreciated him and all our times together, because deep down I knew that one day I'd have to say goodbye.

Friday was that day. As he laid there on the living room floor, with all our hands touching him, and our friend, Dr. Christa Williams of Caravan Vet, having administered the merciful barbiturate, I was happy to be with my loved ones and to have ZZ's life flash before me, and happier still to say that I know we did him right.

He had a good life, filled with love and adventure, and he brought us closer and pulled us through so many good and bad times, and his memory and the gratitude that we shared for being all together to send him off were a gift that will live on. "Always keep a diamond in your mind," as the great soul singer Solomon Burke put it, and as such I've squirreled away my Zero diamonds for safekeeping, and most are already bearing sweet nostalgic fruit.

So, faithful column readers, here is my advice after a weekend of writing, reading, listening to sad music, and crying, beyond all the usual carpe diem and gratitude/presence jive. What I've come to know firsthand during the past few days applies to all sorts of loss, but this one goes out especially to the dog lovers. Take it from me and Z: do your dog right and do it now, because the day will come when you won't have the chance to, and on that day you will feel the loss deeply in your bones, so much so that you'd give just about anything to have that little guy put his snout in your lap and beg for one more lap around the lake together.

2018

7

. . .

FALLING IN LOVE WITH
EVERYTHING I HAVE

I'VE BEEN IN LOVE A FEW TIMES AND HAD MY HEART BROKEN
exactly as many, and that's about all anyone ever needs to know
about all that boring passion, drama, volcanic romance, and wisdom
I gleaned by FALLING IN LOVE WITH EVERYTHING I HAVE and living out the Buzzcocks tune "Ever Fallen in Love with Someone You
Shouldn't Have Fallen in Love With?"

Heading to Pete's, I had all this (and many good thoughts about
my good life with my new lover/partner, Mary Beth) on my mind as
I went ninety miles an hour west on Highway 94, which turns into
Highway 90 and then, out of Bismarck, North Dakota, 94 West all
the way to the Yellowstone River and the Crazy Mountains, which
sit magnificently outside Pete's back deck. I got sick of the sound
of my own voice in my head, so I turned up the music and, finally,
dialed up an audiobook.

Driving that wide-open road from the Midwestern flatlands to
Livingston, Montana, I listened to the first half of *Born to Run*,
Bruce Springsteen's inspiring and extremely human and honest
memoir. His voice and story were soothing, entertaining, funny,
and wise. It accompanied me on my way from Minneapolis, this
place that I've loved all my life but that I'd grown tired of due to my

own restlessness, overcrowding, traffic, construction, noise, and the let's-call-this-rut-a-groove repetition of once-beloved social rituals.

I knew I was on my way to grumpy old man territory if I didn't get out of Dodge and clear my mind in Montana, this place of wild-life, nature, freedom, and wonder that I'd been hearing about from Pete for the past five years, so I put my hometown happily in the rearview mirror and hit the road, with Bruce riding shotgun.

As I listened, it occurred to me that discovering Springsteen at age sixteen and hearing all those songs and stories that were so richly peppered by his tales of Asbury Park, the Stone Pony, Madame Marie, Spanish Johnny, the boardwalk, "The fireworks are hailin' over little Eden tonight," Hazy Davey, the Magic Rat, Jimmy the Saint (C'est moi!), Greasy Lake, E Street, and the whole of the starlit Jersey shore in my mind as conjured by Springsteen's records, resplendent in moonlit carnivals, roller coasters, lights, action, danger, and rock 'n' roll, had a profound impact on my young psyche and storytelling.

"Greetings from Asbury Park, New Jersey," indeed, and from the very beginning Springsteen made it his mission to proselytize about his roots and mythologize the Nowheresville, U.S.A. place from which he hailed. As I drove, he delivered a sermon whose passion-ate testimony to love, life, and living life with passion and purpose connected with me three thousand miles away as I drove with my eight tracks and cassettes around Lake Harriet, all the while thinking about the New Jersey Turnpike and Asbury Park as some exotic and magical music Mecca that gave me so much of my favorite music and planted the seeds in me for wanting to do something similar with my own stomping grounds.

Springsteen was a wild and free kid, ten years older than I, and I could almost smell the Atlantic Ocean seawater all the way from landlocked Minneapolis. So began the buds of my transposing all that romance back onto my own hometown ("James Joyce was born in Dublin"). I found Bruce in 1975 and saw him for the first time in 1978 at the Met Center at the start of the *Darkness on the Edge of Town* tour in Bloomington, as the Minnesota Kicks played a soccer game next door. By the time I graduated high school, I was well versed in Asbury Park, New York City, and Hollywood from rock 'n' roll, movies, and television, and I wanted to represent for Minneapolis, whose main cultural claims to fame before the explosion of the music scene here were grain, the *Mary Tyler Moore Show,* and middling sports teams.

Then along came this band the Replacements, and in 2006 when I wrote *The Replacements: All Over But the Shouting. An Oral History,* I did so because I was afraid my favorite band, which had been in mothballs for more than a decade, would be forgotten, while at the same time I wanted to testify about this place we all grew up in. I knew that the baby-boomed '60s and all those neighborhoods spilling over with kids in South Minneapolis helped give birth to the 'Mats, and so I was very conscious of documenting, mythologizing, and lionizing the neighborhood and hotbed from which this great band rose, and careful to detail the streets, lakes, clubs, bars, creeks, and nooks and crannies of the twin towns in something like a re-imagining of 1980s Minneapolis à la 1960s Liverpool.

Prince's death has brought fame to all sorts of similar Minneapolis signposts, which, I must confess, made it feel, as I lit out on my latest incredible journey, like something to fly like a bat out of hell from—something embalmed, a town whose time had come and gone and whose only glory days remain in a rehashing of the past.

Or maybe that was just me.

After a week of peace and quiet, I was looking forward to being home. Now that I'm back, I'm glad to be here and reconsidering so many stories I wrote years ago that are still timely today, be it "The Imagined Enemy," about the anti-Arab racism endured by the Wadi brothers of Northeast Minneapolis; "Repo Men," about a couple of North Minneapolis guys who made their living stealing cars, and me, their ride-along reporter/sometime-getaway driver; and "Menace to Society," about a North Minneapolis mother of five who got sent to prison for five years for signing for a package of heroin that was delivered to her house in the name of her boyfriend, whom she never saw again.

Then there are all the great conversations, deep chats, and

heartfelt exchanges I've been lucky to have and publish over the years, hopeful and timeless stuff, and in that spirit I hope you've gotten something out of my back pages.

Montana was a week crammed full of good conversations with Pete, and a lot of alone time in a space where I could think and breath. Much of my yearning for new freedom and the open road had been sated, and driving home I can say I felt like a changed man. I learned plenty from Springsteen's deep dives into his life, middle age, psychoanalysis, and the human condition, and because he knows the ego and the artistic process better than anyone, he became a trusted source and good road buddy for me, someone who has irons in many of the same fires.

So in honor of road buddies, gurus, rockers, writers, and those of you living your truth, let's conclude this session of the good craic with a few stories of friends, family, and acquaintances that could be Springsteen songs.

Two Hearts Are Better Than One

Twenty-five years after they first heard Bruce Springsteen's "Thunder Road," Pat Widell told his wife, Danni, he had cancer. Then they told their daughters, Lauren and Hannah. Then they told their friends in their Minneapolis neighborhood, including me. There was a lump in his leg. He had to quit his job. Danni held the fort.

Music has been a big part of Pat and Danni's marriage grout. One time when some Jehovah's Witnesses came to his door, Pat, a world-class curmudgeon, invited them in, sat them down, cranked up Van Morrison, and said, "This is my religion." The Witnesses split. They wouldn't hear it, but I could hear him tell that story twenty times and never get sick of it.

I met Pat in 1975. He was my high school baseball coach. He was more interested in talking about music and life than about winning, which was very good, because we were very bad.

"Thunder Road" was our introduction to Springsteen that year. It was a song about youth and freedom, sung by this worldly cat who wrote about girls the way we liked them (smart, strong, sexy, and next door) and about boys we wanted to be like (rebels and Romeos). I was sixteen, Pat was a few years older, and if we ever talked about death, we never talked about it happening to one of us.

He started the chemo two years ago. Some days, Danni would sit there with him. Some days, she'd have to get back to work or drive one of the kids somewhere, and he'd sit in silence or talk with other cancer patients about whatever cancer survivors for another day talk about.

For Pat and Danni, the wildness of "Thunder Road" ultimately took flight in the form of making a home together. Somewhere along the line, all those Springsteen missives about loyalty, love, roots, and passion translated into a larger lesson they passed on to their daughters: follow the open road to your heart's content, but make sure you've got a ride home.

Pat's father died years ago, which I'm pretty sure is why one of his favorite Billy Bragg songs is "Tank Park Salute," a breathtaking eulogy from a teenage son to his dead father. When U2 came in concert around this time last year, Pat played the cancer-victim card to get my extra ticket. We laughed at that joke plenty of times in the weeks before the show, but not that hard, because we were both scared.

In her high school yearbook, Lauren thanked her dad, a salt-of-the-earth sports purist and the smartest caddy the country clubs of Minnesota have ever known, for teaching her how to golf. At the end of the summer, Pat and Danni and Hannah drove Lauren to the University of Kansas, which she attends on a golf scholarship. Lauren took all of her dad's Bob Dylan CDs with her to college, and something else: Pat called me a few days after they got back from Kansas with a lump in his throat bigger than the one in his leg, having just heard a David Gray song on the radio that expressed exactly how much he was going to miss his daughter.

Last month, he started telling me about this Springsteen rarity he'd heard, "The Promise," a melancholy piano ballad that stares down chased and dashed dreams, and splits the difference between settling down and settling for less. It's a great song, brutally honest, and the only way I heard it is because Pat played it for me one week ago today. The cancer's gone.

When I visited him last Thursday, Hannah, an ace student at Holy Angels, was watching golf with her parents. Danni was propped up in front of the TV with a blanket and some magazines. She had surgery a few weeks ago, but she'll be okay. If you try to tell her the surgery is another in a string of unbelievable events they've had happen to them during the past couple of years, she'll wave you out the door with a grin that says, "This is nothing."

Her Valentine of many years walked me to the car. I could have told him so many things—about all these beautiful new babies that have come into the world recently, about every last one of my cousin Johnny's and his wife Rose's beautiful children, about this God-awful funeral we're all going to—but he just kept going on about "The Promise."

He grabbed a shovel and talked excitedly about how he hears the song's admission of fallibility as a sequel to the indestructibility of "Thunder Road." He talked about how weird life is and about how, even when bad things happen now, he gets so much joy out of little things. Then he bent over and, with rock star passion, started shoveling water off his sidewalk. I pulled out of the alley and, just as my friend disappeared from view, the brilliant February sunshine flashed off his bald head.

So what else can we do now, except roll down the windows and let the wind blow back our hair?

2002

Brilliant Disguise

It's Sunday morning and you're on your way home from the big South by Southwest music and bacchanalia conference, resting your cauliflower ears for Springsteen's church service later that night, and all you want is some peace and quiet. You keep to yourself in the Houston airport. When the boarding call comes, you get in line, get on the plane, and make your way to the window seat over the two people in your row, a young mom and her son. You settle in. You and the mom both open your books at the same time.

She's very tan. She instantly reminds you of you and me and everyone we know. Her kid has a PSP and an iPod and a rogue-in-the-making smile. You look out the window, put your head in your book, but she's bright and alive and wants to talk. So do you, it turns out. You put your books down, and she tells you about her stay-at-home-mom life, and how she and her son are on their way to Utah for a ski trip, leaving her husband and their other two sons back in Texas for a week.

The plane takes off as you make small talk about the weather in Texas and Minnesota. Her kid has his headphones on. She tells you about herself. She has never had a drop of alcohol, drugs, or caffeine in her system. She played basketball and lacrosse in college, tennis and skiing now. There isn't an iota of pretension to her, and it occurs to you that she might be the happiest person in the world. She's not wearing a wedding ring; yours catches the light from the sun blazing in from behind the clouds you are tearing through at thousands of miles an hour.

Her name is Amanda. Her grandmother, who died at age ninety-eight, contended that reading and feeding your mind keep you young. She is very polite. Southern belle, raised by a blueblood Boston mother and an Irish American father who called her "kiddo." They're both dead. Dad when she was twenty-two, Mom a few years later. As she talks about them and her sisters, tears well up in her bright blue eyes. One teardrop slowly pools in the eyelid closest to you. You know it's going to fall, and you know what you have to do when it does, even though you're not sure if you should.

After what seems like forever, the tear drops, and you brush it away from her eyelid and her cheek. She thanks you, not taken aback in the least, rolls her eyes with slight embarrassment, and continues to talk about her father. A few more tears fall, but you leave the mop-up duties to her. Her son is listening to the audio book of *The Spiderwick Chronicles*.

She tells you about a boy she used to know. She met him when she was in eighth grade. He was a couple of years older than she was, but they spent the summer biking around a man-made lake in the town that she and her family had just moved to. She was killing time while her family's new house was being built and excited to start her new school. Her family lived in a gated community, his on the outside of town. Hers had money, his didn't.

The talk was easy between them. They became good friends, growing up together, talking about their lives. Near the end of the summer, he asked her to be his girlfriend. She politely declined. He wasn't her type—she's always liked athletic guys—and so she told him she just wanted to be friends. He said he was fine with that.

Over the next few years, they saw each other in the halls at school, and she always said "Hi" to him and vice versa. She was popular and pretty, and he was a loner. She never told her friends about how he asked her out, because that would have been gossipy and disrespectful. After his first semester at college, he came home for Christmas, turned the car on in the garage, and killed himself. She cried for the longest time. She still feels guilty about it, even though she knows it wasn't her fault. Her dad explained to her that death is a part of life and that "it just gets harder, kiddo."

The plane lands and you say goodbye. You tell her kid to keep playing baseball. She wishes you luck on your career. You brush her arm slightly because a hug would be too forward, and then you walk away, back to your life, not knowing what the hell that was all about but that it was nice while it lasted.

2008

Because the Night

Last Saturday night. April 25, 2001. Eavesdropping. One notebook, two clubs. 7th Street Entry and Lee's Liquor Lounge. Four hours. 9:30 p.m. to 1:30 a.m. On stage, roaring guitars, singers, drums. Off, voices. Verbatim. Real time:

God, am I glad to see you! I forgot my ID, but the guy at the door remembered me. I think he's Janie's old boyfriend.

My relatives don't understand.

Nice to be back.

The Turf is our favorite place to go. It's this dive in St. Paul, but that's, like, my favorite bar. Laurie and her brother go there all the time.

Thursday? That already happened? They played already? Did you get a tape of it?

Think about this: I wouldn't be here tonight if it wasn't for you two.

A lot of Tobias Wolff lately. What can I get you?

Do you know Johnny? He'll probably be here later. He's really cool. He makes too much money. He's just like the government. I was going to ask you about the new W2s. If you put "married," you're gonna get killed by the IRS, but I sold a lot of stock this year.

They were charging five bucks for a vodka sour, and the vodka is about this much. A splash of vodka.

I'll be puking halfway home, just like I did at my buddy's bachelor party. I'm really good friends with her significant other, and that's how I know her. These two girls look exactly the same, and they're both pregnant. That's the best place to go for breakfast in the whole town.

Where?

It's called Victor's.

Check it out.

God, is this a great song. Nah, I had enough beer at your house. Between you two, I owe you, like, eight beers.

Light my cigarette?

One winter break, we were living at my house, and I'd come home at 4:30, and he'd still be in bed. Did he have a job? No, it was like winter break or something.

I want to meet this guy. Attitude, attitude, attitude. It's all about attitude. Are you laughing at me right now?

Light. My. Cigarette!

Are you here by yourself? I'm sort of in that manic "Oh-I've-got-a-lot-of-s___-to-do" mode. I don't know. Stressed out. Big time.

I just parked in the Target lot tonight. That's the easiest. Heeeeey! How are you??! This is Katie. This is Margaret. Katie just got back from Italy, so we're just catching up with her. Anyway, the Target lot is the easiest. There was something going on in Blues Alley when we were walking by. Sex on the pool table or something.

That's exactly what I said: "If I win the lottery, I want a million dollars and world peace."

He's so cute. He's *sooooo* cute. He's not that cute.

I hate going there: you can never hear the band. People are always talking over the band. Tracy! Tracy! Tracy! He's been sick for years.

I didn't know that.

You need a vacation. You need to learn to relax, man.

It's like a fourplex brownstone thing. I'm planning on doing it this year; I can't deal with fucking paying rent anymore. I'll live by myself in a one-bedroom apartment if I have to. Whatever happens, I'm not obligated to move.

That band has been together eight months, and they're on the cover of *City Pages*. That's a jinx.

Gimme money. Money, money, money. Buy me a drink.

I haven't seen *Almost Famous*, but I loved *Wonder Boys*. Loved it. Have you seen *Almost Famous*?

Uh-uh.

I recognized her right away, and I was, like, "Whoa! I haven't seen you in a looong time."

So I'm lying in bed the other day and, you know, it was one of those "in" days, and I was sleeping, and then at the window, I heard this, "Mew, mew, mew, mew, mew." And I woke up, and it kept going, "Mew, mew, mew." And I was, like, "You are a horrible, horrible cat."

Dude, I was tired. I wasn't gonna stay all night. I'm not ready to go. At home I do. Wanna come over?

Who's that? I've never seen her before. What's her name? Yeah, she's a cutie. She's got that natural thing. It's like she loves the music, but it hasn't killed her yet, you know?

That's her boyfriend right there. He's in a band.

Last call, last call, last call, y'all.

My brother owns this bar on the Range, and we go there all the time. Let's go. Okay.

'Scuse me. I'm going this way.

Miss Georgia Peach is just like this uber-female. She's this big, beautiful woman. She showed me her belly button at the Turf Club one night.

You hate me. No, I don't. You fucking hate me. I'm a nice girl. I'm nothing but good. Good, good, good. And I love your friends.

You're drunk.

Good crowd. Yeah, especially when there's so much shit going on tonight. We never hang out anymore. Why don't we ever hang out anymore?

Well, I'm from West St. Paul and you're from . . . where are you living now? He slept with her. He slept with her. What would you do if your boyfriend slept with your best friend?

I didn't know she was your best friend.

Call me. I will. You never will. I promise. I want adventure. And I love your friends.

You're drunk.

Hi, baby.

Let's go, people! Time to go! The bar is closing.

Gretchen had her birthday party at the Towers. That's the last time I saw you. Then I decided to go to grad school.

Gabba gabba hey! You can never plan for that.

Let's go, let's go. Time to go. The bar is closing.

Don't ask me again. Don't ask me that again. Don't ask me to remember. Rob, you are a bitch.

Yeah, I am a bitch.

Excuse me, is this your beer?

It's all about you, isn't it?

After you.

I saw you at Al's last time, and I was, like, "Next time I see you I'm gonna remember your name." How's it going?

It's going as good as it was when you asked me an hour ago.

Did you catch anything?

Five walleye.

I was, like, "You guys suck."

Let's go! Time to goooo! Okay, ladies, time to go. Guys, take it outside. The bar is closed. Let's go.

There's a party at Al's. Al's? Let's go! I'm gonna go over there right now and open the door. Party at Al's!

What's the address? Dupont? Emerson? I thought he moved to St. Paul. The party's on Dupont.

What's the address?

Dupont.

But what's the address?

Dupont and Twenty-seventh. Or Twenty-eighth.

We can walk there! We can sing songs as we walk there.

What kind of songs?

Gordon Lightfoot. I hope not.

Someone stole my cigarettes.

2001

I Wanna Be Where the Bands Are
(The Autograph Man)

"You're not prepared for this. Nobody ever is," says Jim Ashworth, standing on the steps of his tiny St. Paul home. Inside, the cramped entryway bursts with wall hangings, including vintage sheet music, paintings of the racehorse Dan Patch, a life insurance form signed by Jimmy Durante, a photo signed by Amos and Andy, and an album signed by songwriter Sondre Lerche.

"Interesting guy. I met him at the [Electric] Fetus," says Ashworth, a sixty-four-year-old retired teacher and lifelong St. Paul resident. "Over a year later I met him at the Fine Line. He looked at me and said, 'I remember you from the record store.' Mark Mallman did the same thing: 'I remember you! Taste of Minnesota!'"

He's hard to forget. Ashworth can routinely be spotted in the shadows of clubs—a balding, gray-haired man walking amongst the hipsters with a Sharpee in one hand, a record bag in the other, and a single-minded determination on his face. He has been collecting autographs since he was a teenager, when his letters to Mae West and Groucho Marx extracted signed photos. That act turned into a hobby, which is now a collection, which now numbers in the thousands.

You don't have to look hard to find memorabilia from hockey, baseball, and the *Titanic,* but his home is dominated by rock. His favorite band of all time is Sweet, and his favorites of the moment are the Redwalls and the Kaiser Chiefs ("Not only are they very good, but they're very nice"). Stuffed alongside myriad signed artifacts by the Rolling Stones, the Who, the Doors, David Bowie, and you-name-it are locals Flamingo, Johnny Lang, the Suicide Commandos, the Suburbs, Soul Asylum, Plastic Constellations, and his current fixation, Melodious Owl.

The house of Ashworth may be the only place on the planet where countless "To Jim's" and "Your friend, Floyd Patterson" dance with the ink stains of River Phoenix, Bob Dylan, Kurt Cobain, Ray and Dave Davies, Garrison Keillor, the Partridge Family, the Clash, Sammy Hagar, Lucille Ball, Joe Louis, Salvador Dali, Marc Bolan, Siouxie and the Banshees, Amelia Earhart, John Philip Sousa, Patti Smith, Sylvain Sylvain, and the Hives.

"The main thing is, if you get 'em in person, you get to know 'em a little bit and visit with them," says Ashworth, his eyes winking through wire-rim specs. His slight frame swims in a Doors T-shirt, offset by a crucifix hanging around his neck. "Even if you buy them, it's a connection with these people."

Aerosmith, Hanson, Joan Baez, the Troggs, Robert Plant, Bill Murray, the Knack, Foghat, Freddie Mercury, the Marx Brothers, Leon Durham, the Boomtown Rats, Ray Bolger, KISS, Hayley Mills, Ike Reilly, the Raveonettes, Josh Hartnett, Ruth Gordon and Bud Cort ("My favorite movie is *Harold and Maude*"), George Burns, Norman Rockwell, Milton Berle, Roy Rogers, Gentleman Jim Corbett, Cheap Trick, Savoy Brown, Michael Jackson, Bo Diddley, George Gershwin, Lew Alcindor, Kareem Abdul-Jabbar, and James Dean.

"I'm like a sponge," he says. "I just absorb. I don't sell anything. Some people who collect cars, they buy one and sell another one.

But when things come here, they stay here. A lot of people don't understand why you'd want four or five albums signed by the same person, but to me, it's art. An artist can draw four or five different pictures and sign them all, but they're all different because they're different pictures."

"These are probably the most beautiful signatures I have," he says, holding two posters elegantly inscribed by Mikhail Baryshnikov. The artwork overwhelms every wall of the house, as well as the insides of kitchen cabinets, bedroom floors, and the bathroom door (Peter Frampton's *Frampton's Camel*). Part of why he lives alone and never married, he says, is because it would have interfered with his passion for collecting.

The end display is fine, but it is the thrill of the hunt that keeps Ashworth going. At the moment, his white whales are Richie Valens, Clark Gable, and Humphrey Bogart. He "nails" his subjects at gigs, estate sales, auctions, and book and record stores. Sometimes he tries the mail. When the Mirage club closed a few years ago, he scored signed posters by Cinderella, Danger Danger, Mr. Big, and dozens of the hair bands he knows and loves.

He likes originals. Mickey Mantle's high school basketball photo. Troubled Mets star Darryl Strawberry, on a rare one-off LP called *Get Metsmerized!* ("I said, 'Now I know why none of you guys were singing stars,' and [Strawberry] laughed.") A *Harry Potter* movie poster signed by J. K. Rowling. A poster signed by the entire 1980 USA Olympic hockey team.

His two biggest prizes are a note from Lewis Carroll that he procured for $2,000 and that is stashed, seemingly carelessly, under a pile of records and magazines, and Buddy Holly's 1958 New Mexico fishing license.

Ashworth also fishes. And plays bridge and attends St. Paul Saints games. But his obsession is autographs, every one of which tells a story.

Brian Wilson signed *Pet Sounds* with a barely legible "B W" ("I think he was on medication at the time," Ashworth says). Joe Mauer signed a high school photo with "Go Cretin." The J. Geils Band's Peter Wolf, among others, drew on-the-spot artwork. "I told [Motley

Crue's] Nikki Sixx, 'I used to be a math teacher. I think you're the only one I know in music that has a number for a name.' He said, 'I think you're right.' *Flaming Lips*, that was their first album, and he [Wayne Coyne] wanted to show it around. He said, 'There were only about a thousand of 'em. I don't even have one.' I was on the bus with Nazareth, and the manager took my album and went in the other room and brought it back with an obviously forged signature of the lead singer. You know, why not just not do it?

"I asked Elvis Costello if he remembered playing at the Long-horn, and he said, 'I certainly do, is it still there?' I said, 'Unfortunately, no.'

"Lou Reed said nothing.

"The only time I've ever asked anyone for their autograph and they've lost their cool was when I asked John Cale to sign this"—Ashworth holds out a copy of the Velvet Underground's first album—"and he pushed it away and quit signing altogether. You'd think that forty years or whatever would take care of any grudge or whatever.

"Remember Carol Wayne? She was the weather girl on Johnny Carson. She died in an auto accident, so that was a tough auto-graph." The photo, by the way, is a nude. "John Fogerty said, 'I've met you before!' I said, 'I wish, but we've never met.'

"My aunt knew [wrestler] Gorgeous George, so I got that. Ted Nugent's niece went to Como [Park High], where I used to teach, so I was able to get that. One of my former students is Jack Nicholson's caretaker out in Colorado, so I asked his mother to get me a picture. She said, 'You have to wait for the right time with Jack.' About three years later, she called and said, 'I have your picture.'

"I retired six years ago, and I'm busier than I've ever been. If you have interests, you just find things you enjoy, and you stay busy. Like yesterday, I could have spent all day chasing [Negro League star] Buck O'Neil down. If you're teaching or working somewhere, you can't do that."

As he speaks, the full-to-bursting walls of Ashworth's home press in. He may be at an age when splurging his savings and pension on autographs is his right, but he admits that he's starting to won-der what will become of it all when he's gone. "I'm hoping to get a student or someone to come stay in the extra room and help take care of the place," he says. "I'm trying to get stuff organized. My only family is my brother, and he just hopes he goes before I do so he doesn't have to deal with it. I think he sees it as a mountain of accumulation, whereas I treasure each thing."

2005

She's the One

The SuperAmerica at Fortieth and South Lyndale is my go-to convenience store, and I usually blow in and out of the place like a thief in the night, head down and trying not to bother any of the clerks or other jittery creatures of the night and day with idle chit-chatter. Still, I think we're here to connect with one another, to compare notes on the big nutty journey of life, so last Tuesday, I was taking my time and feeling good, and I took a shot.

"How's your night?" I asked the woman behind the counter. She didn't remember me, she never does, but I've liked her since our first exchange about a year ago, when I chatted her up and discovered she was new to town, originally from Alabama. Tough cookie with a warm smile.

"Not bad, kind of slow," she said, then she said what I've heard her say to every customer, no matter how busy the business or long the line, and sweetly, "How you doing?"

In the moment it took for her to ring me up, in my head I ticked off a long list of reasons Why I Should Not Make Small Talk with Her, and instead should just clam up and be on my way, living as we are through these turbulent times of mixed messages, stranger danger, racial profiling, class wars, erupting gender norms, and the overall general malaise, suspicion, and misanthropy that come with being a real, live, bleeding human being in 2015.

Seriously, would she think me a fool? A flirt? Pathetic middle-aged white dude? Would she shut me down?

"Can I ask you a question?" I asked. She sized me up.

"Sure."

"Do you like basketball?" I guessed, introducing that most universal of topics this side of the weather—sports. Her eyes lit up.

"I do!"

"Did you see that game last night?" I asked, meaning the NCAA men's championship thriller in which Duke's Tyus Jones took over in the last three minutes to beat Wisconsin. The whole damn country had been talking about what a great game it was all day, and here we were, too.

"That . . . was . . . awesome," we harmonized, and then I, after briefly representing our polar opposite feelings for Duke, asked her if she played basketball. She said she used to, but she's too old to play now, for god's sake, but she occasionally still plays football with her kids. I asked her if she played in high school or college.

"I was the first female high school football player to play for a boys' team in Chicago."

The guy behind me was getting antsy and another regular was happily jabbering in her other ear about her selling him another winning lottery ticket, so I stepped to the side. She reported her pioneer athlete status with great pride. Seriously? She nodded.

"Bloom Township Alternative High School. I was quarterback, I was wide receiver, I ran track, I was fast. No other girls ever thought about going out for the team; I played on the boys' basketball team and I played on the football team. I actually opened up the door for a lot of people, because a lot of girls were really good and wanted to play, but they were scared. I cleared the way for a lot of them, and that following year there were five more girls on the team.

"I played football, but only for a year, because I found I was pregnant and they wouldn't let me play. Same thing with basketball. I was in the middle of a game and I started feeling hot and strange, and it turns out it was because I was pregnant.

"I opened up a door for a lot of people, and I caused some trouble, too. You know the boys, how they like to smack themselves on the booty? They liked doing that to me, too, so I started smacking them back on the booties. Sometimes I think that's the only reason

I tried out—there were a lot of gorgeous boys on the football team and I just wanted to touch on 'em. So it worked out, and I was good at what I did."

Her name is Cynthia Johnson, and as far as she knows she's not related to the Cynthia Johnson who sang "Funkytown," about her newly adopted hometown Minneapolis. She grew up in Alabama, Wisconsin, and Illinois, and now she's newly married with two of her eleven children in tow. Her oldest graduates from college next month. She works as many jobs as she can to support her kids, including shifts at SuperAmerica, which is something of a neighborhood social hub due in no small part to Cynthia's calm demeanor and positive vibrations.

"It's a community store, so it's a lot of good people that come in here," she said, grabbing three packs of cigarettes off the top shelf for an agitated and raspy-throated customer. "I'm always telling 'em I'm going to put some couches in here and have a social group, because a lot of the regular customers just come in to socialize and they need some comfort."

Her coworker pulls her aside and together they survey a potential shoplifter's patterns. She works with the calm of an air traffic controller as she multi-tasks, trouble-shoots, runs the cash register, and sells pop, water, gum, magazines, newspapers, snacks, gas, cigarettes, lighters, and junk food. She likes sports, she's an avid crocheter, and she recently crocheted fifteen blankets for some lucky military vets. She doesn't have time for anything but work and home these days, but she'd like to go sightseeing sometime soon.

She's looking forward to her kids' college and high school graduations.

"It took a long time to get to where I got, because I was a messed-up child. I went through a lot of different things in life," she said. "I was troubled, I went through a lot of different experiences. I was at peace when I first started out here ten months ago. I'm still trying to capture myself; I fell short a little bit. I just got married, I've been married for five months. I'm still a work-in-progress and a learning experience—for myself and to others."

2015

Reason to Believe

Whether we like to admit it or not, there is a little bit of Karen Iffert in all of us. During the day, Iffert is a fifty-three-year-old mother of three who works at her church putting together the bulletin and brochures and attending to other duties. At night, she retires to the Eagan home she shares with her husband, Richard. In one of the back rooms, there is a sewing machine and an ironing board, but the main occupant is Neil Diamond. His bushy brows stare down from posters, pillows, album covers, CDs, cassettes, key chains, coffee mugs, T-shirts, buttons, and even a customized clock.

"It was a clock that I had, and I just put the picture behind it," Iffert said of the '80s-era Diamond photo wedged behind the idle hands. "It doesn't keep time very well, but I guess it's always Neil time."

Now more than ever. Next weekend, Diamond will set up shop at Target Center in Minneapolis for three nights. Which means that this is zero hour for Iffert and the rest of her cronies in FOND (Friends of Neil Diamond), the international Diamond fan club. "There's going to be a lot of fans coming here that I'll know. Thirty or so. I've got friends coming in from New Hampshire and Des Moines, and a gal at work, and we're going to the first concert together," she explained. "And then I have another friend in Minneapolis, and we're gonna meet there. We'll try and see if we can be at the hotel, which will remain nameless, because I really don't know what it is yet. But somebody always finds out.

"We'll get there either when he comes or when he leaves for sound check, which is about four o'clock. His schedule is on the money. And then we usually go out to eat or something, and then go to the concert. And then probably back to the hotel for when he comes back. That's when you can catch him, and he'll stop and talk and stuff like that." Iffert has this Diamond mining down to an exact science. Over the past ten years, her obsession has necessitated pilgrimages to Chicago, Nashville, and Iowa. With this weekend's triple header, her concert count will total twenty-nine—a pittance, she pointed out, when compared to fans she saw profiled on TV recently, who were celebrating their four hundredth Kenny Rogers concert.

And what does her husband think?

"I don't know," she admitted. "It's hard to read sometimes. Basically, he and a lot of men friends think it's kind of ridiculous. I get a real charge out of people who say, 'You're going to all three concerts? And maybe another one someplace else?' And I say, 'Yeah. Didn't you go to the last three or four Vikings games?' Oh, but that's different.' 'Well, why is that different?' And there's no answer."

In the living room of the Iffert home, the only collection on display is one of Hummel figures. The rest of the decor is all-American postwar suburbia: a ceramic dog, plush couches and matching chairs, baby pictures (all three of the Iffert sons are now out of the house), and a few craftsy knickknacks.

The only concession to Karen Iffert's obsession is the toy frogs, which Diamond fans have adopted as mascots in reference to the "frog who dreamed of being a king" lyric in "I Am, I Said," that litter the house. Other than that, it's almost as if her infatuation has been banished—perhaps grudgingly so—to a secret room. Likewise, when talking about it, she is careful not to appear too gone. She answers questions coolly, analytically, almost as if she's trading recipes. She never threatens to leave her husband for Diamond or to abandon her life in Eagan to follow the *Tennessee Moon* tour.

But behind her composed demeanor, there is a fanatic yearning to be set free. "I told a friend I wanted to come off as enthusiastic and mature," she said with a laugh. "So leave out any reference to 'teenybopper,' which I hear a lot. And 'shrine,' which I also hear. It's a collection. If you call it a 'shrine,' I'll cancel my paper."

Still, there is one picture on the back room's wall that betrays Iffert's goal of enthusiastic maturity. It was taken in the lobby of a Chicago hotel a few years ago, after a Diamond concert. Diamond is all put-on good-guy star pizazz, while the woman he has his arm around—Karen Iffert—is a far cry from the woman standing before me. Her face is a blossoming flower of glowing cheeks, a broad, rapturous smile, and a sparkle in her eyes that suggests a trip to Eden.

To some, there is only one word for a person in such a portrait.

Groupie. "I've heard that, and I'm past that," she says. "A few years back, someone called us the Diamondheads. But it doesn't bother me.

"I guess there are lots of things in life that keep you grounded. Certainly your family, and maybe your religion, and your politics and everything else." Iffert grew up in Nicollet, Minnesota (population: 800), between Mankato and St. Peter. She was "a stargazer fanatic from grade school on," who was hooked on early rock 'n' roll, specifically Bobby Rydell and Elvis. But when Elvis died in 1977, Iffert turned her affections toward Diamond. Her most prized possession is one of three personal Diamond autographs, a handwritten thank-you note for a gift of 1941-era magazines Iffert sent the singer for his fiftieth birthday.

"My collection is peanuts compared to other people's," she said. "There's a gal out in New York who is auctioning off her whole collection, including one of his shirts, which she wants $1,100 or $1,200 for."

The most extraordinary part of Iffert's stuff is the exhaustive newspaper and magazine clip files she has compiled, all housed in eight large scrapbooks and four photo books. Each is meticulously cataloged and dated, sporting Diamond press notices and photos from all over the world. It is here that Iffert gets most of her satisfaction: cutting, pasting, photocopying, or tracking down, by networking with other fans, an article she may have missed.

Why is she so focused on the clip file? "That's a good question. Maybe, for me, I just latched on to something that I wanted to know more about. And now it's—I wouldn't call it an obsession—but if I know there's an article or something out there, I would like to have it."

So whether we like to admit it or not, there is a little bit of Karen Iffert in all of us. All music lovers have felt that ache to be as close to their heroes as possible. Some merely want to say thank you; others want to tap that energy. Most people grow out of it—usually because the real world scoffs at such indulgences. But for everyone who has ever felt the way Iffert feels about Neil Diamond, that feeling is the feeling of being truly alive, of stripping away all pretense, of giving yourself up to the music, and feeding the part of your soul marked *fan*. It is, in the end, about unfettered passion.

"I have a friend who has been a friend for a long time, and she is not a fan of anything," said Iffert, sipping a Diet Coke. "And she always says to me, 'I just think it's so great that you can be so passionate about something.'"

The first time Iffert came face to face with Diamond was in 1989 in Chicago. He walked through a hotel lobby and waved. Since then, there have been a handful of other meetings, all of which have been fulfilling, if typically fleeting. "He's always been so nice," she said. "Friendly and willing to stop. And I guess nobody is—I am not, anyway—looking for anything more."

Standing in her back room, Iffert showed off a few more pictures of Diamond she snapped. In one, she noted the tired expression on his face and sympathized with his life on the road, talking almost as if she knows him intimately. But after all this—the fan club, the pilgrimages, the hours of devoted clipping and pasting—does Neil Diamond know who Karen Iffert is?

"It's not anything that maybe if you were walking down the street, he'd say, 'Oh, Karen,'" she conceded. "But I think he recognizes the people that he sees from concert to concert, as much as anybody like that could. You don't expect him to [remember you] unless you were involved in the business, or something like that."

By this time next week, Iffert's collection will have grown slightly larger. At the Target Center concessions booth, she plans to invest in a baseball cap (with the frog logo), a *Tennessee Moon* T-shirt, and a tour booklet. The merchandise will undoubtedly help appease her case of *The Neilies*—a term coined by an Australian fan club member for the disenchantment that settles in after Diamond leaves town. And since she has no immediate pilgrimage plans, the upcoming shows in Minneapolis are her only chances for a fix.

"Yes, there's a letdown. When it's over, you want it to go on. But it's such an unreal fantasy thing," she said. "It's like you're on a high. I am, anyway. I just get a high for three days, and then you have to come down from that and go back to work and stuff. If you were an entertainer, you would live that all the time. But for people

who just go about their business and work at a bank or whatever
you might do, it's definitely—what did you call it? An escape? Yeah,
I suppose, though I never thought of it as that. It's a little vacation
from reality, I guess."

1996

Drive All Night (Desperately Seeking Denise)

He had just moved his mother—the most important woman in his
life, the woman he'd lived with his entire life—into a nursing home,
and he had recently had his heart broken by a woman he calls "a flirt
who played a game with me." His dad died twenty years ago. He's
"never been intimate with anybody," but when a complete stranger
kissed him on the night of February 28, 2004, he fell in love with
her "on the spot."

The Minnesota Music Café, on the East Side. That's where forty-
six-year-old St. Paul native Kevin Kupferschmidt met a woman he
knows only as "Denise." She had brown hair and "a great shape." She
wore slipper shoes. He remembers as much because he watched her
feet as she danced in front of him. He thinks she looks a little like
an actress from *The Gilmore Girls,* a photo of which he downloaded
and looks at constantly on his cell phone.

She was celebrating her forty-fourth birthday but was feeling
bad about getting older. He is, he says, "a caring person," and he
cheered her up by saying she has a pretty face and looks ten years
younger. She gave him "the sweetest kiss I've ever had in my life."
She asked what he did for a living, which "showed she cared." She
took him by the hand, led him out on the dance floor, and taught
him how to dance.

"It was the most fun I've ever had dancing," Kevin says, sitting
in the office of the silent grade-school gymnasium where he works
nights, surrounded by volleyballs, basketballs, gym equipment, and
team schedules. He's wearing a shabby sweatshirt with "Roseville"
on the front, tennis shoes, and turtle-shell-frame glasses. His words
come out of him slowly, lacquered by a nervous, protective laugh.

His ex-roommate Barry had something to do with that night. Barry told Denise that Kevin was lonely and that he needed someone. Kevin gave her a rose, on Barry's suggestion. He called her "a sweetheart," because she was so "caring and loving." *Sweetheart.* She liked that.

He talked to her for fifteen minutes. She hugged him four times. She kissed him three more times. The third was the charm. She looked into his eyes "romantically," he says, and he knew "it was meant to be" and that "she was the love of my life."

He gave her his business card—he teaches tennis and works for the park and recreation system in Roseville—and she sprayed him with her perfume and said, "This is something to remember me by." As she left the bar, she told him she had a boyfriend. He touched her shoulder, "to thank her and let her know I had a good time." Kevin told his mother about her and gave his mother two of the hugs Denise gave him. He wanted his mother to feel the love that had transpired between them. His mother had always wanted him to get married and have kids, but that never happened. "She was a wonderful mom," he says. "She did a lot of great things for people. She was a great cook, too." His mother died the week after he met Denise.

He placed his first ad in the "I Saw You" section of the *City Pages* classified ads a few days later. "Hi, Denise. It's Kevin. Met at Minnesota Music on 2-28-04, great night! Gave you a rose, you taught me to dance. We had some romance. Please call to talk. Denise, you're sweet, can we again meet?"

He heard nothing. He has placed a version of his ad in every issue of *City Pages* every week ever since. Two years, more than one hundred ads, to the tune of $1,500. Last week it ran in the "Message Center" category. "Denise: Miss you. Sweetheart . . . love you true, only took one tender kiss, touch, yeah, miss sweet kiss, company much, what's phone? Keep in touch, MMC 2-28-04, dance, talk, more? Kevin is lonely, need you only, much."

He thinks about her every day. He looks for her at bowling alleys, coffee shops, anywhere people gather. He thought he saw her at Pappy's in Stillwater one night, but it wasn't her. He saw a brunette at the Minnesota Music Café another night, approached her, and asked her what her name was. She wouldn't say. She was drunk and ran out the door.

He doesn't think he's "a stalker," because these days the object of his obsession can be found only in his mind. Kevin doesn't talk to anybody about her anymore, because nobody understands. They don't understand how a love like that can happen, how he can't forget her, how she came into his heart that night to stay.

He used to talk to Barry about her, but not anymore, "because Barry thinks I've lost it—ever since after I got the tattoo." He got the tattoo on his upper arm a year ago in Lake City: an etching of two hearts, the names Kevin and Denise, and the words "You're a sweetheart."

Kevin knows that eventually he'll have to move on. Not yet, though. He's talked to regulars at the Minnesota Music Café and they think she was from out of town. They've never seen her before or since. He's canvassed all the bikers at the bar about her. No one knows who she is. He has sent e-mails to the KS95 deejays about his search. One of the deejays read one of his e-mails on the air. No reply.

He has a dream. He'd like to see her one more time. He'd like to have one more dance, thank her, and give her a hug. He's "not a forceful person" or "one to show off." He doesn't "have high expectations," he says, but he thinks she deserves "someone who would love her and give to her." He's not interested in any other women. She's the one. He thinks they're a good fit.

She inspires him. Kevin has been writing poetry and songs, and singing karaoke. Everything he does is for and about her. His goal is to sing in a band, but "if that doesn't work out, radio's a backup for me." He's taking guitar lessons. He's been working up a version of Counting Crows' "Accidentally in Love" from the *Shrek 2* soundtrack. He bought her a gift, just in case he sees her again: a stuffed frog holding a sign that says "Kiss me."

2006

Glory Days

The week of September 15 started the way every week has started for Frank "Bud" Woolsey since last August. His wife, Dorie, drove him to Lakeland Dialysis on Forty-third and Nicollet in South Minneapolis, where at 6:00 a.m. he walked through the back door, past the signs that say "Oxygen Closet" and "If You Need Assistance Walking, Please Ask," and where, amid the sounds of pumps and monitors and the murmurings of first-shift nurses and orderlies, he settled into the big green patent-leather recliner he's been occupying every Monday, Wednesday, and Friday for the past thirteen months.

First the nurse hooked up Dwayne, Bud's next-door dialysis neighbor. Then she propped up Bud's left arm and slipped two needles into the vein in his wrist. The needles were attached to two tubes, which were attached to the dialysis machine, a yellowing contraption that looks like a garage-sale robot. By 6:15, the blood in Bud's arm was being moved from his vein to the dialysis machine, which removes waste and extra fluid and returns the blood to his body; it's the same procedure that some two hundred thousand Americans with kidney disease use as a last resort until their kidneys either kick in or give out.

For the next four hours, Bud sat in the recliner, where (when he isn't reading or napping) he's had a lot to think about: good life, great wife, nine kids, twenty-two grandkids, five great-grandkids. His days as a star baseball and basketball player at Washburn High School. His days working at the old Nicollet Hotel on Hennepin Avenue. His days as a semi-pro baseball player. His days as a Navy torpedo bomber pilot in World War II. His days, most recently, working part-time at the neighborhood funeral home, and the fact that, even if his kidneys do recover, the dialysis will eventually affect his eighty-year-old heart, and his days will be numbered.

On September 15, the nurse took the needles out of Bud's arm and put a bandage on his arm to stop the bleeding. Dorie picked him up and took him home, where he took a four-hour nap, which is what he needs to do, because the dialysis takes so much out of

him. So much so that when he started the dialysis, his daughter
Joanie, a nurse, told everyone but Bud that it would be the end of
her father's lifelong love affair with golf. Bud started golfing when
he was eight years old. When he was a young man, he augmented
his team sports with golf. When he was a father and a salesman,
he took every Friday afternoon off for golf, or his "therapy," during
which he'd forget all his worldly problems. So immersed was Bud
in the Tao of golf that he started making his own golf clubs, first for
himself, then for Dorie and the kids and the grandkids.

"Golf has always been a connection for my Dad and me," says
Scott Woolsey, forty-eight. "All my life, through all of the shit I put
him through, no matter what, we could always go play golf. And
whatever differences we had, in a way, they were always forgotten
out there."

Joanie was right. When Bud started the dialysis, he had to give
up his golf. Ten itchy months went by, the longest he'd ever spent
not swinging a club. Then, in May, Scott took him to Hiawatha Golf
Course. It was a disaster. Bud was unsure of himself; he was swinging with his upper body only, his knees hurt, and when he left the
course that day he was scared he'd never play again. So he stopped,
and when he did, something inside him died.

A couple of months ago, Bud's best friend, Bob Johnson, started
bugging him. "C'mon, let's go golfing," Bob would say to Bud, but
Bud put him off. His legs were too weak and he couldn't hit the ball,
he'd tell Bob, and he didn't want to embarrass himself; he didn't
want to play if he couldn't play at the level he'd played all his life.
But Bob, who played high school baseball and basketball with Bud,
wouldn't take no for an answer. They started a regular Tuesday game
at Arbor Point, a nine-hole course in Inver Grove Heights. The first
two months Bud was beyond frustrated. He couldn't play the way he
used to, and what's more, for the first time in his life, he was using
a motorized golf cart. But at the end of August and beginning of
September, it started coming back. Even though he wasn't as sharp
as he was before, Bud was starting to hit the ball decently, and his
drives were straightening out. His therapy was returning. He was
having fun.

On September 16, Scott accompanied Bud and Bob to Arbor Point. On the second hole, Bob reached into his bag for his eight-iron. He pierced the earth with the sharp end of a tee and balanced a freshly scrubbed ball on the other end. And with wrists that had been tied to a life-saving device twenty-four hours earlier and would be again twenty-four hours later, with new-old blood pumping through his veins, with a heart that hadn't yet gotten the word that it should be toast by now, Bud Woolsey took a swing. The ball shot off the tee and rose high into the blue heavens.

"It landed right on the front of the green," says Scott. "He went, 'It's on,' and turned around and walked away. I was standing on the tee box. I went, 'It's goin' in!' I've played golf maybe five hundred times with my dad, and I don't know how many times I've said, 'It's goin' in, it's goin' in!' I just watched it roll and roll and I'm going, 'Hey, Pops, that's goin' in! It's goin' in!'

"And he just kept walking away. And then I started screaming, 'It's in! Hole in one, Pop! Hole in one!' And he just turns and looks at me and says, 'It probably rolled off the back [of the green].' I said, 'Dad, it went right in the hole, I saw it go right in the hole! It's in!' He was pretty nonplussed about it. Me and Bob were much more excited about it. But then when he got down to the green, he pulled it out of the cup and held it up to the imaginary crowd, like he'd just won the Masters."

2003

Back to Minneapolis

I got in the car at six in the morning to leave Livingston, said my "I'll be back . . ." goodbyes to Montana in my rearview mirror, grabbed a coffee, and popped in the last chapters of *Born to Run*.

Listening to Springsteen recount his path to becoming a musician, wrestling with love, marriage, divorce, depression, antidepressants, and the highs and lows of playing live music and being on stage, and navigating the ins and outs of the creative process provided me with the same good companionship his songs provided me with in my youth. I'd been working on this book all the while, so it was fitting that my Montana trip culminated in the moment when I saw the first freeway road sign back to Minneapolis just as Bruce landed back in his hometown of Asbury Park, standing on the shore, looking at the ocean and praying. And so I prayed the "Our Father" along with him, driving fast to get back to the ones I love.

Now here I am telling my story to you, and here he was, one of America's best-ever storytellers, telling me his, and telling me why it's important to tell our stories, our one great big story. I drove and listened, and an hour outside Minneapolis, Springsteen ended his book and our road trip/lifetime journey together. As Montana's mountains gave way to the Badlands of North Dakota and now the swamps of Minnesota, I hugged the slow lane as other motorists raced by, savoring the last pages as the familiar billboards and other ticks of my home state filled my bug-stained windshield.

"I wanted to understand in order to free myself of [my story's] most damaging influences, its malevolent forces, to celebrate and honor its beauty, its power, and to be able to tell it well to my friends, my family, and to you," said Bruce from my Subaru Forester speakers. "I don't know if I've done that, and the devil is always just a day away, but I know this was my young promise to myself, to you. This, I pursued as my service. This, I presented as my long and noisy prayer, my magic trick. Hoping it would rock your very soul and then pass on, its spirit rendered, to be read, heard, sung, and altered by you and your blood, that it might strengthen and help make sense of your story. Go tell it."

And so I have, in part, and so I will continue to—tell my story, our stories—and I hope you see something of yourself between these covers.

ACKNOWLEDGMENTS

This book would not exist without all the great people in my life. Thank you:

To my mother, father, grandfather, grandmother, uncles, aunts, brothers, and sisters, whose letters from decades ago I keep and whose writing voices I only now recognize make up my own voice, passed down like freckles, red hair, and the Irish craic.

To my sister Minnow, for being an inspiring example of hard work and a rigorous mind, and for taking me on an unforgettable trip to Ireland. To my brothers Jay and Terry, for their love and support and for always being there to riff with me, help me flesh out ideas, have a beer, chew on life, and sing songs. To my sisters Peggy and Molly, for their love, encouragement, curiosity, humor, and shared love of history. To my kids, Henry and Helen, the lights of my life, for loving me, understanding me, and hanging out with me. And to their mother and my dear friend, Jean Heyer, for our strong family bond and for her love of family, books, and social justice.

To my partner, Mary Beth Hanson, for all the love, talks, laughs, encouragement, and shared love of books, reading, music, and social justice, and to the Hanson/Suikonen/Giang family for all their love, food, music, and support.

To my nieces and nephews—Matty, Chooch, Sara, Maddy, Gil, Hanna, Scott, Abby, Gabe, Ian, Pook, and Sara—for always asking what their crazy uncle is up to and for actually listening to and caring about the answer.

To Erik Anderson, my editor at the University of Minnesota Press, for his sharp mind, generous heart, endless enthusiasm, and vast knowledge of all good things. To Brad Norr, for the beautiful cover design for *Fear and Loving in South Minneapolis*. To Heather Skinner, Daniel Ochsner, Maggie Sattler, Louisa Castner, Laura Westlund, Doug Armato, Shelby Connelly, and the rest of the killer crew at the University of Minnesota Press for believing in this book and this writer, for keeping the flame alive for independent publishers, and for working so hard to publish through the pandemic.

To Tommy Mischke, Joe Henry, Mary Lucia, Bill Green, Sarah McKenzie, and Bob Collins for their friendship and inspiration over the years and for the good words.

To my fellow Fellows and staff from the 2003–2004 John S. Knight Fellowship at Stanford University, whose journalism and storytelling lessons provide ongoing inspiration.

To all my editors and the journalism colleagues I've had the pleasure of working with over the years, especially David Brauer, Randall Findlay, Jim Meyer, Burl Gilyard, David Schimke, PD Larson (*Minnesota Daily*); Roger Bull (*Florida Times-Union*); Elizabeth Foy Larsen (*Utne Reader*); Tom Bartel, Kris Henning, Brad Zellar, Monika Bauerlein, Daniel Corrigan, Steve Perry, Jennifer Vogel, Dan Heilman, Judith Lewis, Terri Sutton, Britt Robson, Beth Hawkins, Brian Pobuda, Michael Tortorello, Dylan Hicks, Keith Harris, Phil Tippin (*City Pages*); Walker Lundy, Pat McMorrow, Sue Campbell, Amy Carlson Gustafson, Don Effenberger, Jim Tarbox, Bob Shaw, Chris Hewitt, Brian Lambert, Jayne Blanchard (*St. Paul Pioneer Press*); Bobby Armstrong, Dennis Armstrong, Jim Foster, Jimmy Younger, John Habich, Jeff Wheeler, Kent Youngblood, Patrick Reusse, Jerry Zgoda, Steve Aschburner, Sid Hartman, Jon Bream, Chris Riemenschneider, Tim Campbell (*StarTribune*); Erik Lundegaard, Ross Pfund (*Super Lawyers*); Susan Albright, Corey Anderson, Pamela Espeland, Peter Callaghan, Briana Bierschbach, Greta Kaul, Walker Orenstein (*MinnPost*); Sarah McKenzie, Dylan Thomas, Zac Farber, Janis Hall, Terry Gahan, Zoe Gahan (*Southwest Journal*).

To all my friends, fellow songwriters, and music lovers of the

Mad Ripple Hootenanny, for providing me with so much heart, joy, music, laughs, and inspiration over the past fifteen years.

To my buddy Pete Christensen for the Guru Lounge years, the hermitage/writing retreat in Montana, and all the great talks.

To Michael Croy, my agent and friend, for helping me stay on task.

To all my pickup basketball buddies for our weekly sanity-providing runs, even though I'm not sure any of you guys know how to read.

To all the readers who have ever sent me a note about something I've written: our correspondence has been nothing short of an honor. Special thanks for friendship, collaboration, and encouragement to Peter Jesperson, Dave Ayers, Rick Schreiber, Paul Kaiser, Ike Reilly, Doug Collins, Kathleen Hansen, Nancy Roberts, Laurel Lindahl, Paul Westerberg, Dan Kowalke, Mazelle Amani Zulema, Johnny, Joey, and all the Osterbauers, Beth Barron, Doug Bratland, David Tanner, Joe Fahey, Ann Bremer, Diane Mach, Martin Zellar, Kim Walsh, Amber Lampron, Neal Shore, Bob McDonald, Jon Woll, Shannon Lynch, Sara Garcia, Vishnu Ram, Stephanie Heyer-Walsh, Dennis Hanna, Barb Brown, Dave Brown, Chris Mars, Chrissie, Emily, Slim and all the Dunlaps, Eliza Blue, Joel Bremer, Kathleen Lomauro, David DeYoung, Marc Perlman, Caleb Garn, Stook!, Paul Lundgren, Therese Linderholm and Mary Beth Gossman, Tony and Rita Pucci, Brad Colbert, Ed McFalls, Stephen Cohen, Sonia Grover, Steve McClellan, John Swardson, Paul Odegaard, Martin Devaney, Hans Schumacher, James Loney, Elizabeth Winter, Andrien Thomas, Heidi Thomas, Nicole Helget, Erik Koskinen, Tony Nelson, Dennis Pernu, John Louis, Molly Maher, Terry Gydesen, Susan Hamre, Laura Poehlman, Amanda Falloon, Fran and Tom Willford, Tom Hazelmyer, Joseph Pettini, Rebecca Marx, Craig Paquette, John Brennan, Lisa Zwier, Kelly Hammer, Ken Goldman, Katy Vernon, Shawn Stelton, Debbie Donovan, Jim McGuinn, Joe Tougas, Sarah Morris, Patrice Fehlen, Mike Michel, Steve Smith, Kathleen Stockhaus Lee, Jim Hanneman, Lindsay Paine, Todd Smith, Sean Leo Collins, Michael Hardwick, Colleen Martin Oake, Brian

Oake, Brian Drake, Mare Lennon, Chad Hartman, Scott Schuler, Jon Clifford, Martin Keller, Mark Engebretson, Bill Batson, Julia Klatt Singer, Andrea Swensson, Bill DeVille, David Huckfelt, Brianna Lane, Greg Neis, Scott and Laura Burns, Samantha Loesch, Brianna and James Fitzgerald, Rick Widen, Kevin Martinson, Pat and Danni Widell, Charlie Varley, Rick Ness, Steve Olson, Marissa Saurer, Chris Brueske, Mark Twain, John Irving, Charles Bukowski, Louise Erdrich, Toni Morrison, George Saunders, Prince, Richard Yates, Thomas Moore, Ta-Nehisi Coates, Thomas Merton, Jeff Tweedy, Emily Dickinson, Henry David Thoreau . . .

To all the poets, songwriters, musicians, and writers who have filled my ears, mind, and heart all these years, and who in turn have given me the courage to write from a similar heart base.

To all the good listeners and good readers who value the arts of good listening and good reading.

To all the sources who make up the stories in these pages and to all the folks I have interviewed who have granted me the honor of telling their stories. It has been all my pleasure.

PUBLICATION HISTORY

1. Stay Warm

"Stay Warm," *Southwest Journal*, January 13, 2015.
"Twenty-five Years of the Good Craic," *Southwest Journal*, August 12, 2015.
"'It Feels Like a Brighter Day,'" *Downtown Journal*, August 11, 2016.
"Citizen Berquist: The Man with the Van," *City Pages*, August 31, 2005.
"Misanthropes for $500, Alex," *City Pages*, September 29, 2004.
"Confessions of a Commodore," *City Pages*, July 7, 2004.
"The Santa Claus Diaries," *City Pages*, December 27, 1989.

2. Nature City

"Stop and Smell the Rose Gardens," *Southwest Journal*, April 22, 2010.
"Lucky Us," *Southwest Journal*, July 16, 2014.
"Summer of the Super Sunsets," *Southwest Journal*, September 14, 2012.
"Seize the Light," *Southwest Journal*, February 2, 2012.
"Loving Lake Harriet," *Southwest Journal*, July 19, 2012.
"Harriet Lovejoy Was Here," *Southwest Journal*, May 14, 2018.
"Nightswimming," *Southwest Journal*, July 19, 2011.

3. Family Ties

"From Colombia, with Love," *St. Paul Pioneer Press*, August 6, 1995.
"Thanks Given," *St. Paul Pioneer Press*, November 22, 1999.
"Finding Henry," *City Pages*, November 12, 2003.
"Police Off My Kid's Back," *Southwest Journal*, October 23, 2014.
"Fire Alarm Fluffy," *City Pages*, September 8, 2004.
"An Ambulance Chaser Is Born," *Southwest Journal*, March 4, 2010.
"Letter to a Young Soccer Parent," *Southwest Journal*, October 4, 2016.

4. I'm Only One

"Thanks for the Skerch, Dad," *Southwest Journal*, March 10, 2008.

"Why Sylvia? Why Now?" *City Pages*, August 6, 2004.

"Gold Experience at First Avenue," *City Pages*, February 25, 2004.

"The Tao of Spring Forest Qigong," *MinnPost*, March 29, 2013.

"Krista Tippett and the Wisdom of *On Being*," *MinnPost*, January 4, 2013.

"Fear and Loving in South Minneapolis," *Southwest Journal*, April 29, 2011.

"Walking the Path," *City Pages*, October 19, 2005.

"Being the Buddha at Mile Eight," *MinnPost*, October 4, 2010.

5. Hootenanny

"Hootenanny," *MinnPost*, December 1, 2008.

"Peace, Love, and Bobby Sherman," *St. Paul Pioneer Press*, June 22, 1998.

"Rings of Fire (Brothers United)," *City Pages*, March 17, 2004.

"Sing Out!" *St. Paul Pioneer Press*, February 8, 2002.

"The First Dad Rock Column in the History of Rock Criticism," *St. Paul Pioneer Press*, March 4, 2001.

"This Week's Best Bet: Shhh . . . ," *St. Paul Pioneer Press*, June 8, 2001.

"Dan Israel and the Struggle," *St. Paul Pioneer Press*, October 15, 2000.

"*That Thing You Do!*" *St. Paul Pioneer Press*, October 7, 1996.

"Inside the Hollow Square: Shape Note Singing from the Heart," *St. Paul Pioneer Press*, August 6, 1998.

"Gather 'Round, Children, and Ye Shall Hear a Tale of Standing in Actual Physical Line for Tickets," *St. Paul Pioneer Press*, September 13, 1996.

"In Praise of Great Expectations," *St. Paul Pioneer Press*, September 19, 1997.

6. Famous Lasting Words

"A Lesson before Dying," *Southwest Journal*, February 20, 2018.

"Famous Lasting Words," *Southwest Journal*, November 9, 2011.

"Working Stiffs," *City Pages*, July 2, 2006.

"Tears in Heaven," *St. Paul Pioneer Press*, July 19, 2001.

"Family Man," *City Pages*, June 22, 2005.

"Notes from Karl's Bench," *Southwest Journal*, June 29, 2016.

"The Day David Bowie Died," *Southwest Journal*, January 12, 2016.

"The Funeral Singer," *MinnPost*, December 8, 2008.

"Zero Our Hero," *Southwest Journal*, October 28, 2018.

7. Falling in Love with Everything I Have

"Two Hearts Are Better Than One," *St. Paul Pioneer Press*, February 14, 2002.

"Brilliant Disguise," *Southwest Journal*, March 24, 2008.

"Because the Night," *St. Paul Pioneer Press*, June 1, 2001.

"I Wanna Be Where the Bands Are (The Autograph Man)," *City Pages*, July 6, 2005.

"She's the One," *Southwest Journal*, April 21, 2015.

"Reason to Believe," *St. Paul Pioneer Press*, July 8, 1996.

"Drive All Night (Desperately Seeking Denise)," *City Pages*, March 15, 2006.

"Glory Days," *City Pages*, October 1, 2003.

Jim Walsh is an award-winning author, journalist, writer, and songwriter from Minneapolis. His writing has been published in *Rolling Stone, Village Voice, St. Paul Pioneer Press, City Pages, StarTribune, MinnPost,* and *Southwest Journal,* among many other publications. He is author of *Gold Experience: Following Prince in the '90s* (Minnesota, 2017); *Bar Yarns and Manic-Depressive Mixtapes: Jim Walsh on Music from Minneapolis to the Outer Limits* (Minnesota, 2016); *The Replacements: All Over but the Shouting. An Oral History;* and, with Dennis Pernu, *The Replacements: Waxed Up Hair and Painted Shoes. The Photographic History.* He is the singer/songwriter for former bands REMs, Laughing Stock, and the Mad Ripple and is leader of Jim Walsh and the Dog Day Cicadas, as well as the ringleader behind the singer/songwriter showcase the Mad Ripple Hootenanny. He lives in South Minneapolis.

Tommy Mischke is a writer, musician, podcaster, and radio talk show host from Minnesota. He wrote a weekly column for *City Pages* and hosted *The Mischke Broadcast* on KSTP; most recently, he was host of *The Nite Show* on WCCO Radio. He hosts the podcast *The Mischke Roadshow.*